TWO STUDIES OF FRIEDRICH HÖLDERLIN

MERIDIAN

Crossing Aesthetics

Series founded by the late Werner Hamacher

Editor

Stanford

University

Press

Stanford

California

TWO STUDIES OF FRIEDRICH HÖLDERLIN

Werner Hamacher

EDITED BY Peter Fenves and Julia Ng

TRANSLATED BY Julia Ng and Anthony Curtis Adler

STANFORD UNIVERSITY PRESS
Stanford, California

"Version of Meaning: A Study of Hölderlin's Late Lyric Poetry" was submitted to the Freie Universität Berlin in German in 1971 as a master's thesis under the title "Bild und Zeichen in der späten Lyrik Hölderlins" © 1971, Berlin.

"Parousia, Stone-Walls: Mediacy and Temporality, Late Hölderlin" was originally published in German in 2006 under the title "Parousie, Mauern. Mittelbarkeit und Zeitlichkeit, später Hölderlin" © 2006, Tübingen.

Printed in the United States of America on acid-free, archival-quality paper

Library of Congress Cataloging-in-Publication Data
Names: Hamacher, Werner, author. | Fenves, Peter D., editor. | Ng, Julia, editor, translator. | Adler, Anthony Curtis, translator. | Container of (expression): Hamacher, Werner. Bild und Zeichen in der späten Lyrik Hölderlin. English | Container of (expression): Hamacher, Werner. Parousie, Mauern. English
Title: Two studies of Friedrich Hölderlin / Werner Hamacher ; edited by Peter Fenves and Julia Ng; translated by Julia Ng and Anthony Curtis Adler.
Description: Stanford, California : Stanford University Press, 2019. | Series: Meridian : crossing aesthetics | 'Version of Meaning' was submitted to the Freie Universität-Berlin in German in 1971 as a Magisterarbeit under the title Bild und Zeichen in der späten Lyrik Hölderlin. 'Parousia, stonewalls' was originally published in German in 2006 under the title Parousie, Mauern : Mittelbarkeit und Zeitlichkeit, Später Hölderlin. | Includes bibliographical references and index.
Identifiers: LCCN 2019015389 (print) | LCCN 2019019231 (ebook) | ISBN 9781503608399 | ISBN 9781503608399 (cloth: alk. paper) | ISBN 9781503611115 (pbk.: alk. paper) | ISBN 9781503611122 (ebook)
Subjects: LCSH: Hölderlin, Friedrich, 1770–1843—Criticism and interpretation. | German poetry—19th century—History and criticism. | Idealism, German.
Classification: LCC PT2359.H2 (ebook) | LCC PT2359.H2 H26 2019 (print) | DDC 831/.6—dc23
LC record available at https://lccn.loc.gov/2019015389

Cover painting: Franz Karl Hiemer, *Friedrich Hölderlin* (pastel, 1792), Wikimedia Commons

Cover design: Rob Ehle

Typeset by Kevin Barrett Kane in 11/13 Adobe Garamond Pro

Contents

Translators' Preface

"Version of Meaning" is Hamacher's master's thesis, which was submitted to the Freie Universität Berlin under the title "Image and Sign in Hölderlin's Late Lyric Poetry." This original title was later crossed out and replaced with the new one in Hamacher's hand. The copy of the thesis that is part of Hamacher's literary estate also bears a number of other markings and corrections by hand. For the translation, I have taken the corrected version as the fair copy; where it diverges from the original, I have made a note of the change in the endnotes.

The thesis is also Hamacher's engagement with a number of thinkers both contemporaneous and not contemporaneous with Hölderlin. Most prominent among these is Derrida, but there is also the (unnamed) presence of Freud and Lacan as well as that of Benjamin, Adorno, and Heidegger, not to mention Fichte and Hegel, all of whom generated unmistakable idioms of their own. Wherever necessary, I have sought out existing translations of specific terms that are accepted by the current scholarship so as to maintain a level of intertextual comprehensibility for the reader—thus, for instance, *Tathandlung* has been translated as "fact-act," *Setzung* as "positing," *Wirklichkeit* as "actuality," *Verkehrung* as "perversion," *darstellen* as "presenting," and *verstellen* as "blocking and hiding." *Doppeldeutigkeit* has been rendered as "double-interpretation" in order to draw attention to its kinship with Derrida's *double séance*. At one point *das Gemeinte* is translated as "that which they intend" in a discussion of the turning of meaning (*Bedeutung*) against sense (*Sinn*), which is possibly an allusion to Frege via Husserl.

A particular challenge was presented where Hamacher's discussions of specific words that appear in Hölderlin's verses are guided by a philosophical interlocutor, named or unnamed, who also uses the word (or a closely related one) but in a more terminological fashion. This was especially illuminating to consider as a translator, as it became evident only through a comparison of, for instance, the word *hemmen* as it appears in "Voice of the People" (StA 2: 52; PF 241), and the way that Hamacher mobilizes *Hemmung*, in an interpretation that is perhaps inflected by Lacan, to say that the poem "itself," which first describes how the Heavenly "*hemmen*" the human course to ruin in the externalized sense of "obstruct," oscillates and eventually distorts into a deferral of its own ostensive meaning. In the process of such terminological distortion, what was merely an external (and externalizable, cathectable) blockage, or *Hemmung* as "obstruction," gets in its own way and acquires the more ambiguous (and psychoanalytic) sense of "inhibition," which refuses the easy symmetricization of poem and meaning into outside and inside, or form and introspection. Similarly, in "The Rhine," a "double-interpretation" of the *Theilnahme* that "another" undertakes and, in doing so, complies with the demand to "feel [. . .] in the name of the gods," plays itself out in Hamacher's text. "Another" "participates" by answering to the demand to "feel" on the part of the gods, and, through this "participation"—*Theilnahme* in the sense of *partager* and not vicariousness—"inscribes a difference into the self-identity of the gods in such a way that the other participates in this self-identity," *and* inscribes difference "by taking from the gods a part of their identity" (35–6). In both of these cases and more, the poems become refashioned through their "laying out" in interpretation, so much so that for certain poems, it was necessary to almost entirely retranslate them, rendering them almost independent of their established philological birthing ground.

Lastly, I have opted for a style that prioritizes fluency and so have included the original in brackets, particularly where the interplay between cognates and shared roots (e.g. *weilen*, *eilen*, *verweilen*, *Weile*; *Verfehlten*, *Fehl*, *fehlen*, *Verfehlung*) is crucial to the syntactic and semantic development of Hamacher's argument. This has a twofold advantage. First, by avoiding the creation of new words where Hamacher himself did not do so in the German, one avoids giving the impression that Hamacher wrote or thought in a rarified language, or indeed a language that would have policed a categorical distinction between academic German and the German of the everyday. Not only do such boundaries produce a false dichotomy that reproduces a type of esotericism belonging to a period of German philology with which Hamacher did not identify, but the flipside of such a dichotomy is a crass materialism that Hamacher did not condone. And second, fluency allows me to capture, as well as one can do this in translation, one of the key traits of Hamacher's writing: its rhythm. Hamacher valued above all the ability of translations of his work to capture its rhythmic quality, its spatial figures, its pauses and breaks, and its openness to allowing the sense of his interpretations to unfurl from the propensity of words to curl, bend, or stretch themselves of their own accord to the point of defamiliarization. "Version of Meaning" is a very early example of what would become far more pronounced in his later essays, but the hope is that this translation nevertheless registers an incipient step in this direction.

—Julia Ng, Goldsmiths, University of London

Published more than 30 years later in the *Hölderlin-Jahrbuch*, "Parousia, Stone-Walls: Mediacy and Temporality, Late Hölderlin" presents the translator with challenges that are continuous with, but also somewhat different from, those of the master's thesis. While I too have sought to bring out the rhythms—and counter-rhythms—of the text and have valued readability, I also found that in order to capture the dynamics of Hamacher's language, I had to submit, at least to a degree, to tendencies that forced the translation in a different direction. German allows a more intensive, inward-turned, hermetic mode of expression than is usually possible in English. Eschewing referential value for systematic value, cognate words form a constellation whose meaning develops in reciprocal engagement. Hamacher's essay utilizes this tendency with a singular virtuosity, resulting in sentences like the following—well-formed, beguilingly classical and luminous, rigorous in their reasoning, yet utterly disorienting: "*Halt, Haltung, Erhaltung*—support, bearing, maintenance—are gained by evasion [*Ausweichen*]: by a lateral movement of likening and transition, by a diversion [*Abwendung*] that displaces consciousness, soul, and spirit *next* to themselves and into the field of crude externality, thus making possible their encounter with themselves in this sideways way [*in diesem Seitwärts*]" (155). Nearly every word here finds its meaning—its support, bearing, and maintenance—outside of itself, in a circuit of meaning that wends its way not only through Hamacher's essay but also through Hölderlin's poetic oeuvre and the broader intellectual-historical context. Indeed, the intensive rather than extensive, almost solipsistic tendency of philosophical German—the promise of a language that, built from its own atomic elements, would offer a perfectly expressive conduit for meaning—is brought to the point where it turns back against itself, betrays itself, and becomes exposed to an intractable residue.

The German *abwenden*, literally a "turning away," is itself formed from the combination of *wenden*—"to turn"—and the prefix *ab*, the equivalent of the Latin *a/ab* and the Greek *apo*. Here at least English, by way of Latin, seems to offer a literal equivalent in "aversion," and yet, for reasons that are hard to pin down—it is precisely with these molecular incongruences that translation runs up against the intrigues of language—"aversion" does not quite work. It too much suggests an apotropaic movement, a logic of avoidance, of warding off disaster, of the magical incantations of phobic affects, rather than a simple turning away from the path that should have been. *Abwendung*, aversion, is, as it were, averted from itself: from the *straight*, "literally correct" path: the literal, literally, becomes a diversion.

Abwendung, moreover, turns in multiple directions, starting out from the two roots of which it is composed. On the one hand, it evokes a number of words that are cognate to it through *wenden* and yet whose semantic connection is not always obvious. These include not only *Rückwendung* ("turning back") but also *notwendig* ("necessary," but literally "need-turning," what's needed to turn away the need of the moment) and, indeed, *verwandt* ("related") and *verwandelt* ("transformed"). And, perhaps not least of all, *Wände* ("walls"), as in the striking formulation: "Nothing winds along these walls [*Nichts wendet sich an diesen Wänden*]" (162). Hamacher's essay thus reveals itself as being full not only of twists and turns but of turns that, turning away, diverted from their more literal turning, converge, transformed, in a new way of thinking the relation of meanings and of what it might mean for words to be *cognate*. Nothing less is at stake, indeed, than a new sense of the natal, the genetic—and hence also, to use Hölderlin's own word, the "national." All this turns on the question of time: it is the question of the generation of time, of the generation of the horizon in which generation itself is possible. The structure of time, in its genesis, is diversionary: the "faithless" diversion of time from time.

The root *wenden* turns in one direction; *ab* turns in another—branching out into a slew of words that share this prefix: *abbrechen* ("break off"), *abgeschlossen* ("closed"), *abgetrennt* ("detached"), *abgestorben* ("obsolete"), *abheben* ("set in relief to"), *Abirrung* ("aberrance"), *Abschied* ("leavetaking"), *absehen* ("disregard"), *absonderlich* ("peculiar"), *absterben* ("die off"). Here, alas, the translator must renounce all hope of preserving the semblance of etymological connection: the English language takes its own paths. More significant, though, than the mere existence of this new series of related words is how Hamacher's essay, through this accumulation of affinities—of word turned to word—brings the prefix to the point where its sense becomes detached from that of the roots to which, in the ordinary and prosaic operation of language, it remains subordinate. The *ab* is itself diverted, detached, divorced from *wenden*, and yet if this divorce annihilates the faith that words could have a literal meaning ultimately grounded in a reference to objects—that meaning can be reduced to extension—it also, oddly and ironically, sunders the word into two parts that in fact, in their molecular isolation, belong together more intimately than ever before. For indeed, both *wenden* and *ab* converge in the lateral gesture, the "sideways way," that is the way of space, time, language, and being.

There is also, speaking in broad strokes, a third turn that things take. The branches of meaning do not remain restricted to literal cognates and immediate resemblances. A further order of associations comes into play. These belong to translation, which itself, as the translation of the German word *Übersetzung* recalls, hinges on a law of *lateral* displacement. Consider, for example, *Abwendung*: *Wende* translates as "verse," "trope," "strophe." Thus it elicits the matter of poetry and poetic language in the most general—universal or categorical—sense. Hamacher's essay, recalling the title ("Version of Meaning") with which he will rechristen his master's thesis, reveals itself as not just an extended if tacit commentary on Heidegger's claim that Hölderlin is the "poet of poets" but an attempt to descry where this insight might have led had Heidegger not insisted on thinking poetry as *Dichtung*, *dictare*—a phatic world-founding saying—rather than as "mere" verse.

"Parousia, Stone-Walls" is free of polemics and never directly confronts the myth, still promoted by Heidegger, of Hölderlin as a prophet-poet. Yet there is at least one point, indeed at the apex of the essay's rhetoric, where, with incomparable understated precision, it brings the myth of Hölderlin as *vates* and as father to a new Germany to ruin. Regarding the poem "Half of Life," Hamacher writes:

> And in the verses, 'The stonewalls stand / Speechless and cold, in the wind / The weathervanes [*Fahnen*] clang,' the winter of this caesura stands still: the 'stone-walls' stand therein as a crude fact of time and language standing and standing still. In them nothing else is said than that only a cold wind remains of the 'living breath' of communication (StA 6: 184). Of the pronoun *you* in 'you lovely swans' and 'you dip' only a *clanging* remains; of the poetic *swan* and its doubling in the lake only *vanes*, a '*nefas*' (StA 5: 197; StA 4: 150)—not echoes, still less remembrances, only shrill relics, traces, distorted residues. (161)

The caesura, the counter-rhythmic interruption, turns itself to winter, a winter that stands still in the complete destitution of the "living breath" of communication; indeed of any sort of prophetic order, which, so Hamacher writes a little earlier, could "still mediate between past, present, and future, between world and language, between language and itself." Poetic language has turned to "relics, traces, distorted residues." This strange and catastrophic turn of events is, moreover, orchestrated through one word in particular, the *Fahnen*—not flags, but weathervanes. Throughout his poetry, the various winds of the earth—the very idea of a wind—entangles the spatial, the temporal, and the linguistic; the physical and the spiritual, movement and stasis are invested with meaning. Winds are winds of history. And hence one may suppose that the weathervane is itself a figure for a prophetic apparatus. Here, though, the *vanes*, which could (through a doubtless false etymology) evoke a *vates*, yield, in a gesture at once perfectly inexplicable and perfectly justified, to a *nefas*—to the ineffable, to that which refuses speech, or is forbidden to speech. What allows this to happen is perhaps only the fact that, amidst the stonewalls' menacing silence, the weathervane, rather than being liberated by the enveloping silence to its proper and authentic prophetic speech, becomes a mere clanging. Not just the mere sound of the word, but its noisy distortion.

This essay's way is, for the most part, not the way of neologisms and extravagant invention. By promising a better language, the neologism remains within the order of approximation. Instead, Hamacher intensifies the ordinary modes of signification, bringing these to the point of shattering. His more violent interventions, as seen, often take the form of breaking a word apart—dislodging the preface or root, letting it turn against the intention of the word to which it belongs. In a few instances, though, he does something more—or less: exposing the word to an almost imperceptible deviation. This is the case with *Veranderung*, *Selbstveranderung*. These would be perfectly normal words, were it not for the missing umlauts. They should read *Veränderung*, *Selbstveränderung*—"alteration," "self-alteration." This microscopic diversion—the word for "alteration" itself being altered, as though the word for alteration or indeed self-alteration could not quite remain faithful to itself—turns out a word that will capture the most basic gesture of Hamacher's essay. Not only does it evoke a proximity between "alteration" and *Wanderung*, "wandering," the errant movement of a river, the pedesis of language, but it redoubles on the peculiarity of the German *ver-*, which, while analogous to the Greek *para-* as well as *pro-*, seems to pervert their straightforward spatial metaphorics and in this way, in an oblique move, turns the self not against, but to the side of itself. I was almost tempted to leave *Veranderung* untranslated—yet another ghastly residue. Instead, I took the liberty of rendering it as "dissamblance," (130, 135), bringing together "semblance" and the echo of "amblance" in "ambulation," seeming and walking, into a passing disarray. I will leave the reader to judge whether this liberty, the "necessary arbitrariness" of the translator, can justify itself.

—Anthony Curtis Adler, Yonsei University

Acknowledgments

The editors are grateful, above all, to Werner Hamacher, who, shortly before his death, granted permission to publish a translation of his master's thesis. In addition to providing auxiliary documents concerning Hamacher's plans to revise his thesis, Shinu Sara Ottenburger, the executor of Hamacher's literary estate, supported our expansion of the volume to include "Parousia, Stone-Walls." Sabine Doering, president of the Hölderlin Society, granted us permission to publish a translation of this essay, which first appeared in the society's literary journal. Eva Geulen, Director of the Leibniz-Zentrum für Literatur- und Kulturforschung (ZfL), provided one of the copies of the master's essay used for the production of this volume. Irene Albers, professor of romance philology and comparative literature at the Peter Szondi Institute (Berlin), who sent us numerous pages from another copy of the master's essay, generously provided otherwise unavailable information and documentation concerning its provenance. Dr. Robert Zwarg promptly responded to our urgent requests concerning Hamacher's papers in the Deutsches Literaturarchiv in Marbach. Members of the Special Collections of the University of California, Irvine Libraries made available five letters that Hamacher sent to Paul de Man between 1974 and 1978. We thank Jonas Rosenbrück for preparing the index.

Beyond thanking Susannah Gottlieb, Inbo Gottlieb-Fenves, and Zoli Gottlieb-Fenves for their assistance and patience, Peter Fenves would especially like to thank Ursula Rütt-Hamacher for authenticating the handwritten title of the thesis as well as Sophie Hamacher and Johannes Hamacher for facilitating communication with their father. Julia Ng would like to extend thanks to Herbert Kopp-Oberstebrink of the ZfL, who generously provided information concerning Hamacher that was preserved in the Jacob Taubes archive there, as well as to Markus Hardtmann, whose insight and counsel made for an altogether better translation. Anthony Curtis Adler is grateful to Barbara Natalie Nagel and Daniel Hoffman-Schwartz for their insight regarding several intractable passages and to his wife, Hwa Young Seo, for her support throughout.

List of Abbreviations and Note on Citations

F	Fichte, Johann Gottlob. *Sämmtliche Werke*. Ed. Immanuel Hermann Fichte. 8 vols. Berlin: de Gruyter, 1971.
SK	———. *The Science of Knowledge (Wissenschaftslehre).* Ed. Peter Heath and John Lachs. Cambridge: Cambridge University Press, 1982.
EL	Hölderlin, Friedrich. *Essays and Letters*. Ed. and trans. by Jeremy Adler and Charlie Louth. London: Penguin, 2009.
HS	———. *Hölderlin's Sophocles: "Oedipus" and "Antigone."* Ed. and trans. David Constantine. Hexham, UK, 2001.
HSP	———. *Hyperion and Selected Poems*. Ed. Eric Santner. Trans. Richard Sieburth. New York: Continuum, 1990.
PF	———. *Poems and Fragments*. Ed. and trans. Michael Hamburger. 4th edition. Manchester: Carcanet Press, 2017.
StA	———. *Sämtliche Werke.* Ed. Friedrich Beißner. 7 vols. Stuttgart: Kohlhammer, 1943–1985.
A for 1781 edition B for 1787 edition	Kant, Immanuel. *Kritik der reinen Vernunft*, reprinted in vols. 3 and 4 of Kant, *Werkausgabe*. Ed. Wilhelm Weischedel. 12 vol. Wiesbaden: Insel Verlag, 1960; *Critique of Pure Reason*. Trans. Paul Guyer and Allen Wood. Cambridge: Cambridge University Press, 1998.
S	Schiller, Friedrich. *Werke*. Frankfurt am Main: Insel Verlag, 1966.

Whenever parenthetical references to German texts are not followed by references to English editions of Hölderlin's work, translations are the work of Julia Ng ("Version of Meaning") or Anthony Curtis Adler ("Parousia, Stone-Walls"). Modifications of published translations are indicated by "mod." Julia Ng's translation of the "third version" of "Der Einzige" (The Only One), as reconstructed by Friedrich Beissner for the Stuttgart edition of Hölderlin's writings, appears as an Appendix and is used throughout the volume.

TWO STUDIES OF FRIEDRICH HÖLDERLIN

Introduction

Versing, Ending: Hölderlin in 1971

est-ce commencer par la fin?
—Mallarmé

tō tósō ónoma bíos, érgon dè thánatos
—Heraclitus

A book is a totality that begins with an author—it closes, however, not with the end of the book as the conception of the author but with the death of death. This was the thesis of a short article composed around January 1968 and later published under the title "Culture et écriture: la prolifération des livres et la fin du livre" (Culture and writing: the proliferation of books and the end of the book) in the journal *Noroit*, in which Jacques Derrida sought to apply some of the insights from his recently published work, *Of Grammatology*, to a question opened up by contemporary information science: what becomes of death after the closure of the Book of Life?[1] Prompted in part by the discovery that life writes itself, as it were, in cell DNA and in cybernetic programs, at a scale impossible to comprehend for any given individual, Derrida wonders whether the exhaustion of the idea of a divinely authored nature implies that our capacity to bring things to an end has also exhausted itself. Perhaps the very concept of ending must come to an end and with it end the notion that the end of presence is the end of life as such; never before, Derrida writes, has it been more apparent that systems organized around presence, and around "alphabetic" cultures, behave as modes of domination and exclusion aimed at all that is deemed "analphabetic"—not just the masses of humankind who have no access to literacy but also those whose languages fall outside of "phonetic" systems. In *Of Grammatology*, Derrida identifies logocentrism as an ethnocentrism organized around the metaphysics of phonocentrism; in "Culture and Writing" he describes how phonocentrism, like a book, presumes a temporal and linear totality of spoken discourse such that, insofar as it expects to be read and understood as the reflection of the living word of a living author, it also presupposes an adequation or *homoisis* of present reality and represented reality, of the thing in itself and the thought of the thing.[2] In *Of Grammatology*, attention to the graphic, hieroglyphic supplements to signification present a challenge to this model. In "Culture and Writing," this challenge is presented by *l'outre-livre*, the Mallarméan idea that the book should have its leaves unbound and emerge, in each *séance* of their rearrangement and reading, as a book anew. The *outre-livre* is, in the words of Mallarmé, an "Orphic explication of the earth."[3] Its rhythm, impersonal and therefore living, is a trace of interruption from within the philosophical, logical, theological domination that perpetuates itself through forms of reproduction or inheritance held together in the name of the father. In other words, the end of the Book reveals another end of the book, one that discloses from a non-presentist, non-expressive place the possibility still of bringing things to an end.

A version of this thesis—that the end of the book is the death of patronymity—was also the topic of a guest session Derrida led in the summer semester of 1968 at the Department for General and Comparative Literary Studies (Seminar für Allgemeine und Vergleichende Literaturwissenschaft, AVL), founded three years earlier by Peter Szondi at the Freie Universität Berlin. The department had been conceived with an expressly anti-nationalistic intention against a background of what some would remember as shame at the role played by German philology under fascism, which *Germanistik* had yet to fully, or indeed even begin to, work through by the mid-1960s.[4] Unlike his counterparts in *Germanistik*, Szondi had a network that consisted mainly of exiled scholars who were outside Germany and had access to other traditions of literary criticism and theory, in particular comparative literary studies at Yale and the aesthetic theory of the Frankfurt School. His research seminar reflected this international orientation, frequently hosting guest lecturers from the United States, France, and Switzerland. Those who attended remembered it as a space for theoretical experimentation unencumbered by the territoriality and hierarchy they saw as typical of national literatures. Derrida's aforementioned visit to the department, his first, took place in early July of 1968 and was devoted to "the end of the book" and related themes in Mallarmé; he returned a year later, in the summer of 1969, to lead a colloquium on the topic of "the concept of mimesis in two passages from Plato's *Philebus* and Mallarmé's *Mimique*." These visits to AVL were, in effect, the introduction of Derrida and poststructuralist theory to Germany and German-language literary studies.[5]

Szondi's project of pushing the boundaries of what was deemed acceptable for literary studies appealed to students and younger colleagues who were interested in the work of contemporary French philosophers, particularly Derrida. One of these students was Werner Hamacher, who had entered the department in 1967.[6] It was here that Hamacher composed his first extended scholarly work, initially entitled "Bild und Zeichen in der späten Lyrik Hölderlins" (Image and sign in Hölderlin's late lyric poetry), which he submitted to the Freie Universität Berlin as his master's thesis in December 1971. Hamacher's choice of topic may have reflected his expectation that its evaluator or even its supervisor would be Szondi, who had recently published *Hölderlin-Studien*.[7] But above all, in 1971, Hölderlin was perhaps the most fitting topic for anyone to have selected who thought at all about hastening the death of patronymity from its interior. The revival of interest in Hölderlin, which had begun half a century earlier with Norbert von Hellingrath's establishment of the first historical-critical edition of his works and his discovery of the then unpublished and unknown poetry from Hölderlin's "late" period, had been accompanied from the outset by the admonition that these hymns and fragments, far from being the products of an unwell mind, in fact contained the most significant of his technical and conceptual achievements—that is, if one possessed the key to their intelligibility. In a lecture that he gave in Munich in 1915, a year before his death at Verdun, Hellingrath specified where this key was kept: it was an "innermost ember" embedded in the "deepest" level of the "German essence." Hölderlin, whom Hellingrath described as "the most German of Germans," produced hymns whose hidden message was entrusted "only to a select few," would only "come to the light of day in a secret Germany," and was destined to remain "perhaps never penetrable by non-Germans."[8]

The extent to which this George-School paradigm of Hölderlin as the "pure" poet, to whose will and mystery acolytes surrendered themselves, persisted even after the two world wars can be measured by the furor that ensued following Pierre Bertaux's address to the annual meeting of the Hölderlin Society in 1968, convened on the occasion of the 125th anniversary of Hölderlin's death. In his lecture on "Hölderlin and the French Revolution," Bertaux not only advanced the thesis "that Hölderlin, in his heart of hearts, was and always remained an enthusiastic supporter of the French Revolution and a Jacobin"—a point that was, in itself and as Bertaux himself admits, uncontroversial, having been made by various scholars before him and being evident from Hölderlin's correspondence.[9] Bertaux, a professor at the Nouvelle Sorbonne who had once been told that no Frenchman could hope to comprehend Hölderlin, started out by addressing his audience of listeners in Düsseldorf, who themselves had spent lifetimes studying Hölderlin, with an inversion of Hellingrath's dictum: it was not the Germans who held the key to understanding "the most German of German poets" but the French. "What can a German understand of Hölderlin," he asked, if Germans "lacked the one prerequisite" for doing so, namely a "visceral familiarity with the history of the French Revolution and with the revolutionary pathos that the French possess"?[10] The address, which immediately provoked heated discussions during and after the conference and captured the attention of the press for a long while afterwards, was a self-conscious parallel action to the efforts made by the May 1968 student movement in Germany to seek in Hölderlin a legitimizing standard-bearer for their own struggle against the reactionary forces of capitalism. For those looking to Hölderlin for an exemplary revolutionary hero, both his "poetry" and his "madness" were, as manifestations of the disequilibrium between thought and action, encoded modes of resistance that immediately translated poetics into praxis.

Similarly, Bertaux argued, one finds the intention for such a translation in the opening lines of "Stimme des Volkes" (Voice of the people). In the verses "The voice of God I called you and believed you once, / In holy youth; and still I say it!" (StA 2: 51; PF, 239, mod.), the "you," according to Bertaux, evidently refers to the "voice of the people," which the poet immediately identifies with the "voice of God" in an expression of enthusiasm that would only have been shared by the Jacobins and for the new republican ideas of freedom, equality, and fraternity.[11] The simplicity of this expression, so Bertaux, only enhances the sense that Hölderlin was by temperament "freely born," the "arcadian" and "archaic" character of his ideal an indication that he, like all successors of Rousseau, was "internally ready for action, and was just never presented with the right opportunity."[12] Citing Hellingrath on the inseparability of Hölderlin's life and works—for Hölderlin, there was but one world, in which "poetry is reflection . . . , a mirror image of the times and of the nature of things"—Bertaux interpreted various excerpts from the poetry in toto as a manifesto of Hölderlin's political convictions and hopes for a Swabian republic circa 1799.[13] Correspondingly, Bertaux took the existence of a "late" period of Hölderlin's poetry not as evidence of a psychopathological breakdown but as a reaction to the "turning point" of 16 March 1799, when General Jean-Baptiste Jourdan declared that the French Revolutionary Army would quell rather than support the republican insurgency then brewing in Swabia. From this point on, Hölderlin turned towards articulating a new lyrical form that corresponded with his sense of living under enemy rule; the lyrical-mythical characteristic of his "late" poetry became the form in which the poet felt he could encode and conceal his political message and preserve it for future generations—or for the secret friend in possession of the interpretive key, Isaac von Sinclair. Later, in his 1978 biography, Bertaux would go as far as to argue that Hölderlin feigned insanity in order to escape arrest for his alleged involvement in the Sinclair plot.[14]

Bertaux's inadvertent restaging of the aesthetic ideology of the "secret Germany" of the 1910s inspired a brief but significant episode of left-wing popularization that unsettled the monopoly that the "establishment"—or, more precisely, the Hölderlin Society—had held over Hölderlin reception since its founding under "Reichsminister Dr. Goebbels" in 1943.[15] This was nowhere more apparent than during the celebrations of Hölderlin's two-hundredth birthday two years later, in 1970, when Hölderlin seemed to fully reemerge as the "leader" of the people, albeit a people that vocalized its discontent with the "reactionary falsification" of Hölderlin at the hands of the Hölderlin Society and its National Socialist remainders in ways that were ever more direct, both within and beyond the confines of the society.[16] The publication of Bertaux's talk in the *Hölderlin-Jahrbuch* and, in extended book form, with Suhrkamp in 1969 had paved the way for open debates on Hölderlin's politics; as the summary of the discussion published in the 1967/68 volume of the *Jahrbuch* already attested, it was time for "Hölderlin interpretation and therefore the Hölderlin Society's self-understanding [to] enter a critical phase requiring methodical reflection."[17] Bernhard Böschenstein, who had written his dissertation on the "Rhine" hymn (whose apostrophe to Sinclair Bertaux had interpreted as evidence of a surreptitious call to arms[18]) and who by 1967 had become one of the editors of the *Hölderlin-Jahrbuch*, noted that after the shock delivered by Bertaux's address, "it has become necessary for German Hölderlin research to recall its failures, the correction of which would fall upon the shoulders of younger generations."[19] And in 1970, it was a young Martin Walser, who had studied under Friedrich Beissner and had communist inclinations at the time, who delivered the keynote, which was eventually published under the title "Hölderlin zu entsprechen" (Corresponding to Hölderlin). Distancing himself somewhat from Bertaux's polemical shorthand, Walser was careful to cast Hölderlin as a mediator, "singing, on the side of the revolution, no doubt, but singing."[20] Nevertheless, he thereby also recast Hölderlin as a future-oriented thinker in a time of stagnation, whose role it was to mediate, by way of "harmonic opposition" [*harmonische Entgegensetzung*],[21] the presence of an alternative precisely where opposite parties caught up in a stalemate had brought the historical process itself to an end.[22]

Walser's lecture closed on the notion that, for Hölderlin, it is anathema to hold that mastering a goal is synonymous with arriving at the end of history; he pointed out, referring to a verse from Hölderlin's "Celebration of Peace," that instead history moves in the direction of a "now [where] / Dominion [is] nowhere to be seen among spirits or mortals"[23] (PF 525). Certainly, neither spirits nor mortals could have been said to hold dominion over the other the day before Walser's address, when, on March 20 1970, a group calling itself the "secret tübingen jacobin club" gathered at Hölderlin's grave site for a parallel commemoration of his birth. Attired in red Jacobin caps with tricolor cockades, the participants laid a wreath made of barbed wire on the grave, dedicating it "to the suppressed revolutionary." Displayed across a banner was a quote from "Empedocles": "You can't be helped / If you won't help yourselves."[24] Speeches were delivered calling for the "liberation" of Hölderlin from the "claws of the reactionaries" and drawing parallels between Hölderlin and Marx. In the wake of these two events—Walser's address and the graveside action—that both, to varying degrees, defied the "establishment," Hölderlin also emerged as a figure in public life; in the months that followed, the Deutsche Akademie der Wissenschaft, the Deutsche Akademie der Künste, the Deutsches Nationaltheater in Weimar, and the Schiller-Nationalmuseum in Marbach all convened events at which Hölderlin's "anticipatory capacity" for the "overcoming of the theory-praxis relation through art" was proclaimed, by and on behalf of not only scholars but also poets and cultural functionaries.[25] By 1971, "Hölderlin" was thus well on his way to becoming a pop-cultural, albeit short-lived, icon of the post-68 generation; beyond that, Hölderlin's model of "harmonic opposition," hitherto regarded purely as the organizational foundation for his poetology, now redefined his poetry as the horizon for thinking, and mediating, the advent of another state.

In the third of the essays collected in his *Hölderlin-Studien*, "Überwindung des Klassizismus" ("Hölderlin's Overcoming of Classicism"), Szondi, too, had invoked "harmonic opposition" as the "tension" to which "spirit" had to become adequate by maintaining a mediating "elasticity" towards the foreign.[26] Walser, however, dismissed Szondi's "interlinear mumbling" for downplaying Hölderlin's appeal for social-historical transformation,[27] while Bertaux did not refer to Szondi except to suggest that what Szondi identified as the "extreme precision and thoroughly thought-through character of Hölderlin's use of language"[28] allowed for "each word of the poet [to be grasped] in its full meaning, full content and [full] seriousness" as a "testimony" [*Aussage*] to his presence of mind.[29] Bertaux finds a synonym for this hearing-grasping of the word in the verb *horchen*, "listening to," which is related to *gehorchen*, the "listening to" by virtue of which one submits to the will of a higher authority, and which Bertaux uses to translate the "listening to [*akoúsantes*]" with respect to the *logos* that Heraclitus, Hölderlin's "master," exhorts his addressee to do: "listen not to me, but to the *logos*" (*ouk emou, allà tou lógou akoúsantes*),[30] he writes in Fragment B50, and "say, in agreement with the *logos*, that all things are one" (*homologein . . . hèn pánta einai*).[31] Thus, for Bertaux, there is no doubt that the fragment "Das untergehende Vaterland" (The declining fatherland), to which the editors of the Stuttgarter Ausgabe gave the title "Das Werden im Vergehen" (Becoming in passing away), and which is ostensibly about a poetic problem (namely, the artistic imitation of dissolution in lyric, epic, and tragic forms), has as its "actual object . . . a dialectical analysis of the situation of a society in the transitional period between one and another determinate shape."[32] During this "transition" [*Übergang*], Hölderlin writes, "spirit and sign" are a "harmonically opposed one" (StA 4: 286; EL 275, mod.); for Bertaux, this further reference to Heraclitus—to Fragment B51, which describes "how a thing at variance agrees with itself [as] a harmonic turning back, like that of a bow or lyre" (*hokōs diapherómenon heōutō homologéei; palíntropos harmoníē hokōsper tósou kaì lúrēs*)[33]—describes in nuce the law of the Hegelian dialectic.[34] This law, however, which also determined the "decline of the fatherland," was one that Germans were destined to feel with "fear" because, from the post-1799 perspective, they had failed to apprehend national decline as the moment in which "the possible enters reality"[35]—the possibility of *patrie*, which is reserved for the free.

Szondi, though, had insisted on the centrality of the "mediation of oppositions" for Hölderlin's conception of the "free use of that which is one's own" (StA 6: 426; EL 208, mod.) in order to show that, contrary to the image perpetuated of Hölderlin after 1918—as "law-giver of Germanness" (however concealed), as bound by national duty to give himself up to "beautiful passion"[36]—Hölderlin was precisely not "the poet who writes as he must write, having submitted to his personal and historical mission."[37] This image had more recently been perpetuated by Martin Heidegger and Beda Allemann, who, for Szondi, also fail to recognize the nuances of language that distance the poet from the poetry and so distort Hölderlin's careful separation of the national from its origins into a nationalism yearning for realization. Allemann, who was Heidegger's disciple, saw in Hölderlin's letter to Böhlendorff from December 1801, in which he famously outlines his poetology in terms of a philosophy of history, the affirmation that "occidental man must turn back [*zurückbiegen*] in the direction of his proper element, sobriety"[38]—a "turning back" that is not contained in the letter, which nowhere speaks of either an "occidental turn" nor a "return to the fatherland," but is, rather, beholden to Heidegger's notion of Hölderlin's *Kehre* away from metaphysics,[39] which in turn has its counterpart in Heidegger's 1951 remarks on Heraclitus's Fragment B50.[40] There, Heidegger gives a translation of "listening to the *logos*," *allà tou lógou akoúsantes*, as "*aber seid horchsam der lesenden Lege*"[41] by inventing the word *horchsam*, or "being in the mode of listening-obeying," for *akoúsantes*, in order to denote the relation to a "law" that, in his commentary on "Remembrance" [*Andenken*], determines a "right direction" for the poet: the "return to what is proper to one, a return that can only be made as a journey out into what is foreign" but "remains turned toward the homeland."[42] Allemann's *zurückbiegen*, which can mean both "turning back" and the "bending back" of a bow—as can the word *palíntropos*—likewise misconstrues "harmonic opposition" as obedience to a law of return, understood as the appropriation of "one's own" at the expense of the foreign. For Szondi, however, conceiving of *palíntropos harmoníē* as return obscures the most important fact of all: that for Hölderlin, there was no certainty at all of returning to a primal or pre-existing homeland. What is one's own must equally be "learned" and is the "hardest part"; in fact, Hölderlin predicts that, eventually, "the properly national will become ever more the lesser virtue" by which the poet might attempt to surpass the Greeks.[43]

In other words, unlike the critics against whom he sets himself, Szondi seeks to establish an image of Hölderlin that cannot be reduced to the tendency to turn against the foreigner in order to recover a pre-existing permanence in the progression towards a future. Rather than being the poet-leader who is *horchsam* to a law of "patriotic reversal" and amplifies the authoritarian confidence with which his critics have exploited him for the sake of the historical moment, Szondi's Hölderlin is "anxious" about how he stands up to the achievements of the ancients—and is, in that precise sense, modern.[44] Szondi thus seeks out other forms of "harmonic opposition" to account for this "anxiety" and the necessary "elasticity" of the mind with respect to the manifold—a "harmonic opposition" conceived not as law, but as jointure, in the sense of one of the meanings of *harmoníē*—which would then also do away with the presumption that literary reality stands in an a priori relation of adequation with historical reality. For this, Szondi turns in the first instance to Adorno, whose criticism of Heidegger's racially inflected treatment of the "foreign" in the poem "Remembrance" he calls upon in support of his argument that the Hesperian poet encounters his own proper origin as a foreign element, only thereby gaining "freedom," which is distance from his origin.[45] In another, later essay from *Hölderlin-Studien* entitled "Gattungspoetik und Geschichtsphilosophie" (Poetics of genre and philosophy of history), Szondi again calls upon Adorno in an analysis of the alternation of tones that also culminates in an interpretation of the letter to Böhlendorff. "Parataxis," which Adorno retrieves from Hellingrath's description of the *harte Fügung* (hard jointure, or *harmoníē austērâ*) that is characteristic of Pindar's style, describes how the late hymns' structure of reciprocal tonal dissolution points to a philosophy of history beyond even that of the Böhlendorff letter, one that does not aim at the mirror symmetry between ancient and modern nor at the appropriation of the foreign element but is instead based precisely on the failure to hit those targets.[46]

Parataxis—the "formation of a flowing continuum of images" on the basis of the "autonomy of . . . metaphors with regard to what they signify," the "inversions of periods" and then "the logic of [such] tightly bound periods, one following on the next, . . . characterized by [a] compulsive and violent quality for which poetry is to provide healing and which Hölderlin's poetry unambiguously negates"[47]—is how, for Adorno, Benjamin also understood the structure characteristic of the late poems in relation to the philosophy of history contained in them: as Benjamin writes, "human beings, heavenly ones and princes—crashing down from their old orders, as it were—are linked in a series to one another [*zueinander gereiht*]."[48] Benjamin's *Zueinanderreihung*, which he also describes as "intensive interpenetration" [*intensive Durchdringung*] and "violent belonging" [*gewaltige Zugehörigkeit*], is a function of an "infinite chain of series in which the poetized [*das Gedichtete*]," the synthetic unity of intellectual and perceptual orders towards which the poem tends, "unfolds."[49] It is this "series" that is infinitely expansive or contractive and in which the structure of relations, but not the identity of individuals, can be grasped that Szondi describes, citing a late Hölderlinian hymnic fragment, as "the apriority of the individual over the whole."[50] Thus also the "thoroughly thought-through character" [*Durchdachtheit*], with which Szondi describes Hölderlin's poetry overall in his earlier essay on "Celebration of Peace,"[51] does not indicate the adequation of the subject's intention to a reality encoded in the poem nor even the identifiability of the one who is named "the prince of the festival" within the mythopoetic universe; rather, it suggests that the curve of the bow that is traced by "opposition" or "turning back," the *palíntropos* determining the course of history, is anything but the shortest distance between two points and is not fixed in direction, shape, or extent. It is, in a word, "elastic," and it is this "elasticity," in which the poet's intention must be abandoned and the legislating subject sacrificed, that makes Hölderlin a modern poet who has more in common with Mallarmé than with Goethe or George.

Hamacher's master's thesis opens with a methodological statement that, by and large, follows Szondi's lead: it discusses how *not* to read Hölderlin. Within the first few pages, Hamacher lays out much of the same terrain in which Szondi's *Hölderlin-Studien* moves: existing literary scholarship, he writes, has mobilized parts of Hölderlin's poetology to "legitimate the claim that the late lyric poetry exhibits a consistency of meaning" (20), a consistency that presumes that texts refer to a "transcendent meaning" that is consistent in itself, is knowable, and offers itself wholly and unambiguously to the interpreter in the poetry. Hamacher cites Szondi's "Poetics of genre and philosophy of history" for its characterization of the "late poetry" as containing, in whatever form, a "theory of Hesperian reversal," but he also refers to the obverse of the image promoted by the entire tradition of Hölderlin reception from Hellingrath to Bertaux when he dismisses the project of "emphasizing . . . e.g. the monographic intentions of a politically engaged writer" at the expense of the "textuality" of the poetry. Thus, first, the "late lyric poetry" is a contested category for Hamacher; the divination of a political "intention" in it relies on a contrivance of its adherence to certain logical connections—the "law of synthesis," notably, which lends to the poetics the character of a "theory of reversal." Second, however, the "late lyric poetry" is in fact "based on the subversion of logic," such that the only way in which it might nevertheless express any sort of synthetic unity is by abdicating its very claim to synthetic unity. Even "Voice of the People"—the very poem in which Bertaux contrives an identity between *vox populi* and *vox dei* by suggesting that the poet expresses sentiments only Jacobins would have shared—presents such a difficulty, for in it the correspondence established between the voice of the people and the voice of God is linked to an element (the "rushing" of the rivers) that is not also linked to the "I say" of the poet (21). Thus, in fact, "adequation" between gods and human beings is presented here as being in decline; where there is adequation there is also doubt; and these two routes of the poem, adequation and doubt, distort one another, frustrating the path of logical distinction; at the very point where logification finds articulation in the poem through the yearning for identity, the movement of that very yearning pulls autonomy, self, and its telos "toward the abyss" (StA 2:51; PF 239, mod.; 23). This "unbound," the place where alone the identity of voice, saying, and logical structuration is to realize their identity, is itself "the product of their reciprocal distortion" (23). Thus, as Adorno pointed out, Hölderlin's language presents an "affront to Idealism's doctrine of the substantiality of meaning."[52] Even the shortest route that the voice might take, the route between its process of signification and what it signifies, is deferred and distorted, paratactically, by the very process of synthesis, and synthesis itself is never attained.

Yet the debt to Szondi and Adorno is not without qualification. In his treatment of "Celebration of Peace," Szondi demurred at identifying the "prince of the festival," arguing instead that the poem follows the course of an epiphany and that "God appears of his own accord in the poem."[53] Hamacher directs a highly critical footnote at this notion that the appearance of God might occur "in" the poem rather than as a fictional contrivance of the poet; in fact, he argues, nothing about the celebration in "Celebration of Peace" lends itself to any such semantic associations with revelation or manifestation of being as "epiphany" might suggest, since the "festival" at which gods and mortals gather in the poem, far from being a moment of plenitude and presence, is in fact "structured by the delimitations of immediate presence and by obstructions introduced through the intervention of death" (38). Similarly, Adorno fails, in conceiving of parataxis as a "flowing continuum of images" capable of linking gods and humans, to capture the interruptive, distorting figure of Hölderlin's syntax, whose movements "evade" the linearity of any one form (43). No presence is uninterrupted by absence, no appearance uncloaked by the "doom" (38) of death, and therefore no appearance, in either the historical or the natural world, is subsumable under the concept of self-generation or progression towards an identity; rather, the structure of history is determined by these obstructions to vision and will. At one point, Hamacher notes that this Hölderlin, who conceives of "the relation between mortals and immortals [as] withdraw[ing] from every attempt at a synthesis," is "not so much . . . the student and friend of contemporaneous dialecticians as . . . someone familiar with pre-Socratic philosophy, particularly that of Heraclitus" (36). Hamacher cites Fragment 62 to illustrate this ("Immortals are mortal, mortals immortal, living one another's death, dying in one another's life"[54]), though he remarks that even this paradox tends too much to "reconcile opposites in a circular process" (37) to fully capture the refusal of synthesis presented by the "irreducible ambiguity of difference" (37) that Hölderlin has in mind. There is, however, one fragment of Heraclitus that articulates its own "collision" course towards self-disintegration, which, though Hamacher does not cite it, he must have had in *his* mind, for it bears out his point exactly: *tō tósō ónoma bíos, érgon dè thánatos* (Fragment B48), which is distinguished for the fact that the word for "life" (*bíos*) is differentiated from the old word for "bow" (*biós*) only by the accent, which was not written in Heraclitus's time—such that the fragment reads both "the name of the bow is life; its [life's] work is death" and "the name of the bow is bow; its [the name's] work is death," and whether "death" is the work of metaphor or tautology, whether death is the product of life or of a process of self-cancellation, is left entirely undecidable. This undecidability between death-as-end and death-as-circle seems to be a suitable way to comprehend the "well-allotted fate" (StA 2: 145; PF 505) that falters, in the "Rhine" hymn, between "wanderings" and "memory," providing respite that is sustained by the boundary between mortals and immortals yet declining to synthesize the difference that the work of the name displays. To this "rest," this "harmony which the Heavenly and mortals approach in one another [and which is] indebted to delimitation, to the affirmation of a difference," Hamacher gives, in contradistinction to "parataxis," the name *Aufenthalt*.

Aufenthalt can mean "sojourn," "dwelling," or "inhabitation." It appears in the "Rhine" hymn in both its temporal and spatial aspects and has therefore been translated as "term and site" (StA 2: 144; PF 507). As harmony indebted to delimitation, it represents the interruption that halts the inclination of mortals to travel down the path towards dissolution; only when obstructed from their own end are mortals able to "turn around" the distance of the gods to their own end. But this interval, the "'time-image' of history" (39), is therefore also not a "clearing" [*Lichtung*] that remains "unproblematically self-identical" as the "place of origin of identity and negativity," itself immune to irritation or negation (as Heidegger argues). *Aufenthalt* is, rather, related to *behalten*, "to retain," which in "The Rhine" describes the route and the destination of a life as a "bearing in mind," in the *Gedächtnis*, which bends, diffracts, and curves the time of the meeting of gods and humans (the festival) in the direction of a mournful interval and in the mode of passing away. History, in other words, "is the mournful interval between the living and the dead, where the dead is at the living and the living is at the dead" (45). What this description suggests is a rigorous and specific form of Christology qua philosophy of history, which Hamacher develops in the central chapter of the thesis, devoted to the three versions of the poem "Der Einzige" (The Only One). With respect to the interval that is world history and the "holding up" of mortals on earth, Christ is absent; Christ's absence, *Fehlen*, is "felt" as a "fault" [*Fehl*]. This fault is double, moreover, as not only does he fail to appear, but his death introduces an epochal break separating Greek from Christian history. In the first version, this double fault is an indication of the "historical self-overstepping" represented by Christ's life and death, a "misconduct" [*Verfehlung*] that introduces a new measure for history. The third version then introduces "that element of Christ's achievement, of the demigod who is missing from the plastic order of the Greek gods, which corresponds in all transgressions of positive legality to the Greek principle of space, form, and law: that element, therefore, [as] that [which] also makes possible the hymn to him, the moment of its articulation" (71). In other words, contrary to both epiphany as the model for the poem (Szondi) and "patriotic reversal" as the model by which the worldly steps in place of the spiritual (Allemann), Hamacher argues that "presence" in the poem itself relies on a lack—a lack, moreover, into which Christ allows himself to lapse through self-denial as a condition for his fulfillment as the *logos*. Evading the choice between presence and absence, Christ represents a break in the law that finds permanence "because the distance from presence and absence has, as their condition, become a figure" (84); he "situates the condition of the law at a place where not only the law itself but also its entire dichotomous order is broken" (83). As Hamacher points out, Christian history, based on the transgression and fault in the order of presence, thus also relinquishes phonologism or indeed "the logic . . . of the self-present and living word" (81); what this life is only remains in the graphic traces of the word in the wasteland.

In other words, Hamacher discovers in the very model for how we understand occurrence and historical time (insofar as we subscribe to the Christian account of history) the incipience of a refusal of that model, a refusal that takes the form of its primary agent, Christ, tracing out its trajectory by acting out in each instant the transgression of that very trajectory. Christian history is the history of an illegitimacy; its fault, the founding of history on the permanent break with an order that tolerates only either presence or absence, is therefore also the "indicator" [*Anhalt*] of where that order begins to subvert itself. Nowhere is Derrida's mark on the thesis more evident, in fact, than in the analyses of the graphic mark both "in" and "on" the poem: first, where Hamacher discusses the similarity of the letters *d* and *el*, and *ch* and *f*, when handwritten (69), which disturbs the order of meaning that is buttressed by syntax and pronunciation—the linear teleology of phonologic discourse—and second, where the distribution of the phonemes comprising the name of the river "Ister"—"Ist" and "er"—texturizes the poem in such a way as to disturb the very structure of the "now"-time of the "Hesperian" song: such that, over the course of the poem, even the seemingly shortest path to meaning, the "it is" [*er ist*], bends, "almost backwards," even as it veers towards what is nearest, towards a path whose end "no one knows" and which must end only in turning the ontological proposition into a question: "is it?" [*Ist er?*] (102). If the "it is" "depicts the condition for the spirit's and the highest's self-experience and self-reproduction, it [therefore] also depicts the condition of their impossibility; it abandons the constitutive form of being and cognition while at the same time it carries out its deconstruction" (106). This analysis has repercussions for the theory of "Hesperian reversal," which, in an analysis of "Celebration of Peace," Hamacher now reconceives as a species of Platonic *epistrophē*, or the reversal of direction that occurs precisely in the interval in which we wait for death—that interval called *this life*—and whose movement deconstitutes maturation and progression. In the version from John, which Hölderlin echoes in notes he made for a sermon on the Letter to the Hebrews, such cosmic reversal is a moment of the double movement of God's approach, on the one hand, and the reversal of God's course during his absence, on the other, a double movement that underlies the possibility of being in the first place. What Hölderlin's hymn enacts, however, is the revolutionary potential of such a reversal that, rather than restore original unity, indicates the futility of doing so by way of pointing to the "allegorical" character of the return of the gods (91). In "Celebration of Peace," the Heavenly are allegorized and, as such, abandon their own movement;

divine presence is "in" the poem only as such an allegorization that unsettles the notion of an autonomous movement of the divine and abandons it to the position of a derivative. Thus, as in the poem "Bread and Wine," the reversal takes on the form of postponement; the reversal towards the point of a new beginning, where rebirth coincides with new life, is transposed into a wilderness in which this reversal, in the figure of Christ allegorized as Bacchus, survives only in the shelter of the Hesperian shadow.

According to Hamacher, what has been called Hölderlin's "eschatological anticipation" (95) has no other goal than to transplant the notion of reversal away from its self-reproductive ground, where the regeneration and dissemination of the basic (Christological) structure of history as eternal return might continue unabated in the name of the father, and into an infertile place, where it can be made apparent that certain conceptions of how to bring about the new, including revolutionary newness, have been nothing other than the same forms of power and domination that have secretly reproduced themselves under the protective cover of the "new." To capture Hölderlin's affirmation of the "nonorigin" of meaning in text and history, Hamacher translates Derrida's concept of "dissemination" as *Entdeutung*, or de-interpretation: a dissemination of the seeds of meaning that at the same time deconstitutes its ground, the idea of the self-sufficient subject, by dispersing these seeds, the *logos spermatikos*, as wastage, without re-collecting them for the purpose of their self-propagation (112–3). What such de-interpretative traits do in the poetry is to derange—in the Derridean sense of dislodging the priority of sense over the excess to sense—the process of gathering meaning from the poem. They also derange—in the further (and also Derridean) sense of dispersing the poem's textual elements across the page—the meaning gathered from interpretation into its spatial configuration. In one regard, then, Hamacher treats Hölderlin as Mallarmé, running his texts through a *double séance*—the process to which he gives, in a couple of places, a name that he derives by radically decontextualizing a term taken from the discipline of prosody, "to scan" [*skandieren*], and reconstituting it in the sense of "to re-cite" (24). In another regard—and this is indicated by Hamacher's reference to the "dispersion of life and its reproductive possibilities," insofar as they are "conceived as the *conditio* of history"—the derangement of Hölderlin's poetry, which spatializes sense and lets history emerge from the wastage of all the self-reproductive capacities of dominant systems of signification, is described as a "baroque trait in Hölderlin's late texts" (110). For this notion, Hamacher again has Benjamin in mind, no longer the Benjamin of "Two Poems of Friedrich

Hölderlin" but, rather, the Benjamin of the *Origin of the German Mourning Play*. This Benjamin, who is concerned with the *conditio* of history after the end of eschatology—the end of ending, the death of death—describes how, in undomesticated eruptions of swerves and evasions, the baroque drama aspired, awkwardly, to realize the transfiguring apotheosis of concepts through the *ponderación misteriosa*, the intervention of God in the work of art, only to have its ponderous equipment collapse their over-elaborated constructions into ruins. Similarly, Hamacher's Hölderlin splits concepts from their names and correspondences, turning them, as Adorno put it, into "*capita mortua* of the aspect of the idea that cannot be made present."[55] This Hölderlin swerves towards an allegorical image of the world with one enduring, "versing" purpose: to point out the utter inadequacy of the poetic word relative to the propagation of reality. In doing so, Hamacher, as the "re-citer" of Hölderlin, recovers a place to which all that is abandoned in the process of the predication of being—nonsense, singular marks, errant phonemes, the excess of mourning and remembrance—flees: a place from which the condition of impossibility of the spirit's and the highest's self-experience and self-reproduction is depicted and the poem, as the *conditio* of history, carries out their deconstruction.

Following Szondi's death in the fall of 1971, the institutional and intellectual context within which the thesis had roamed underwent a disruption that, for Hamacher, changed its orientation in an irrecoverable way.[56] As discussed in the afterword to this book, the original plan for Hamacher's doctoral dissertation, which was to have been an expansion of certain themes first presented in his master's thesis, gave way almost accidentally to a dissertation that would eventually become the long preface to his critical edition of Hegel's early so-called "theological" writings and bear the title *pleroma*.[57] This is one of the reasons why Hamacher's thesis was, in this form, perhaps never meant to be a book, as was also true for its replacement, which was nevertheless able to fulfill an institutional function and eventually (almost two decades later) appear *as* a book in French and English translations—but never in the original German, where it remains an introduction to drafts, fragments, and a proposal written by a thinker who perhaps never wanted them to appear in book form.

Another reason concerns a question about whether the refusal that

Hamacher uncovers in his thesis—the potential to negate the existing order by concentrating the historical into a self-deranging force—would in fact amount to something like political action. This potential was, of course, formulated by Jacob Taubes, who was an active presence at AVL and a close advisor of Hamacher's, particularly after Szondi's death. Taubes understood Jewish (read: Pauline) messianism as an antagonistic, radically historicizing force that signals the insuperable nullity of worldly institutions in the proximity of redemption. In doing so, he famously took the opposite position from that of Gershom Scholem, who saw Jewish messianism precisely as a symptom of the lack of transition between history and redemption. Taubes only published his opposition to Scholem after 1982, but he first articulated it in May 1968, during a guest seminar led by Scholem at Szondi's invitation on the topic of Benjamin's semi-autobiographical fragments, "Agesilaus Santander"—fragments upon which Scholem's and Taubes's divergent accounts of Jewish history would be constructed, refracted through the question of the relation of Benjamin to Carl Schmitt. Taubes, for his part, understood the decisively post-*Christum* relation to historical time that he shares with Schmitt as a state of being "in liebendem Streit" (in loving strife), a phrase from the opening strophe of Hölderlin's poem "Heimkunft" that he traces back to Heraclitus—specifically, to Fragment B51, in which the *palíntropos harmoníē* of the bow and lyre might well describe the counter-striving jointure of *katechontic* and anti-*katechontic* forces that Taubes, following Schmitt, believed to be holding world history at a revolutionary turning point.[58] Taubes also saw Marxism as belonging to the same redemptive tradition, which he seems to have communicated to Hamacher at some point before the end of 1981. In a letter responding to Taubes, however, Hamacher writes that "the Marxism of which you speak, in spite of its negation potential, would never possess the force necessary to cancel the prohibition and found a new brotherhood"—the prohibition, that is, that forbids entry into "a location [*Ort*], . . . even if it is not called Eden."[59] Years later, a similar concern seems to have informed the composition of "Parousia, Stone-Walls": the condition of a new brotherhood, being epistolary, was bound to the barren place of sheer temporalization, meeting nothing but a stone wall.

Never meant as a book and never transformed by its author into one, the master's thesis nevertheless presents a response to a specific moment, a moment to which the "proper" form of response was not the book but, rather, precisely what the thesis remains: a thesis without synthesis, held in place not by a self-legislating subject—a "master"—but by the original tension of bow and lyre, life and name, spirit and sign. This original tension refuses to harmonize into adequation or homology or anything but this refusal "itself," where this "itself" is thinkable and actual only insofar as it "enters into the element of [its] impossibility" and "accepts [its] impotence as the uncertain and unknowable condition for [its] efficacy" (108). This refusal, which in the thesis discharges the move to "suspend . . . those moments that suppress the revolt in its object" (21), became a lifelong preoccupation, wandering not only, some thirty-five years later, into an expansion on the communicative-epistolary conditions of political theology in the only essay Hamacher published on Hölderlin in his lifetime ("Parousia, Stone-Walls") but also into the essays on historical time in Benjamin ("Now," "Guilt-History," "Intensive Languages," "Das Theologisch-Politische Fragment"), the critique of messianism ("Lingua Amissa," "Uncalled," "The Relation," and "Ou, séance, touche de Nancy, ici" in its several iterations, each also resisting the book form in its own way), and "language-justice" ("The Right Not to Use Rights," which also exists in several iterations, "The One Right No One Ever Has" and others recently collected into the volume *Sprachgerechtigkeit*).[60] There is a tragic edge to the project that aims not at totalization but at the finitization of all the infinite possibilities connected with it, insofar as each moment of its jointure counter-strives towards its own dissolution and loss. But in tragedy, an inconceivable place is also discovered: a mere possibility, a becoming-historical that is the condition of every actualization, a calling of all established law into question without attempting to realize another order. In derangement, a time and space open up that register as the annihilation of all self-continuous forms of time and space. From this trace of a disappearance, Hamacher's Hölderlin suggests, there may be a capacity to finally bring things to an end.

—Julia Ng

I Version of Meaning

A Study of Hölderlin's Late Lyric Poetry

MASTER'S THESIS BY WERNER HAMACHER, DECEMBER 1971, BERLIN[1]

That the understanding writhes [*sich krümmt*] that research never
Arises

—Hölderlin (StA 2: 606)

Time to bid that very instructive exploitation adieu.

—Mallarmé[2]

I. Interpretation [*Auslegung*]

The efforts of literary research, be it in textual criticism or the history of genres, methods of interpretation, or aesthetics, are oriented, even if they do not intend this explicitly, towards the construction of a logic of poetry. And if this is its goal, then the main achievement of such research must be found where it succeeds in demonstrating that the chaos of entangled references [*Bedeutungen*] and contradictory or merely equivocal forms is structured by a synthesizing meaning [*Sinn*]. Unlike that of other classic writers, Hölderlin's poetry occupies such an exceptional place in the scholarship probably because it provides an opportunity for such a demonstration but, moreover, because it presents perhaps the most serious challenge to the theoretical foundation of that demonstration: the possibility of discovering meaning [*Sinn*] from a text. In response to this challenge, literary scholarship sought to find in etymologically determined ambiguities a rebirth of the original force of language; to restrict overdetermined syntactical figures and meanings that were controversial for their context to the unambiguous and unequivocal; or simply to suppress the textuality of Hölderlin's poetry while emphasizing instead e.g. the monographic intentions of a politically engaged writer. Themes or questions of the poetic process are left out inasmuch as they call into question the category of meaning [*Sinn*]—that is, what is left out is precisely those places where Hölderlin's poetry is concerned with the conditions and forms of constituting meaning [*Bedeutung*], and especially the forms of its subversion. For the allegorical distortion of meaning [*Sinn*], the suspension or splitting of meaning, concerns the very constitution of literary studies insofar as it must presuppose that a text refers to a transcendent meaning [*Bedeutung*] or manifold of meanings that can be grasped as consistent in itself and is therefore knowable. But this position is one that must suppress the critique that Hölderlin's late texts in particular level against Idealism's concepts of language and cognition, if only not to jeopardize its status as a discipline [*Wissenschaft*].[3] The part of Hölderlin's poetology in which it itself belongs to Idealism and postulates the law of the synthesis of material and meaning [*Sinn*] for poetic art was necessarily used by literary scholarship to legitimate the claim that the late lyric poetry exhibits a consistency of meaning [*Sinn*].[4] But for the poetics that can be described as post-Idealist, and which contains in a variety of forms a theory of Hesperian reversal, criticism is unable to appeal to the law of synthesis.[5] Like the poetics whose procedure the late lyric poetry itself adopts, and the poetics that is thematized in it, the late lyric poetry is based on the subversion of logic, such that it can no longer serve the construction of logical connections without being subjected to a restriction that already implies the sacrifice of the criteria of scientific rigor and logic. The first to have formulated the affront that Hölderlin's language presents to Idealism's doctrine of the substantiality of meaning [*Sinn*] was Adorno. Regarding the "sacrifice of the period," he writes: "Poetically, this represents the sacrifice of the legislating subject itself. It is in Hölderlin, with that sacrifice, that the poetic movement unsettles the category of meaning for the first time. For meaning is constituted through the linguistic expression of synthetic unity. The subject's intention, the primacy of meaning, is ceded to language along with the legislating subject."[6] Where language is no longer regarded as the vehicle for the subject's intentions or for the intention for logic, something happens to meaning [*Sinn*] that interpretation can represent only under the condition that it sees the status of science as a theory concerned with the construction of structures of meaning unsettled by its own object, the poetic process. Correspondingly, the interpretation of those aspects of Hölderlin's late lyric poetry that are connected to a critique of mimesis, of language, of "comprehension," and of epistemology, would by implication itself have to be a critique of the intentions of the science that turns to this critique. And in its own process, interpretation will have to be aimed at the suspension of those moments that suppress the revolt in its object and, to the extent that it is logic, it will have to aim at its own deconstruction.

Yet interpretation may strive for an equality with its text, for an imitation of the text, only in a restricted manner if it does not want to slide into a concept of adequation that reproduces the logic that was dissolved in the relation between exegesis and writing. Adequation—between legends [*Sagen*] and their interpretation, between gods and men—is presented by Hölderlin as being in decline in an ode that does not yet belong to the late period, in other words the period after his sojourn in France—"Voice of the People":

> The voice of God I called you and believed you once,
> In holy youth; and still I say it!
> No less indifferent to our wisdom
> Likewise the rivers rush on, but who does
> Not love them? (StA 2: 51; PF 239)

In one fell swoop the structure of the poem, which is decisively determined by the position of the I in the thematic and linguistic tangle of its presentation, is undone when the rushing of the rivers is restrictively linked only to the correspondence between the voice of the people and the voice of God, but not also to the correspondence with what the poet says [*sagt*]. The distance of the I from its own belief hinders it just as little from articulating this belief as the distance of the rivers from "our wisdom" could prevent someone from loving them. Motivating the saying and an identification of the *vox populi* with *vox dei* is a love that does not bother with "wisdom." On every level, in the relation of the voice of the people to the voice of God, and again in the relation of the rivers to the saying and to the *vox populi*, and in the relation of the speaking I to its own belief, equality reproduces itself by the force of this love. But this equality is not positively articulated anywhere because the doubt of wisdom, the difference between those things that are being equated, which is held fast within this doubt as the other route that does not correspond to the one travelled by the rivers, conserves itself against the synthesizing compulsion of saying as the possibility of its representation:

> Always too my own heart is moved
> When far away I hear those foreknowing ones,

The fleeting, by a route not mine but
Surer than mine, and more swift, roar seaward (StA 2: 51; PF 239)

The two routes, of love and of wisdom, of adequation and of doubt, determine the course of the poem not as paralleled routes that are themselves brought back into adequation but rather as routes that cross and distort one another. If the third strophe, which is introduced by a causal particle, tries to achieve a rational, reflective grounding for the route of the rivers and for the differing route of the knower:

For once they travel down their allotted paths
With open eyes, self-oblivious, too ready to
Comply with what the gods have wished them,
Only too gladly will mortal beings
Take the shortest route back to the All;
So the river falls—not movement, but rest it seeks—(StA 2: 51; PF 239, mod.)

—if the I tries with logical justification to apprehend the motivation of the course of the poem, it falls—also as "mortal" and travelling down its "allotted path"—outside of its own route, just like that from which it knows itself to be differentiated, and it displaces the route to which it had turned as its object: under pressure from the dictum that it is the "shortest route" that mortals take, the period has to represent not whatever speedy course is taken by the rivers into the *sea*, but rather the fall over the cliffs into the *abyss*, as the movement, which is now no longer even that of rivers, but of the river. The "original" telos towards which the rivers strove as mortals strove towards the All, however, is not only surrendered in the second instance, but is itself signified at this other place in the allegorical halo that surrounds the object of intention, a place that is designated by the abyss. And it is signified precisely in that in which it is surrendered: for whoever seeks "rest" in the abyss will not find it in the sea. This distortion, however, does not only affect the route of the rivers and of love; it also affects the route travelled by logical distinction. The inadequacy of what it explains to what should be explained shows it to be going down the wrong path; the logical hypostasis of the subject by way of its own love and its own saying, decisively expressed by the formulation "my route," is frustrated by the illogical moment in which its "wisdom" and the logification it undertakes are articulated thanks to that same yearning for identity that prescribes to the river its "other" route. Where the autonomy and the direction of the route prevail, be it the route of the yearnful river, or of the knower, or even of the voice of the people, where the movement of the self and the movement that aims for identity are asserted, that is precisely where autonomy, the self, and its telos are implicated in a movement that makes them disappear:

> For . . . too ready to
> Comply with what the gods have wished them,
> Only too gladly will mortal beings
> Take the shortest route back to the All;
> So the river falls—not movement, but rest it seeks—
> Drawn on, pulled down against its will from
> Boulder to boulder—abandoned, helmless—
> By that mysterious yearning toward the abyss (StA 2: 51; PF 239, mod.)

What the mortal subject takes with its willful act, that in turn is that by which the subject is itself taken, as object. This double tendency of the formulation "only too gladly will mortal beings / Take the shortest route"—which [in the German] can also read "only too gladly will the shortest route take mortal beings"—is introduced by the verses that follow: "The unbound attracts, and whole peoples too / The longing for death takes. . . . " (StA 2: 51; PF 239, mod.). Wisdom's route, which proves to be directed by the shortest route, which is to say by the route that becomes such under pressure of its logification, meets with this other route that it transforms and that transforms it in a single figure, in the fall through the abyss. This figure destroys the identity of both. For the abyss, the unbound, towards which the desire of the voice, of saying, and of logical structuration strives as the place where their identity is to be realized through distinction or through synthesis, is itself the product of their reciprocal distortion.

It is not the fact that it complies with "what the gods have wished" but the fact that it is "too ready" and "only too glad" to comply that changes the route into a fall with such rigorous abbreviation; the voice of the people, which wants to realize its identity as the voice of God, seeks it in silence; the poet's words find their actual subject, the connection between *vox populi* and *vox dei*, at the place where they withdraw from representation. Both voices—and both are spoken of—want to acquire the abyss as the place, and "rest" as the condition, in which the difference between the process of their signification and what is signified by them disappears; but with this difference they themselves disappear. Already in the second strophe the rivers are therefore emphatically apostrophized as "the fleeting"; to introduce the relation between their disappearance and their signifying function, "those foreknowing ones, the fleeting" are described in an earlier draft as "full of interpretation [*die Deutungsvollen*]" (StA 2: 487). Their yearning foreknowing and interpretation must extinguish themselves, and the process of designation that completes itself in them must be an erasure of the sign, when the difference that the sign establishes is paced through by the desire for identity and compliance with foreknowledge. This difference spreads itself out as the landscape that the river must cross through, and it contracts with the abbreviation of its route in the abyss. The identity with what it articulates, the presence of the voice of God, wants to reach the voice of the people in the absence of voice, in "rest [*Ruh*]," and "reaches" it in no other way than as a voice that is different from its own "original" goal, distorted by the attempt of the concept to structure its route. This "rest" does not grant the intended compliance, and in it no goal is attained; rather, "against their will," the route of the voice is re-cited [*skandiert*]. The first version of the ode lets the fall into the abyss transition into an ascent of clouds to the sky and into their return to the "birthplace" of the river, to the place where its voice raises itself instead of falling silent. It is a landmark, a point of reference. There the voice of the people does not find itself again as the voice of God, but instead must, broken by the fall, begin with precisely the path from which it sought to withdraw. "Crying," it returns, and the movement, yearning and "full of interpretation," must repeat itself as that which is in mourning, remembering the unattainability of that for which it strives and the irreducibility of difference. - The second version of the poem localizes remembrance not in the tearful return to the place of birth, but where a "holy end" is met, be it the river, peoples, or cities. The paratactic process, which persists over five strophes, locates it in the fall at the end of contingent structures themselves:

> these too
> A holy end has stricken; the earth grows green,
> And there beneath the stars, like mortals
> Deep in their prayers, quite still, prostrated
> On sand, outgrown, and willingly, lies long art
> Flung down before the Inimitable; and he himself,
> The man, the artist with his own two
> Hands broke his work for their sake, in homage to those on high. (StA 2: 51; PF 239–41, mod.)

For the sake of affirming the fall and the stasis of the fragmented, the natural-historical image of the river as well as the image of the voices and of the poet's speech are dropped; their living, continuous flow, which—significantly, even if only in a draft, is described as being driven by "divine yearning" (StA 2: 488)—sought its compliance, its fulfillment, in death and in "the unbound," falls, and is only broken by it, in another place where it petrifies into material form. There a resolutely determinate concretion, as manifest in the single color ("green") of the poem and the alliteration in the "still . . . beneath the stars," meets with the shattering of form in a figure in which totality and cohesion, in which alone meaning could come to realization, and the harmony of opposites, which the poetological writings from the Homburg period demanded, are relinquished. The hubristic verticality of the return to the All, of the fall into the abyss, and of the shape of "valiant towns" (StA 2: 51; PF 239) yields to the horizontal, in which the works, far removed from all height and all depth, are alone on the even earth to be equated with what lies prostrate: those deep in prayer. And it is not the day, in which the significant one travels its route "awake" (StA 2: 488) and "with open eyes" (StA 2: 51; PF 239), but the night, into which the light of divinity shines as little as its voice resounds in it, that is the period of time in which the pretension to revelation that is evident in human works extinguishes. Yet it is not that the gods, imagined as "given," autonomously acting subjects, had withdrawn from the world in which it was now night; rather, night is the time when, like the distorted and fragmented articulation of yearning, like the incongruence of *vox populi* and *vox dei*, the gods' distance from whatever mortal beings intend them to be is manifest. For the route of the voice strives for the gods as for the All, for the unbound, which is not held back at any distance from their self and not separated by any difference from their own self. Just as the living flow of speech breaks off and petrifies into an artwork in ruins, just as the fall into the unbound is held back in utmost reserve when faced with those on high, God's voice nevertheless also comes, though not as the voice of the people, but, distorted once again and as the artwork in ruins, to a standstill "before the Inimitable." Instead of merging together into the unity of its appearance, his light is therefore dispersed into stars. Correspondingly, the gods should not be regarded as fixed entities that provide for themselves an expression in different shapes that would leave their being untouched; rather, through the actions of human beings or, more precisely, through the realization of their mortality, the gods are introduced into a process of deferrals and dispersions in which not only the identity of their expressions but also their self-identity disintegrates. Identity *articulates* itself: this means that it represents itself through the discontinuous process of a synthesization that distorts, defers, and differentiates it from its own self. This ineluctably [*unaufhebbar*] ambiguous act of articulation, in which the wish for identity produces, in the shattering of expression itself, the difference that it wishes to reduce, is achieved by the voice of the people, by its history, and also by the work of the artist to the extent that the mimetic impulse that drives this voice realizes the impossibility of mimesis. In it, the possibility of speech that is meaningful and present to itself is destroyed. For while the living flow of the voice, which sought to overcome the distance from its goal by way of the shortest route, meant to find in this goal its actual destination, its identity as the voice of God in the speechless presence of that which is signified by it -, in the fragmentary work, by contrast, in which the river is arrested by virtue of its fall, the shattering of the possibility of an identity brings with it the shattering of the possibility of significant speech and meaningful form as well. Meaning is affected by its yearning for compliance and fulfillment to such a degree that in becoming the moment of articulation, it alone represents the admission that what it strives for is unattainable.[7] In the poetic process, this lesion of meaning finds expression in the fact that the river metaphor breaks off abruptly, and then the talk of the peoples is broken off and transitions into the work of the artist; in the fact that what was previously "against their will" is now "outgrown, and willingly"; and that the "Inimitable" and "those on high" are positioned by syntactic parallelism in such a way that they refer to both the gods and the stars: an ambiguity that extends into the following strophe, insofar as the intervals of the night can be that which prolongs "a man's course" (StA 2: 52; PF 241). The work that proceeds in such a manner with its meanings follows that which is shattered in the middle of the poem.[8] Here is the place in which the closing strophe of the second version can be incorporated into the interpretation. Just as in the entire second half of this version, the concern is no longer with the course taken by the legend [*Sage*] that is the voice of the people, but rather with how those who hear this legend react to it, with the relation of the children to the deeds of their parents, and with the repetition of the legend. Following the description of the self-annihilation of the Xanthian people, the poem turns to reflecting on the connection between the deed, how it is understood, and its repetition:

So their descendants heard, and no doubt such lore
Is good, because it serves to remind us of
The Highest; yet there's also need of
One to interpret these holy legends. (StA 2: 53; PF 243)

Just as the river falls into the abyss in order to cross over into unboundedness, so the Xanthians seek freedom in "holy aether" (StA 2: 53; PF 243). The poem now concludes the representation of the downfall of the later Xanthians with a reference to Brutus, who sought to hinder their self-destruction: "It is not wise to fight against heroes" (StA 2: 53; PF 243). Yet the final strophe itself nevertheless gives no advice, even though it reiterates, however fleetingly, its distance from the legends. For the poem cannot be saying that the "reminder of the Highest" is not to be renewed, nor can the text be concluding by simply consenting to the repetition of the legends. Unlike the first version, the poem refrains from establishing a general maxim in which meaning, whose shattering it articulates thematically as well as in terms of its process, would have to reconstitute itself. *Interpretation* [*Auslegung*], by contrast, which the text demands through its suspension of any unequivocal position and through the etymological link with how the broken works *lie* [*Liegen*],[9] designates that act—be it of the artist, or of the interpreter—in which the intention of meaning, conceived as identity, logical distinction, or mimesis, is interpreted as the extinguishing of intention, the relinquishment of meaning, and in which the verticality of "comprehension" (viz "understanding" [*Verstand*])[10] is interpreted [*ausgelegt*] as shapelessly lying prostrate [*Liegen*]. If the destruction that exegesis visits upon forms and actions leaves logical construction and eschatological intention in ruins, however, it does so not as an act intervening from without, not as a form of expression belonging to a transcendental subject. The hand that constitutes the sign is the same hand that destroys the sign; desire (itself), which drives back into the abyss and into the All, travels the route of distortion, insofar as the realization of its telos, for which it strives in death as the self-presence and place of freedom, reverses itself and lays out [*auslegt*] in ruins what its meaning [*Sinn*] wants to comply [*erfüllen*] with: a break with itself and with the pretention of a self.[11] The pathos of salvation history changes into a mortification of meaning to be laid out in ruins by interpretation.

Thus the "shortest route" is laid out in interpretation [*ausgelegt*] and stretched out in length by virtue of its own course, which crosses over into lying prostrate [*Liegen*]. It is in this way that the poem, whose route proves itself in this context to be, like the route of the mortals, its own laying out, its own interpretation [*Auslegung*], represents human love in its counterimage, the love bestowed upon humans through the gods:

> Yet they, the Heavenly, to men remain well-disposed,
> As we love them so they will return our love
> And in order that he long enjoy the
> Light, will obstruct [*hemmen*] a man's course to ruin. (StA 2: 52; PF 241, mod.)

The length expressed in the phrase "in order that he long enjoy the light," which this strophe sees realized through the obstruction of the shortest route, finds an even clearer exposition in an earlier version:

> Yet they, the Heavenly, to all mortals remain well-disposed
> and return love equal to the love we give them
> and gladly prolong it
> and . . . (StA 2: 490–91)

The equality of the love of humans and gods—which is asserted here in the most rigorous opposition to the inequality and inimitability that was just described—can be seen from what is revealed by the mirror symmetry arising around the "equal" in the one version and the "so" in the other version, as though along an axis. It is precisely what the inimitability of the gods expresses and what the suspension of meaning produces: distortion. Laying itself out here, it is figured as the prolongation of the route whose radical abbreviation it nevertheless represents at the same time. The dialectics, whose concept, if left unproblematized, could all too easily explain this movement, is, unlike the Hegelian variant, not a dialectics of fulfillment or compliance, and therefore not synthetic, but rather a dialectics of distortion, one that is itself distorted. For the shortest route leads to the ruination of its telos, not to this telos itself; and it can be regarded as a "moment" of the prolonged route only to the extent that on this route the destruction is brought to a completion not as dying off, not as a pure negation of meaning and of the impulse for identification, which it would have to reproduce as its reverse image, but rather as its obstruction and as its deferral: deferred into the middle between living and dead meaning. Obstruction, inhibition [*Hemmung*], is that figure in which intention towards the highest life and the degradation into the amorphism of death merge, not in their synthesis but in their distortion. It is the distortion of the self that falls out with itself with no possibility of sublation: distorted, the shortest route gets in its own way and lays itself out into that which the first version calls "the more curved route" [*die geschwungnere Bahn*] (StA 2: 50).[12] It does so in such a way, however, that it turns into the other form of difference that it was extended in order to reduce. - What this intermittent obstruction-as-inhibition does to meaning, then, can be most obviously seen in the fact that the content of the first two verses of the strophe in question is delayed and is opened up only in retrospect, namely by the formulation "And in order that he long enjoy the / Light, will obstruct a man's course to ruin"; in the fact that the implications of comparing the love of gods and humans, the double relation to the fall as well as to lying prostrate, dissolve its simple symmetry and make its consummation possible only in "obstruction-inhibition," in which falling and lying prostrate reciprocally interpenetrate. The calculus of these formulations can be measured if one contrasts them with the first version of these first two lines of this strophe, which still represented the obstruction-inhibition coming from heaven as opposition to the path of the mortals: "Yet the Heavenly, well-disposed to the mortals, impede their hasty return" (StA 2: 490).

The double meaning of the shortest route, that is, the fact that it can mean both fall and deferral, and the ambiguity of the meaning of the break, which means both the intention for the presence of meaning and the distortion and inhibition of this intention at the same time, is developed more radically in the strophe that follows. The double movement is no longer allegorized in images that successively follow upon one another but rather in their simultaneity.

> And not the eagle's fledglings alone their sire
> Throws out of eyries, knowing that else too long
> They'd idle—us the Ruler also
> Drives into flight with a prong that's fitting. (StA 2: 52; PF 241, mod.)

The phrase "too long they'd idle" can be connected with the length of the route that humans, obstructed by the gods, take; if the image of the eyries is read in isolation from the context of shattering, it can be related to a rest that precedes every route, even the shortest ones. Correspondingly, to be driven out with "a prong that's fitting" means to be driven into life and at the same time out of life, out of a long idling, and into death. This doubled and self-contradictory movement—or, as what was probably Hölderlin's latest hymn put it, "Life is death, and death is a kind of life"[13]—is the route that leads into death as into life, and into life as into its death; this is the obstructed route. Its course is not a continuous one leading to its fulfillment or compliance in extinguishment, and it is not meaningful as living speech, nor does it aim at a self-identical sense; rather, its course is discontinuous, always already affected by the break, the laying out of interpretation, and the obstruction-inhibition, and as such it is the *articulation* of a sense, its representation, and its hindrance. As inhibited themselves—and the comparison of their love with the love of humans implies that they themselves are "inhibited" by the ruination of works—the gods are, along with sense, rest in the All, and whatever else might be intended, no longer in the position of a transcendental signified. As moments of articulation, they, too, are drawn into the process of distortions and breaks, in which the coherence of meaning, the self-sufficiency of the concept, disintegrates because it is painfully hindered in the course of its constitution—which has no end, but rather is always already re-cited by it—by inhibition and by the outside into which it is driven.

> So their descendants heard, and no doubt such legends
> Are good, because they serve to remind us of
> The Highest; yet there's also need of
> One to interpret these holy legends. (StA 2: 53; PF 243, mod.)

The postulate in the last strophe that holy legends are in need of interpretation is neither directed against repetition nor simply affirms it. For interpretation can certainly be seen as being realized in the repetition of the downfall of ancestors that takes place in the downfall of their descendants, and without such repetition and repeated obstruction, interpretation would not take place. However, it must also be grasped as interpretation, as a laying out: that is, not as the reconstitution of an original unity, not as the way into the "expanse [*Freie*]" (StA 2: 53; PF 243, mod.) or into the All, but rather as that intention for sense in which sense, and intention itself as well, do not fulfill or comply with themselves but rather wreck, obstruct, and lay themselves out in interpretation. Repetition is interpretation insofar as it is aimed not at identity but at its articulation. Not the suppression of the yearning for synthesis, but rather its implementation leads to the distortion that meaning requires for its representation and in which its primacy of synthetic unity is revoked. To determine the route travelled by the voice of the people, the route of legends, the route of history as that which, by virtue of its intention, however, deviates from it, and thanks to its signifying function goes against its tendency, obstructed and broken, to arrive at the situation in which the difference from the goal is experienced in suffering and actively produced—: that is interpretation, as postulated by Hölderlin's poem and achieved by the poem (itself). This is because its advancement, the poet's speech, is guided by the same yearning and is met with the same distortions and the same allegorical incoherence as are the routes and shapes of the other voices.

II. Crooked [*Krumm*]

In his letter to Isaac von Sinclair on Christmas Eve 1798, Hölderlin writes:

> But then it is a good thing, and even the first condition of all life and of all forms of organization, that no force is monarchic in heaven and earth. Absolute monarchy will always cancel itself out, because it has no object; in the strict sense it has never even existed. Everything is interconnected, and suffers as soon as it is active, including the purest thought a human being can have. And strictly speaking an *a priori* philosophy, entirely independent of all experience, is just as much a nonsense as a positive revelation where the revealer does the whole thing and he to whom the revelation is made is not even allowed to move in order to receive it, because otherwise he would have contributed something of his own. (StA 6: 300–301; EL 117)

The argument presented here against absolute monarchy and positive revelation appears almost four years earlier in a letter to Hegel as an argument against Fichte's theory of the absolute I—an argument that forfeits none of its rigor and force to the author's plea to his reader, in the second half of that letter, "to regard the argument as not worth writing down" (StA 6: 156; EL 48, mod.): "[Fichte's] absolute I (= Spinoza's substance) contains all reality; it is everything, and outside it there is nothing; therefore for this absolute I there is no object, for otherwise all reality would not be in it; but a consciousness without an object is not conceivable, and if I myself am this object, then as such I am necessarily limited, even if only in time, and therefore not absolute" (StA 6: 155; EL 48). It is from a related criticism of Fichte's *Foundations of the Entire Science of Knowledge* that the philosophical fragment "Judgment and Being" (StA 4: 216; EL 231), which was written in the same year, presumably derives. Against Fichte's equation of the absolute I as the one and only connection between subject and object to which the term "unity" could be ascribed, Hölderlin's fragment defines "being as such" (StA 4: 216; EL 231) as the non-separatedness preceding every possible separation in subject and object. By constructing such an unthinkable unity of subject and object, inaccessible to any judgment or conceptual knowledge, he avoids the aporia of the absolute's objectlessness. But because "being as such" designates the unity before any separation of subject and object, it does not fall under the concept of monarchic force. - If the letter to Hegel is concerned with the criticism of the idea of a "monarchic" origin, and the fragment on "Judgment and Being" with the construction of an origin as the irreducible unity of subject and object, then the letter to Sinclair is concerned not with primordial unity but rather with unity as the result of the relation between subject and object: unity is understood as "anything made, every product," as are "the purest thought" and "revelation" (StA 6: 301; EL 117). As a consequence of the insight into the produced character of the mediating instances between heaven and earth, there emerges that insight that will determine the whole of Hölderlin's late lyric poetry, an insight that is already formulated here in all its strictness: "that no force is monarchic in heaven and earth" (StA 6: 300; EL 117). But if no force is monarchic, then the same applies to the force of the gods and also of God. Not only for the sake of revelation but also for their own sake, those who reveal are dependent on that which is other to their selves: the immortals depend on the mortals, the immediacy of infinity on its dissolution in finitude. Programmatically speaking, the "physical" need of gods is probably depicted for the first time in "The Rhine."

In answer to those who "strove to become the equals of gods," the central strophe of the hymn reads:

> But their own immortality
> Suffices the gods, and if
> The Heavenly have need of one thing,
> It is of heroes and human beings
> And other mortals. For since
> The most Blessed in themselves feel nothing
> Another, if to say such a thing is

Permitted, must, I suppose,
Feel, by participating, in the name of the gods,
And him they need (StA 2: 145; PF 505, mod.)

As far removed as the theoretical content of these verses is from the fragment on "Judgment and Being," it is nevertheless very close to the criticism Hölderlin levied in his letters against Fichte and the monarchic principle in philosophy. That is, it is close to the criticism thereof, and not, as has been claimed,[14] to Fichte's philosophy itself. Fichte's grand attempt to describe the self-constitution of the I is dependent on the positing of an absolute I as a synthetic category so that he can resolve the aporia resulting from the fact that this I itself is posited *in* the I and negated at the same time because the not-I is also posited in it; this aporia is to be resolved in the very instance that produces it: in the I as an absolute. In this connection, its synthetic function is not conceived as progressive, as in Hegel, but rather as what underlies every possible antithesis (cf. F 1: 113; SK, 111–12). This synthesis, which alone salvages the identity of consciousness, completes itself in the "original act of the self" (F 1: 107; SK 107, mod.) by way of the "*limiting* of each opposite by the other"; "*to limit* something is to abolish its reality, not wholly but in *part* only, by negation. Thus, apart from reality and negation, the notion of a *limit* [Schranke] also contains that of *divisibility* . . . " (F 1: 108; SK 108, emphasis added). The absolute I thus contains, as posited by itself, a divisible I and a divisible not-I, from which it emphatically distinguishes itself by simply being identical with itself. At first, it appears that Hölderlin's image of the gods was wholly influenced by Fichte's concept of the absolute I; if one takes Fichte's remark that "the self *posits* itself, and by virtue of this mere self-assertion it *is*. . . . It is at once the agent and the product of action; the active, and what the activity brings about; action and deed are one and the same . . . " (F 1: 96; SK 97, mod., emphasis added)—and compares it with an earlier version of the central strophe of "The Rhine," connections do in fact become apparent:

For they go without straying, looking straight ahead
From beginning to predetermined end
And always victoriously, and it is forever the same
With them, act and will.
Therefore the blessed ones do not feel it themselves
. . . (StA, 2: 726)

Yet with regard to Hölderlin's imagery alone: the fact that the gods "go," that there is a distance they have to cover between beginning and end, as much as these might be "the same," indicates that this spatial extension of divine movement, with which the moment of difference is retained already in self-identity, withdraws from Fichte's notion of the presuppositionless identity of the absolute I. The fact that the "blessed ones" do not feel "it" "themselves," or experience the straightness of their going and their sameness with themselves, is reminiscent once again of the criticism Hölderlin levies against Fichte in his letter to Hegel of January 26, 1795: "therefore for this absolute I there is no object, for otherwise all reality would not be in it; . . . therefore no consciousness is conceivable in the absolute I, as an absolute I, I have no consciousness, and insofar as I have no consciousness I am (for myself) nothing, therefore the absolute I is (for me) nothing" (StA 6: 115; EL 48). Therefore, what led the absolute I as the original synthetic act into an aporia is arguably projected as a positive in the gods. Self-experience is possible only under the condition of non-identity. If the Fichtean I posits in itself the not-I as its formal object and thereby posits the divisibility and quantitative determination of its negation and its self, what is significant in view of the relation between gods and mortals as depicted in Hölderlin's hymn about "The Rhine" is the fact that they are not synthesized in an original fact-act [*Tathandlung*] and mortals do not figure as positings of the immortals. The concept of the limit [*Grenze*][15] and of divisibility, as well as that of negation, are, however, also definitive for Hölderlin's conception in a transformed sense. For insofar as the self-experience of those who, being equal to themselves, do not have sensibility at their disposal for their own movement, therefore requires another, this self-experience is dependent on the negation of its self-identity, their straight path on the straying of humans, their immortality on their mortality. It imparts itself to them through the language of humans:

> Therefore the blessed ones do not feel it themselves,
> Yet their joy is
> The saying and speech of human beings. (StA 2: 726)

Through the contrast with the gods who do not stray [*irrlos*], look straight ahead, and are adequate to themselves, the "saying and speech of human beings" might be seen perhaps as non-identical, as straying and detour; for only as a deviation from the path that leads directly from the beginning to the end, only as diverging from the beginning and from the end and always wandering off anew from their rigorous connection, might mortals themselves provide for the immortals the deferral before their end, the difference from themselves that they desire, which is necessary for their self-experience. This difference from oneself is achieved in a decisive passage, the central verses, by the language of the hymn:

> For since
> The most Blessed in themselves feel nothing
> Another, if to say such a thing is
> Permitted, must, I suppose,
> Feel, by participating, in the name of the gods,
> And him they need (StA 2: 145; PF 505, mod.)

At the place where the final version of the strophe turns to the necessity of supplementing the gods, where the poem is supposed to depict how the capacity for sensible experience has to be loaned through the participation of "another"—speech interrupts itself and holds itself back from the goal of the sentence through its limitation: "if to say such a thing is permitted" (StA 2: 145; PF 505). The distance that language thus brings into relation with itself also inserts itself into the speech of the poem, where in the earlier version of this strophe it turns from the need of the gods towards the happiness and suffering that humans receive from their "participation" in the fate of the gods. For what gives pleasure to immortals as difference from themselves is, as mortality, the suffering of human beings: the difference from the happy self-identity of the gods is realized not only syntactically but also thematically in the poem. This difference, which runs through the language and life of human beings, this articulation that makes possible sensible and intellectual experience, must also determine the route of the gods, if one is permitted to elaborate on the thoughts contained in the first verses of this strophe. Only through this articulation can "another" fulfill and comply with its demand:

> Another, if to say such a thing is
> Permitted, must, I suppose,
> Feel, by participating, in the name of the gods,
> And him they need (StA 2: 145; PF 505, mod.)

The other inscribes a difference into the self-identity of the gods in such a way that the other participates in this self-identity, that is, strives to become equal to it and, with heroic hubris, "[d]espising mortal ways / Chooses foolhardy arrogance" (StA 2: 145; PF 505, mod.). It also, by taking from the gods a part of their identity—the assonance between [the German for] "name" [*Nahmen*][16], and "participating" [*Theilnehmend*], dissolves the compound and emphasizes the extractive sense of the taking [*des Nehmens*] —diminishes the sameness of "act" and "will" and in this way limits the immortals. This limitation of self-identity—and this distinguishes Hölderlin's conception from Fichte's—is not preceded by an absolute I that has priority over it and that is removed from every limitation and, without suffering it, produces it in the first place; the participation of another breaks the law, the straight and correct route of the gods, and not only places limits on it but even dismisses the threat that it poses: "sure of their own rights / And of the heavenly fire / Defiant rebels mocked" (StA 2: 145; PF 505). This renunciation of the immortals and diminution of their identity, through which this identity is completed into self-experience to begin with, cannot be harmonized in a system whose structure is determined by the principle of synthetic unity, be this the system of transcendental, subjective, or speculative Idealism. And even the "verdict" that the gods of Hölderlin's poem pass on those who participate and intend equality with the gods can hardly be seen as a synthesizing act:

> . . . but their verdict is that
> He shall demolish his
> Own house and curse like an enemy
> Those dearest to him and under the rubble
> Shall bury his father and child,
> When one aspires to be like them, refusing
> To tolerate anything unequal, the enthusiast. (StA 2: 145; PF 505, mod.)

The "verdict" is that he shall be divided from himself; only where his equality with himself disintegrates, where he dissolves connections and violates both divine and human law, is he the other that the gods "need." The function of a representative, which the phrase "in the name of the gods" attributes to him, thus represents the function of the one who, in the first instance, completes and brings to an end the self-presence of the gods. This self-presence is thus completed through the ruination of both the equality that determines the connection of human life and the identity that governs the life of the gods. It is not so much in the guise of the student and friend of contemporaneous dialecticians as in the position of someone familiar with pre-Socratic philosophy, particularly that of Heraclitus, that Hölderlin would have intuited a consequence for the relation between mortals and immortals that withdraws from every attempt at a synthesis. According to one fragment from Heraclitus, "Immortals are mortal, mortals immortal, living one another's death, dying in one another's life."[17] Yet even the dialectical paradox into which Heraclitus contracts the antinomy between mortality and immortality does not suffice to define the relationship that Hölderlin has in mind. For, if Heraclitus's paradox reconciles opposites in a circular process, in Hölderlin's conception synthesizing is ruled out by the irreducible ambiguity of difference. The difference that mortals introduce into the self-identity of the gods only ever supplements it as a diminishment. Thus, the incompleteness of the self-consciousness of the gods and the non-identity of human beings cannot be sublated. The difference, which in every case is a lesion of the self, is at once constitutive and deconstitutive for mortals and immortals as well as for the connection between them. Even the "one another" in which the mortals and immortals of Heraclitus's text collide must disintegrate with itself. The articulation through which the gods experience themselves and humans participate [*Anteil nehmen*] in their existence thus does not add itself either to a closed circle nor to a context for which the concept of synthesis could be valid. "A well-allotted fate" (StA 2: 145; PF 505), as the subsequent strophe of "The Rhine" calls it, affords the rest that is interrupted by the titanic revolt against boundaries, but offers as little of the equality with the gods that humans intend as it converts differential movement into a synthetic one. The harmony which the Heavenly and mortals approach in one another is indebted to delimitation [*Einschränkung*], to the affirmation of a difference.

> So that this way, that way with pleasure
> He looks as far as the boundaries
> Which God at birth assigned
> To him for his term and site.
> Then, blissfully humble, he rests,
> For all that he has wanted,
> Though heavenly, of itself surrounds
> Him uncompelled, and smiles
> Upon the bold one now that he's at rest. (StA 2: 144; PF 507, mod.)

The drawing of boundaries, the determination of term and site [*Aufenthalt*], and obstruction are the acts by which the gods hinder, for their part, the downfall of mortals and their inclination to flee into the All in the face of the suffering of non-identity. Only where the path of mortals is interrupted [*zäsuriert*] by terms, sites, and delimitations can they turn around the straight path of the gods; only at a distance from their own end can they make possible the distance of the gods to their own end.

> A god, however, wishes to spare his sons
> A life so fleeting and smiles
> When, thus intemperate but obstructed
> By holy Alps, the rivers
> Like this one rage at him in the depth. (StA 2: 144; PF 503, mod.)

This obstruction, this holding fast of and to difference, is the figure that determines the movement of mortals and immortals as well as the form of their coming together in celebration. In the first draft of the hymn that would later be called "Celebration of Peace," there are often word-for-word correspondences with the formulations found in "The Rhine":

> . . . And God smiles
> When not to be stopped but obstructed by his mountains
> The rivers, raging, roar at him in their brazen banks,
> Deep down where no day calls the buried by their names.
> And O that ever, Upholder of All, me too you shall
> Hold thus and spare my soul that all too readily flees,
> Today I celebrate, and vespertine now in the stillness
> All round the spirit blossoms . . . (StA 2: 131; PF 515)

Under no circumstances, then, should it be suppressed—as has happened all too often[18] for the sake of a conception of the celebration as an epiphany—that the constellation into which gods and humans enter together in the festival is structured by the delimitations of immediate presence and by obstructions introduced through the intervention of death, which is announced by the apostrophizing of the rivers as "buried." If the second coming of Christ, whose earlier presence is "quickly . . . obscured" and whose radiant appearance was cloaked in shadows by a "doom" (StA 2: 131; PF 519) and is thus doomed [*verhängt*][19]; if his return is beseeched with the words, "Be present, youth, only now . . . " (StA 2: 131; PF 519), this is not because humanity would "only now" have become mature in the sense of an organic or teleological process, but because in order for his presence to appear as something that can be experienced and "felt" by the gods, this presence must be interrupted by absence. The historical interval between the "quickly obscured" appearance of Christ and his appearance in the "Evening of time" (StA 3: 536; PF 529), in the "Evening of his days" (StA 2: 132; PF 519, mod.) is absolute, however, insofar as there is no appearance other than one that is shrouded in darkness or broken up by darkness in either the historical or the natural world. The caesura that death introduces into Christ's speech; the obstruction that is put into effect on the rivers—but *not* the self-generation of the spirit or its progression towards identity—is what determines the structure of history and of the festival.

> And human beneficence is followed by thanks,
> But godsent gifts for years at first
> By exerting and straying
> So that more mildly in the years that follow
> The lofty ray
> Through holy wilderness shall shine.
> Therefore, divine one, be present now . . . (StA 2: 131; PF 519)

The process of the spirit outlined by Hölderlin, in strict opposition to the process that his Tübingen classmates conceived, is a process of its diminishment and moderation rather than its self-appropriation, self-production, and fulfillment. The law of its route and of its "presence" at the festival is designated not by epiphany but by obscuration. And the spirit progresses not processually, that is, not by teleologically following a predetermined goal, but rather by straying off track, through the spatially determined inadequacy of the path towards the goal. But where gods and humans celebrate their coming together, there they must also take leave of one another; the place where the "lofty ray" meets the beholder over whose eyes "one night" (StA 2: 130) had been spread—that is the evening. That which lies *between* night and light, between presence and absence, between exit and goal, that which as obstruction, deferral, detour, or straying marks the transition of opposites into one another, depicts, at the same time as the condition for the possibility of their relation, the form of negation of this relation. The between affirms difference as the possibility of synthesis and as its hindrance. Thus, the pact to which the "time-image" of history—this intermediary deviation—attests in "Celebration of Peace" is not a pact between "the great Spirit" and "other powers." This "time-image" means, rather, "that between him and others, / A pact of peace there is between himself and other powers" (StA 3: 536; PF 529, mod.). The two "betweens" here are themselves different. They differ insofar as the first "between" serves as a disjunction, while the second serves as a conjunction. Given such a suspension of the identity of difference, it can hardly be maintained that synthesis and interruption come *together* in the between, unless this dissolved unity were, against the grain of the text, to be reintroduced on another level. The difference and the between are instances of a structure that is in no way synthetic, however, only insofar as their organization, which is itself self-differential, has been inscribed [*sich eingeschrieben hat*], with the repetition of the same syntagma in a different place, as a removal that is spatial and for this reason irreducible in the text. The ambiguity of difference also reproduces itself in the "pact" that is placed between the repetitions and, from this place, goes against its lexical definition and takes up the task of division. Here it becomes evident what had to remain hidden from Heidegger and Allemann,[20] who were the first to direct interpretive attention to the topos of the between in Hölderlin: the between is not a category of meaning, but rather a category that is primarily produced through constellations in such a way that it does not describe the state of "Beyng," the "open" [*das Offene*] or "the expanse" [*das Freie*][21] without also blocking and hiding [*verstellen*] it. By contrast, the between, as Heidegger understands it under the title of "clearing" [*Lichtung*], is hypostasized into that place where, extracted from the movement of difference, and thus identical once again to itself, it opens itself up as the place of origin of identity and negativity: "The opening grants *first of all* the possibility of the path to presence, and grants the possible presencing of that presence itself."[22] The breaking through, irritation, or negation of possibility of the opening itself remains unthought in Heidegger. Unproblematically self-identical, its category therefore falls back within the terrain of Idealism and of original synthesis, whose deconstruction is the aim of Hölderlin's texts.

The "sign" laid out in interpretation "in front of us" by means of the "time-image" of history that has come to an end and that refers to an ambiguous "between" and thus not to a logically specifiable phenomenon, insofar as the historical and structural articulation of a difference between humans and gods that is no longer full of suffering is dreamed in the "time-image" and in the "festival-day" that also appears as a "sign of love"—this "sign" is definitely not the signifier of a signified that transcends it; rather, it is a sign of something that itself has the structure of a sign.[23] The between has this structure and is "another" of which the hymn "The Rhine" speaks, insofar as the "great Spirit" and the gods on the whole "can be known" to humans as well as to themselves; they have "proof" of their identity in the "festival-day" with which the poet hopes for a place of difference, "where" the differentiated can gather.

> Yet ultimately, you holy powers, our sign
> Of love for you, and the proof
> That still you are holy to us, is the festival-day. (StA 3: 536; PF 529, mod.)

The differential structure of the sign, which makes cognition possible, but also limits [*einschränkende*] cognition to the cognition of the identical and thus makes cognition impossible, is one of the most significant subjects of Hölderlin's textual production up until the very last of his poems. Corresponding to this structure in the poetic process is the parenthetical structure of Hölderlin's language: the art of the pause, of delay, of inserting in-between construction [*Zwischenbauen*].

> Up there perhaps
> On Monte   , sideways too perhaps
> I stray, come down
> Across Tirol, Lombardy, Loretto, where the pilgrim's home is
>   on the Gotthard, fenced, carelessly, under glaciers
> Poorly he lives, where the bird
> With eiderdown, a pearl of the sea
> And the eagle there calls the accent, before God, where the fire runs because of men (StA 2: 252; PF 685–87)

Like the obstruction and the straying off track, the parenthetical intervening terms have their source in the attempt to defer the reaching of the goal and to insert between beginning and end, between subject and object, a third term that holds the first two apart from one another and at the same time links them, as a figure of difference bearing the character of a term and site [*Aufenthalt*] and of a promise. Thus, the description of the "pilgrim's home" pauses at the caesural insertions between "poorly he lives" and "before God," in order to protect him, as though with shadows or clouds, from the immediate proximity of God. Among other things, what this description places between the two is God's sign, the eagle. The implication of its "calling the accent" is defined by its parenthetical position. "Accent" here does not mean, in the Rousseauvian sense,[24] the expression of passion but, rather, its precise opposite: articulation put into effect through sobriety. The accent of sobriety stands before the pilgrim's proximity to God. It is the "presenting" [*darstellende*][25] Hesperian sign that has its corresponding place in the pausing parenthesis. As the atoning pilgrim strays off track, it is the intermittent accent of the eagle that is the sign that the hymn-fragment demands shortly before, which is to say, it is the discriminating sign:

> To preserve God pure and with discrimination
> Is the task entrusted to us,
> Lest, because much depends
> On this, through a penitence, through a mistake
> In the sign
> God's day of judgement set in. (StA 2: 252; PF 685)

Thanks to the parenthetical series of locations, the syntactic cohesion between "poorly he lives" and "before God" is not only unsettled; the proximity to God, whose "discrimination" and whose harmlessness the interpolation is intended to protect, itself becomes an element of the series through the fact that it, too, is formulated as a location. The proximity to God, *definiendum*, appears through what is supposed to protect from it and determine it, through the parenthesis that it introduces into the parataxis of the straying journey as something belonging to the parataxis itself, *definiens*. God's proximity, embedded in a language that is delay, deferral, and digression, is no longer the telos in which form his hypostasis in the logical proposition would allow him to appear. Hölderlin's concept of inversion is theoretically directed against the logical proposition:

> There are inversions of words within a period. Greater and more effective, then, must be the inversion of the periods themselves. The logical position of the periods, where the ground (the ground period) is followed by the becoming, the becoming by the goal, the goal by the purpose, and the subordinate clauses are always simply attached at the end of the main clauses to which they most closely relate—is certainly useful to the poet only on the rarest occasions. (StA 4: 233; EL 240)

Just as the "inversion of the periods themselves" succeeds in including goal and purpose in the movement towards inversion, and still treats it as a deferring and discriminating movement, so the parenthetical process also succeeds within the period. However, insofar as the syntactic tension toward "living" remains preserved in "before God," equivalent to the way that the inversion is preserved as inversion, and insofar as this one location is not assimilated without remainder to the locations that surround it, so the concept of the series or even that of parataxis cannot be said without serious reservations to capture the figure of Hölderlinian syntax. For both concepts still retain the possibility that the continuity broken by the hierarchical hypotaxis be restored in parataxis and in the linking of gods and humans to one another.[26] And indeed, Adorno speaks of "a flowing continuum of images."[27] The fact that the distinction between the spheres and separation of syntactical structures is also still preserved in serialization is perhaps more precisely described by the concept of syntactic ambiguity. In syntactic double-interpretation [*Doppeldeutigkeit*], hypotaxis and parataxis come together in reciprocal obstruction. What is achieved in this double-interpretation—and double-interpretation, too, remains an insufficient term because the interplay of the two forms does not allow either to exist in its own way—is not a synthesis, or a sublation, in which difference is eliminated. Rather, what this double-interpretation achieves is the interlocking of movements that exclude one another yet always already imply one another, an interlocking that is constitutive for every unit and every syntactical form in this sentence. - If in "before God" there is a syntactical double-interpretation at work, there is in what comes after "before God" a semantic double-interpretation, in the phrase "where the fire runs because of men." Like the light of God, fire runs because of humans; and it runs thanks to the initiative of, and on the paths travelled by, humans, *hominum causa*.[28] The heavenly is dependent on the movement of humans in precisely the act by which it supports them: the configuration of movements that exclude one another and yet imply one another at the same time, movements that evade the linearity of *one* form and are therefore not subsumable under the concept. In them, two kinds of conditional relations are merged together that are irreducible in their syntactical double-interpretation. Only as such inversive movements do they describe the place that follows "before God": "where the fire runs because of men."

Divine presence, self-identity, preserved "with discrimination," makes its way through a sign in which the possibility of its appearance is opened up and the appearance is blocked, that is, is presented as a moment of its own deferral. The secession that leads from the gods' erstwhile but quickly interrupted "presence" to their desired appearance in the evening of time—this deviation from the straight path of light produces the historical prism, and history as a figure, in which the transcendental content of that which traverses this history passes away. The diffractions [*Brechungen*] that this content endures in this medium of historical "wilderness" (StA 2:

131; PF 519) are not straightened out in the utopia that is represented by the festival-day in Hölderlin's lyric poetry; rather, diffraction, curvature, and bending are the constitutive forms for the festival (itself). They are the constitutive forms as a loving *inclination*. Thus, it can be said of the Apollonian demiurge in "The Rhine" that, after he has guided human life with his winds:

> Rests also, and down to his pupil
> The master craftsmen, finding
> More good than evil,
> Day now inclines to the present Earth.— (StA 2: 147; PF 509, mod.)[29]

This inclination of the sun towards the earth describes the arc that defines the route as well as the course of a life led by love and suffering:

> More you also desired, but every one of us
> Love draws earthward, and grief bends with still greater power;
> Yet our arc not for nothing
> Brings us back to whence it came. (StA 2: 22; PF 201, mod.)

It is that singular one through which the highest life, in its proximity to death, is able to touch those to whom it owes its self-experience. The arc, the reversal of intention, that is to say not intention itself but its deviation, is the movement in which the self-identity of the gods or the self-identity that humans yearn for is dissolved; in which lordship and mastery pass away because the inclination of the light belongs neither to the domain of the day nor to that of the night; in the evening, neither the absence nor presence of the gods, neither the moment nor the duration, neither the one nor its opposite determines the scene. And yet both do so each time. Thus, the evening, in which gods and men celebrate the "bridal festival" (StA 2: 147; PF 509, mod.), would be the place and time at which the various jurisdictions separate as at their border, the condition common to them both where they open one another up. The evening would be the between in which they come together and take leave of one another at the same time. At the same time, it is understood not in the sense of identity in the moment, not as pause [*Einstand*] in duration, but itself as "a while [*eine Weile*]" (StA 2: 147; PF 509): a whiling away [*Verweilen*] in which the "hurry" [*eilen*] (StA 2: 148; PF 511) of another but nevertheless corresponding place[30] is also marked:

. . . but those unreconciled
Are changed and hurry now
To hold out their hands to the other
Before the benevolent light
Goes down, and night comes. (StA 2: 148; PF 511)

The relation into which gods and humans enter is, like the relation of those unreconciled, a "marriage" [*Ehe*] that is an "earlier" [*ehe*], a *Bevor*, and attained shortly before the departure [*Scheiden*] of the light and dissolved with it in just as much of a hurry. Or it is "retained" [*behalten*] in the mind [*Gedächtnis*]:

For some, however,
This quickly passes, others
Retain it longer. (StA 2: 148; PF 511)

The "bearing in mind" [*Gedächtnis*] (l. 201) preserves the rights of the "before" [*ehe*] in what comes later. In it, the while [*Weile*] is structurally reproduced as the path of transience [*Vergängnis*], as the between and the bridal festival of the evening. Like inclination, "bearing in mind" is the figure of a whiling away, a lingering [*Verweilen*] of that which is past and has died off. It is the mournful interval between the living and the dead, where the dead is at the living and the living is at the dead.

III. The Trace of Transgression

The mythic landscape in which the festival is located, and where the while and the between are drawn into a geographically circumscribable place, is the extreme west, the place where "the benevolent light / Goes down, and night comes" (StA 2: 148; PF 511): Hesperia. Just as the sun, the allegory of the divine, travels along an arc from east to west, so the spirit in Hölderlin's allegory of history travels in an arc from the morning of the daytime of the gods in Greece through the in-between time of its distance and towards its evening in Hesperia. In its Greek time and its Hesperian time, the spirit experiences, respective to the place of its appearance, a different fate in each time. Hölderlin describes this in the form of a historical-philosophical poetology for the first time in his letter to Böhlendorff of December 1801. According to the model outlined in this letter, for which correlativity or symmetry, as it were, was still definitive for world-historical processes, the "sacred pathos" of the Greeks, the "heavenly fire" (StA 6: 426; EL 207), rescues itself by way of the "Junonian sobriety of the occident," whereas the Hesperian "clarity of exposition" does so through the "beautiful passion" (StA 2: 426; EL 207, mod.) that can be learned from the Greeks. Only in such reciprocal historical synthesis, according to the conception developed in this first letter to Böhlendorff, is the protection against petrification in what is our own and subjugation to the foreign achieved. Shortly after Hölderlin's sojourn in France, this synthetic model, which underlies both the poetology of his first letter to Böhlendorff and the essays of his Homburg period, must have undergone significant changes. Peter Szondi has pointed out important traces of these changes in his study of Hölderlin's "Genre Poetics and Philosophy of History" [*Gattungspoetik und Geschichtsphilosophie*].[31] More decisive perhaps in this regard than explicitly theoretical reflections is the theory that is constituted in the praxis of the poetic texts concerning the historical relationship between Orient and Occident, between divine identity and its articulation in the pathetic or sober speech of humans. In none of the poetological essays does it seem that the problem of subjectivity, whose fate is so significantly tied to the course of all the great hymns, ever gets discussed. The progress of the subject in the lyric, whether this be its idealistic hypostasis or its reduction, its positivity or its distortion, also defines the shape of the poem, just as, conversely, the degree of articulation of the poem's language determines the fate of the subject of this language. This relation of the I to its history and to the forms of its self-presentation is paradigmatic for the three versions of "The Only One"—and for each in a different way. What Beda Allemann points out when he writes that "[t]he hymn is constructed according to the law of patriotic reversal"[32]—this turnaround within the poem is achieved with respect to the figure of Christ and, as though in imitation, according to the example of his action. It is the lack of a figure or shape, the absence of the Christian demigod, that compels this reversal, the turning away from the beautiful plasticity of the Greek landscape and of Greek art:

What is it that
To the ancient happy shores
Fetters me, so that I love them
Still more than my own fatherland?
For as though into heavenly
Captivity sold,

I am where Apollo walked
In the shape of a king,
And Zeus condescended
To innocent youths, and sons in a holy fashion
Begot, and daughters,
The exalted, amid humankind. (StA 2: 153; PF 535, mod.)

The I is bound to Greece as the space not of a former divine presence but of a divine presence that is caught in a plastic shape and could be preserved in it. This divine presence expresses in, as it were, plastic speech—according to the supplement added in the second and third versions, as "stones say" (StA 2: 157, 161; PF 543, mod.)—the progress of the Gods even in the present. "Of Elis and / Olympia I have heard," "Much that is lovely I have seen" (StA 2: 153; PF 535, mod.): audible and visible, the documents of a mythic presence of the gods attain authoritative value for the progress of the I through a landscape in whose name the history of the effects [*Wirken*] of the gods' actions has contracted; the documents also become binding for the song. For the song does not refer to an imageless god or to one of which it is forbidden to make an image, but rather to "the image of God" "as here among the human kind / It lives" (StA 2: 153, 154; PF 535, 537, mod.). In the space of the plastic gods, however, one fails to appear:

. . . and yet,
You old gods and all
You valiant sons of gods,
One other I search for whom
Within your ranks I love,
Where hidden from the alien guest, from me,
You conceal the last of your race,
The treasured gem of the house. (StA 2: 154; PF 537, mod.)

The song of "the image of God" meets its limit in the one who marks the limit of the Greek race of gods: in "the last" of its kind. The Hesperian poet, in Greece in order to investigate the plastic order of the divine, finds the one he loves precisely not in this order; the one whom he calls master, lord, and teacher. A peculiar ambiguity is significant with regard to the poet's love: he loves "the ancient happy shores," the architectonically and thoroughly wrought shape of the space they enclose, but at the same time the one who remains far from this space. The fact that this second love is not absorbed in the first, that an identity is not achieved between the promise of Greek plasticity and the demands of the *logos* that fleetingly took shape in Christ, shatters for the subject the closedness of the Pantheon, and the abundance of the gods appears empty due to the single absent one. The mourning over this double lack, which stands opposite the double love, is articulated in a statement whose proverbial character almost conceals its complexity:

> . . . And now my soul
> Is full of mourning as though
> You Heavenly yourselves excitedly cried
> That if I serve one I
> Must lack the other. (StA 2: 154; PF 537, mod.)

By virtue of the neuter gender of its demonstrative terms—one / the other, *einem / das andere*—the dichotomy of the "either-or" is dissolved: the service that pertains to the "one" has to be seen both as service to the Christ who is named "master and lord" and as service to those who populate the Greek landscape as plastic and present. If "the other" is therefore "lacking," the closedness of the Greek cosmos is also absent along with the one who caused its breach. The dissolution of a world organized by the law of a dichotomous logic, introduced with this statement of the mourning subject, is reiterated by the statement that follows, which confesses to guilt and gives reasons for this confession.

> And yet I know, it is my
> Own fault [*Schuld*]! For too greatly,
> O Christ, I'm attached to you,
> Although Heracles' brother
> And boldly I confess, you
> Are the brother also of Evius (StA 2: 154; PF 537, mod.)

In its admission of guilt, that its love for Christ is too great; in the attempt to give logical structure to the demonstration of its knowledge and of its self-cognition, the I once again gets caught in formulations that undermine, as it were, that which they intend [*das Gemeinte*] by the strength of their intention [*Intention*], perversely turning meaning [*Bedeutung*] against their sense [*Sinn*]. It is therefore undecidable and thus withdrawn from self-"critical" structuration whether the link established in the verse "For too greatly, / O Christ, I'm attached to you, / Although Heracles' brother" refers to the kinship between Christ and Heracles or rather that between the poet and Heracles. It is unquestionable, however, that the restriction of double-interpretation to a determinate sense—as commentators from Stoll to Beissner and Allemann have tried to do[33]—suppresses insight into how this one equivocation functions as well as insight into the essential limitation of logical operations, both of which were formulated by Hölderlin in his "Reflection" on inversions in a way that no other lyric poet of his time did. The subject's hubris and the overdetermination of its confession emerge in the very phrase that, along with the Greek demigod, introduces the principle of measure and of strict distinction. The world-historical achievement of Heracles and Bacchus, that is, the installation of laws and the delimitation of life-threatening excess, remain impotent for the poet who is attached "too greatly" to Christ. Love and mourning for Christ thus overstep Greek law even where they lament that overstepping and reproduce anew in every turn of their articulation the absence of that which had to withdraw from love due to the excess of love. At the same time, they show this overstepping to be one that is founded, with the subject's hubris, in the historical decline of the Greeks' "kingdom of art" (StA 2: 228; HSP 279), in the Greeks' inability to tame excess.

Paratactically serialized, the poet's "bold" (StA 2: 154; PF 537) confession leaves behind the immediate argumentative context to declare that Christ is the "brother also of Evius,"

> Who to his chariot harnessed
> The tigers and right down
> As far as the Indus
> Commanding joyful service,
> First planted the vineyard and tamed
> The fierceness and rage of the peoples. (StA 2: 154; PF 537)

The precision of this statement, of its descriptions of place and action, differs centrally from that which is posited through Evius's actions. If Evius's activities are directed against an excess of freedom and self-destructive agility, the parataxis introduces precisely this positivity of Dionysian action into its boundary-transgressing movement, introduces measure into the lapse of measure, and introduces pausing in the face of danger into "the way of death" (StA 2: 158; PF 545). In the hymn, Greek concreteness becomes a moment of its own lack of measure. The entire strophe—and this structure that has just been outlined remains the same across its three versions—is calculated as the presentation of a transgression of Greek measure that affirms Hesperia: an affirmation that realizes itself in the process of transgression and is already thereby qualitatively different from the plastic figurativeness of Greek affirmation.

> Hindering me is however shame
> From comparing you with
> Worldly men. And yet know I,
> The one who made you, your father,
> The same who . . . (StA 2:155; PF 539, mod.)

Talk of the knowledge of the father who is common to all also disregards the shame that recalls difference, and no less "boldly" than the first time the kinship between Christ and the Greek demigod was established. As with the measure in the preceding strophe, the hindrance that shame presents is overcome as being too weak to withstand the wish to come into proximity with Christ—even if this proximity is only achieved through knowledge. This wish leads, already in the central strophe, to an approximation of the personal pronouns for the poet and for Christ: "*I*'m attached to *you*," "boldly *I* confess, *you* / Are." In this sixth strophe, the wish forces into being a double-interpretation that, though resolved again in the course of the sentence, expresses with an intensification of "boldness" the comparability, if not the equality, of Christ and the poet: "Hindering *me is however shame* / From comparing *you* . . . " (StA 2: 155, emphasis added; PF 539, mod.).[34] The excess of love and of subjectivity even unsettles the syntactic organization of the bastions erected against it. However weak it is, the ambiguity penetrates the expression of shame; the paratactically added statement that *one* father is common to both Greek heroes and the last of their race repeats the injury of shame to the extent that it, too, is directed at the comparability of the demigods. The most extreme hubris of the subject, which is expressed in the phrase "And yet know *I*, / *The one who made you*, your father," is not only naming itself as the knowing subject in proximity to Christ but also admitting, in the articulation of knowledge, the possibility of its paternity of the demigod. The movement of the subject aims at the depiction of Christ in connection with the Greek gods, at the definition of his place in their space and, furthermore, at its own relation to him. The definitional gesture that wants to return the Christian demigod to the Greek domain of fixed measure is thereby peculiarly thwarted by the impulse of love and excess that initiated the gesture to begin with. For the subject turns towards the definition and identification of the one who fails to appear [*Ausgebliebenen*] for the sake of the maximal proximity and intelligibility of the "treasured gem" (StA 2: 154; PF 537); this proximity, however, is possible for the subject only through the polyvalence of its speech, and intelligibility only under the condition of the withdrawal of distinct and conceptual sense. The overdetermination that results from excess and desire explodes the, as it were, spatial and linear movement of syntax and thereby also diffuses the relation to the beloved, whose construction was supposed to be accomplished by precisely this syntax. In this way, the movement of the text realizes what was depicted in the transition from the fourth to the fifth strophe as the connection between the exclusivity of service and the absence [*Fehlen*] of the one who is longed for. The penultimate strophe of this first version turns once again to the same problem, as a problem of the hymn or song itself.

> To One alone, however,
> Love clings. For this time too much
> From my own heart the song
> Has come; if I sing other songs
> I'll make amends for the fault.
> Much though they wish to, never
> They strike, men, the right measure. (StA 2: 155; PF 539, mod.)[35]

The self-accusation of the fifth strophe[36] is taken up again here and transitions into the depiction of Christ's fate as a paradigm for the hymn's procedure. If the exclusivity of yearning is to blame for the "absence" of Christ according to the confession in the fourth strophe, here it is the exclusivity of the hymn and its law of subjectivity in which this fifth strophe recognizes the root of this "fault" and thereby exposes the connection between the two confessions, not only in the etymological proximity of the vocabulary but also in giving grounds for this guilt. Along with this connection, however, the fifth strophe also exposes the connection between Christ's absence [*Fehlen*] and the fault [*Fehl*] of the song. If fault here does not mean only guilty misconduct [*Verfehlung*] and the missing [*Verfehlen*] of a striven-towards goal, but also the absence [*Ausbleiben*], in the song, of the one the I so yearningly tries to reach, the same applies to the non-appearance [*Ausbleiben*] of the "others" that the song was also supposed to be about, whose treatment remains relegated to "other" songs. In this doubling of the missed [*Verfehlten*], the doubling of the "one" and the "other" that is produced by the same excess is repeated: each is at once itself and also the other, the Christian God and the Greek gods are both signified, as both missed [*verfehlte*] and as the object of song. Doubling reproduces itself in the "fault" of the song insofar as in this absence, "other" songs, songs of the "others," *Greek* demigods, are absent [*fehlen*] and insofar as the one for whom the hymn mourns is absent [*fehlt*]: the *Christian* demigod. Thus, because the excess of song exceeds according to two measures in each case, insofar as it holds neither to the law of equality nor to the law of difference between Christ and the others, one must also speak of a duplicity of the song's fault [*Fehl*] as well.

Insofar as the song's law is the overstepping of measure posited as law; insofar as the song dwells neither in the domain of equality nor that of the difference between the Christian demigod and the Greek heroes and yet moves in both, it follows the route of the one it seeks, that of Christ: Christ is the "last" of the race of Greek demigods and gods, and as such is equal to them; as imageless *logos*, however, which does not belong to the space of Greek gods, he is foreign to them. As the figure of the historical self-overstepping that defines the plastic order of gods, Christ's life and death lead towards a double fault [*Fehl*]. The law of history and the law of the song come into agreement in this duplicity. Yet the course of history cannot be regarded as a simply predetermined given, towards which the song might orient its own course as though toward a fact. The historical turn that takes place with the appearance and disappearance of the *logos* is itself a positing or, better yet, the misconduct [*Verfehlung*] of the subject: "I must lack [*fehlet*] the other. // And yet I know, it is my / Own fault [*Schuld*]! For too greatly, / O Christ, I'm attached to you" (StA 2: 154; PF 537). The absence [*Fehlen*] of Christ, as established in these verses, appears to be bound to the movement of the song, a movement that seeks to follow that of the last son of the gods. However, the subjectivity of the song is irrevocably split by the fact that it distances itself from its goal with every step it takes towards it; with every equality it attains, the gulf between those being equated grows larger, and, at the convergence of fault [*Fehl*] and lack [*Fehlen*], there is only a repetition of their negativity. The singer promises to make up for the errant [*fehlgegangenen*] song with other songs, but the promise is—as the moment of precisely this song gone wrong, which the promise does not yet make good—its affirmation. This is all the more so when the verse following the promise dashes the hope for a song free of fault [*fehlerlos*] and failure [*verfehlend*]: "Much though they wish to, never / They strike, men, the right measure." This verse, which like its earlier version, "Much though I wish to, never / I strike the right measure" (StA 2: 746; PF 539) renders the "this time" of the preceding sentence into permanence and refers to the renewed attempt, through the equating of heroes and poets, to depict the song as a heroic undertaking: that is, as misconduct [*Verfehlung*] in which a new realization of measure is announced. For, differing minutely yet nevertheless strictly from the "*what* I wish" that follows a couple of verses later, the formulation of the parenthesis in this sentence reads "*much though* they wish": they strike the "measure" not as they wish to, but in some other way: "But / A god knows when it comes, what I wish for, the best" (StA 2: 155; PF 539). How this striking fault [*Fehl*] comes about, how it "comes"—for it is no longer the intended deed of a subject, but rather a deed in which the subject's intention is extinguished—how "the best," the superlative of that impossible making good that other songs are supposed to bring about, arises: this is anticipated in the fact that Christ, as he "Once moved on earth, / A captive eagle" (StA 2: 155; PF 541) submits to a worldly measure, but also in the fact that he evades captivity through his ascension. The interaction of the structural and textual moments of the far-reaching comparison in which this double movement is depicted marks, against the grain of a crude comparative schema, the internal complicity of Christ's two movements in the "captivity" of the "souls of heroes":

> For as the master
> Once moved on earth,
> A captive eagle,
> // And many, who
> Looked on him were afraid,
> While the Father did
> His utmost, effectively bringing
> The best to bear upon men,
> And sorely troubled in mind
> The Son was also until
> To Heaven he rose in the winds,
> So too, the souls of the heroes are captive.
> The poets, and those no less who
> Are spiritual, must be worldly. (StA 2: 156; PF 541)

Just as Christ escapes from his captivity on earth, so the part of the sentence in which he is still depicted as captive and troubled in mind escapes the strict bond of the comparison. It begins to come loose at the beginning of the final strophe and turns into an independent sequence of statements that is still bound to the comparison in terms of content but is, formally speaking, free. Following upon this syntactic secession is the secession from comparison in terms of content when Christ's ascension into heaven is mentioned, immediately before the reintroduction of the comparison:

> . . . until
> To Heaven he rose in the winds,
> So too, the souls of the heroes are captive. (StA 2: 156; PF 541)

The splitting away of what is being compared does not subject the meaning of the decisive "so too" [*Dem gleich*] to an indefinite irritation; rather, the meaning of the phrase is split up in a precisely determinable doubling. First, the "so too" has to be linked with rising "to heaven" through the mention of a "heavenly captivity" (StA 2: 153; PF 535); second, it has to be linked with Christ's earthly captivity by way of the verse about "a captive eagle." The word that might have served as a *tertium comparationis*—"captive," in which the heroes and the master would have had to come to an agreement—is unsettled in the identity of its meaning through the syntactic secession and the semantic overturning of the comparison: the autonomy of signification comes up against the sense of the comparison and forces it apart in the "actual" [*eigentlichen*] sense and, here, in its opposite. Insofar as they are compared with the captivity of heroes, the two opposed movements of Christ—his movement in captivity, his ascension—undo the comparison as well as the concept of captivity. The equality in which the different are supposed to have come together and in which the separate are supposed to have been bound together is split up into an equality with bondage and an opposing equality with liberation, such that equality is unequal to itself and is set in opposition to itself. Through the secession of syntax and image, the synthetic function of comparison is reversed into a sylleptical function, as it were: both equality and inequality, unity and opposition, are signified in the one phrase "so too." Yet the identity into which they combine in the "so" [*gleich*] is not the identity of Hegelian synthesis, since it does not suppress either of the movements for the benefit of privileging another and thus, unlike Hegelian synthesis, does not have to put a halt to the opposition of its relata by means of sublation. For if, in Hegel, identity is, at one of its lower stages, defined as "a vanishing of otherness"[37] precisely according to the model of the spirit's self-generation and therefore according to its hierarchy of stages, the verses of Hölderlin under discussion here indicate that in the determination of equality, difference does not dissolve; rather, the identity of sense, to whose force the Other in Hegel asserts its rights, is shattered: "The poets, and those who no less/ Are spiritual, must be worldly" (StA 2: 156; PF 541). The "captivity" of heroes is determined and dissolved through the comparison; the "worldliness" of spiritual poets is determined and dissolved through the caesura. The intimate interaction of spiritual and worldly that this statement establishes is signified, through the syntactic proximity of concepts that emphasize their contradictoriness and through the caesura that separates them, as one in which the difference between spirit and world is preserved. If—with good reason—it could be said[38] that the epigraphic concluding formulation establishes the law of patriotic reversal, this cannot mean that the heavenly captivity becomes an earthly one, that the worldly steps into the place of the spiritual; rather, the spiritual poets are worldly under the condition that the two domains are separated. For the subjectivity of the poet, who distances himself from his own yearning with this sober imperative, the double movement of the final lines signifies the decline into a concretion in which alone the possibility of yearning and of excess are preserved. Only where it is weighed down by the burden of worldliness will it be able to preserve itself as a "spiritual" subjectivity that aims at identity. - The categorical imperative of Hesperian poetry, as presented by this hymn, would be this: to signify the foreignness of that which is close to one another; to meet with the excess in that in which it is limited through measure; to simultaneously secure and relinquish meaning as that which both misses and strikes its target. -

---

The stylistic procedure that, through its confrontation with material contents [*Gehalten*], puts into effect such an alteration in the interior of meaning and in the structure of the sign and the position of subjectivity, has been known by a term taken from the poetics of the mature Hölderlin: Hesperian sobriety. Yet while the idea that literary criticism has formed of the meaning of this concept—that sober precision designates the other side of Oriental infinity, and that the Hesperian turn to the national has as its historical task the reconciliation of the two opposing tendencies—finds a firm basis in the first letter to Böhlendorff, it falls flat in regard to the poetics of the later period, which is the period to which "The Only One" belongs. In particular, a closer description of Hölderlin's late conception of Hesperian reversal, such as is set out in the "Notes on the *Antigone*," is presented with the problem of *contraria significatio*.[39] Here the concepts of fate [*Schicksal*] and hitting upon something successfully [*Treffen*] have been sources of contention. According to Allemann's attack on interpreters who relate Hesperian "hitting upon" to "the Occidental creative drive towards heavenly fire," the Hesperian concept of fate is understood as follows:

> Corresponding (to this interpretation of "hitting upon"), "to have a fate" has to be interpreted as the capacity for a heroic-pathetic deed, and "fatelessness" as native sobriety and the Nordic life of a snail. Even just a fleeting verification with the corresponding definitions across the rest of Hölderlin's oeuvre would have long uncovered the complete groundlessness of this interpretation. Since "Hyperion's Song of Fate," "fatelessness" has been an attribute of the Heavenly; . . . *therefore*, fatelessness is a weakness of Hesperian humankind, since it is an attempt to escape from this demand to be worldly.[40]

This interpretation suppresses the double-interpretation of fatelessness and rest, the *contrario significatio* of their concepts, and accepts the consequence that it has to insinuate a self-contradictory concept of *weakness*, in contrast to the obvious movement of the "Notes on the *Antigone*." Hölderlin's text reads as follows:

> [For us,] the Greek ideas alter, insofar as the Greeks' main aim is to grasp themselves, since this was *their weakness*, whereas the main aim in the modes of understanding for our own age is to hit upon something successfully, to have a fate, since fatelessness, *dusmoron*, is *our weakness*. (StA 5: 269–70; EL 330)

If Allemann's interpretation were correct, the weakness of the Greeks would have to lie in what was originally their own and the weakness of the Hesperian in what they first had to acquire through cultivation [*Bildung*], because it was foreign to them. Weakness, however, belongs in both cases to the appearance of something original.

> For everything original, because all potential is justly and equally divided, does not in fact manifest itself in its original strength, but actually in its weakness, so that really and essentially the light of life and the manifestation of weakness are part of every whole. (StA 4: 274; EL 316, mod.)[41]

The Greek tendency to be able "to grasp themselves" is thus directed, in the medium of sobriety, towards "sacred pathos" as the original weakness, which, as the letters to Wilmans[42] emphasize, was necessarily neglected and thus forced the decline of the Greek "kingdom of art." The weakness of the Hesperian must thus lie in two directions: its fatelessness springs from far too great a security; as *dusmoron* it is the fatelessness of the immortal gods. Measure is thus missing [*verfehlt*] from this fatelessness in two ways, and Hesperian art must strive towards this measure, its fate [*Geschick*], in two directions. For one, it seeks to dissolve that which is all too restful, the stagnation of sobriety: just as it turns against what is the Hesperian's own, "hitting upon [this weakness] correctly" also turns against the Oriental creative drive, which, while in the throes of self-bondage and "grasping themselves," neglected the national. Hölderlin's undertaking in his Sophocles translations to "expos[e] more boldly what was forbidden to the original poet, precisely by going in the direction of[43] eccentric enthusiasm" (StA 6: 439; EL 22), and to emphasize the original excess, thus includes the attempt at an historical salvaging of the lost Greek world. This salvaging through linguistic correction, which first becomes possible from an historical distance in Hesperia; this Hesperian turn, which is given to the original through its translation, is the poetic and historical-philosophical correlate to the revolt thematized in the "Notes on the *Antigone*." The translation of that passage in *Antigone* where Creon insists on being true to his oath and Haemon counters, "But you aren't, *if you don't honor the name of God*" (StA 5: 267; EL 327; HS, 93, mod.); where Haemon turns in rebellion away from the law that has become positive and from which the name of God has disappeared—Hölderlin comments on this passage with the following words: "Admittedly, the manner in which time reverses at the centre is not really alterable; similarly, the manner in which a character categorically *follows* categorical time, and *the move from the Greek to the Hesperian*; however, the sacred name under which the highest is felt or occurs can be altered" (StA 5: 267; EL 327, emphasis added). The turn from deadly fidelity to lawlessness is described explicitly as a turn from the Greek to the Hesperian. Yet the categorical reversal that takes place in this stichomythia between Creon and Haemon must—"like any total reversal without any check is not granted to man as a creature endowed with perception" (StA 5: 271; EL 331)—also already contain within it an objectifying moment in which it can affirm its own character without falling into one with the positivity of the law. Hölderlin explains the correction of Sophocles's text as follows: "It was probably necessary to change the sacred expression here, since it is meaningful at the centre, as a serious and independent word, around which all else is objectified and transfigured" (StA 5: 267; EL 327, mod.). As Haemon's objection implicitly includes the demand that God's name be *held* sacred, it must in the reversal from Greek into Hesperian also already be "independent" in the sense of being "*constant*" to itself [*selbst-ständig*]. In Haemon's Hesperian turn, two movements are combined: first, the movement to follow swiftly flowing time in the categorical reversal in order to destroy positive law; and second, the movement to give oneself an indicator [*Anhalt*] with the reversal itself. In it, excess and precision meet: the breaking of the law is aimed at the positive, while sobriety is aimed at excess. Each one alone causes a fall back into fatelessness, into cold order's rest, as the letter to Emerich calls it (StA 6: 388–89), or into the hubristic order of equality with the gods. Like Haemon's revolt, the work of translation is a form of patriotic reversal, and both undertake the attempt to force positive law and the Greekness that was lost due to its positivity "more decisively to earth" (StA 5: 269; 330); this means, however, to cause them "fate" ["*Geschik*"]: to determine for them a fate and make them skillful [*geschickt*] at bearing it. As long what is seen in "fate" is doom alone, however, instead of the doubling of determining and determined,[44] the deed of "the more essential Zeus," who "on his way into the other world, *more decidedly forces down to earth* the natural process which is eternally hostile to man" (StA 5: 269; EL 330), must go unrecognized, and with this also Hölderlin's attempt to salvage the Greek world. His translations aim to supplement the originals with what the originals, compelled by their historical position, had to deny, and through this supplementation they want to reverse their path into decline and turn it toward one on which the Hesperian realizes itself as the form of lingering [*Verweilen*], of intermediary measure [*Zwischenmaß*], and of protection. In the phrase "Hesperian turn," "Hesperian" does not mean straightforward sobriety, as has often been suggested; rather, it carries the sense found in the comparison and the caesura at the end of the first version of "The Only One"; it has the sense of turning the form [*Gestalt*] of Greek positivity, through an exposition of "sacred pathos," toward a figure[45] of deferral, and "eccentric enthusiasm" (StA 6: 439; EL 220) toward a form of "propriety" ["*Schiklichkeit*"] (StA 5: 270; EL 330).[46] - The double work that is to be accomplished by the Hesperian turn towards the double weakness of the Hesperian does not, however, come to light only in the commentary to Haemon's categorical reversal; it is also evident in the phrase "to hit upon something successfully" (StA 5: 270; EL 330). This "something" being aimed at is something external, determinate, and certain [*Feststehendes*], corresponding to the sentence from the "Notes on the *Oedipus*": "Among men, one must above all bear in mind that every thing is *something*, i.e. that it is cognizable in the medium (*moyen*) of its appearance, and that the manner in which it is defined can be determined and taught" (StA 5: 195; EL 317). Such determinate externality must, however, be hit upon by the act of the one who, not being implicated in the distinction of the "something," moves in the sphere of excess. Hitting upon something is mostly depicted by Hölderlin as an act of the gods.[47] In this act, excess bumps up against measure in such a way that measure is marked and wounded by this encounter at the same time as it undergoes its determination[48]—its determination, its precise representation, transforms it into suffering and therefore into the opposite of that which, as a fixed measure, could be certain [*feststehen*] in itself. The Hesperian poetic process is a hitting of the target [*Treffen*] with which the measure is determined and wounded [*verletzt*], and is determined only through injury [*Verletzung*]; as lesion, the measure turns against the positivity of "grasping oneself" [*Fassen*], and as the establishment of measure it turns against the rapidity of the Oriental. Just as "fate" is doubled as determining and determined, so the determining fate, in turn, is divided into a fate that injures and a fate that fixes. - The Hesperian reversal does not take *one* path, unlike what commentators of precisely the last verses of the first version of "The Only One" and the "Notes on the *Antigone*" like to claim. It is the double path of measure and excess, of sobriety and the violation of the law, of decline and preservation, on which Christ moves, on which history completes itself, and towards which the poet must head. As a comparison with the second and third versions shows, what Hölderlin did not achieve to his satisfaction with the first version of "The Only One" was probably the proximity of the second half of the poem with its first half, that is, the far-reaching adequation if not in the structure of meaning, then in the virtually elegiac tone from which almost only the last verses deviate. For Hölderlin, the specific characteristic of Christ's form and his manner of "planting" or "granting" [*Stiftung*][49] and of remaining probably seemed all too little worked out. The second and third versions put into effect with utmost clarity the affirmation of excess and the Hesperian reversal, the law of the hymn, through a change of stylistic gesture between the first and the second half. From the middle of the poem onwards, and thus where the subject appears to be the most exposed, the characteristic style of hymnic appeals striving for great immediacy is retarded by heavy parenthetical constructions, through which individual sentences and words are lent a weight that protects them from the danger of fleetingness and transgression. The new conception of the second half begins with the depiction of Evius's deeds. To the same degree that its periods acquire the material weight of concretion, however, the statements also become more abstract. While Evius's deed is depicted in the first version using the image of the taming of raging animals, in the second version it seems to be elevated to the language of an almost conceptual reflection:

> . . . you
> Are the brother also of Evius, who
> Restrains the deathwish of the peoples and breaks up the snare,
> Well men can see now, so that
> They do not go the way of death and keep the measure, so that
> A man shall be something in himself and fear
> The moment, the destiny of great eras and
> Their fires no less, they strike [*treffen*], and where
> Another goes that way, they also see
> Where there's a destiny, but make
> It safe, resembling human beings or laws [*Gesezen*]. (StA 2: 158; PF 545–47, mod.)[50]

The negation of death, as intended by Bacchus's legislation [*Gesetzgebung*], remains one that fears death, bans its way, and is fixed on it negatively; the risk of excess, which is originally the Greeks' own, is not "freely used"—to borrow from the formulation in the first letter to Böhlendorff—in Bacchus's positing of measure [*Maßsetzung*]. This antinational turn of the Greeks under Evius's regime can thus be disregarded in the hymn by the Hesperian poet's excess, and in history by the last of the demigods. The strict mediacy that is introduced with measure, fate, and history into the relation of God and humans, the "sacredly posited" ["*heiliggesezte*"] (StA 2: 159; PF 547) relation, is injured by Christ.

When the following strophe continues:

> His fury flares up, however; that is, so that
> The sign shall touch the earth, gradually
> Released from eyes, as though by a ladder.
> This time. (StA 2: 159; PF 547)

—it is thus clear that the flaring up derives metonymically from the "fire" that the Greeks must fear according to Evius's law; it is clear that it is the sign of God, divine self-expression, that had to be repressed by the Greek principle of plasticity, measure, and self-preservation. Yet these three verses are too distinctly separated by the emphatic "this time" from what follows, and the mediated character of the flare-up of fury is too "gradual" and "as though by a ladder," for them to be linked to Christ's first appearance, as the secondary literature commonly argues. Rather, as the final sentence of the second version, "But that is ended" (StA 2: 160; PF 549) suggests, they are related to the appearance of the light that rises again, the evening light in a time of the now: this time. "Released from eyes": a glimpse of God, but as one who disappears from the field of vision of humans and is released from eyes. The appearance[51] of God in fury "this time" is one in which fire is not feared, as with the Greeks, but rather transitions gradually into his appearance as into his disappearance in the oxymoron of suddenness and retardation. - The "at other times" in the following sentence distinguishes the first appearance of Christ at the end of the days of the ancient gods decisively from the "this time."

> This time. Willful at other times, immoderately
> Boundless, so that the hands of men
> Impugn whatever is living, more than is fitting for
> A demigod, the design transgresses beyond
> What's divinely ordained. For since evil spirit
> Has taken possession of happy antiquity, unendingly
> Long now one power has prevailed, hostile to song, without resonance,
> That within measures transgresses the violence of the mind. But God hates
> The unbound. (StA 2: 159; PF 547)

The flaring up of fury occurs gradually and undoes the positive measure insofar as it also corresponds to the measure. "Immoderately / Boundless," by contrast, is the process by which the design that becomes efficacious in Christ's death shatters the law of the mediacy between God and humans. If Evius's deed was to bring something to a halt on the "way of death," Christ's dying "transgresses" what is "divinely ordained"; if humans during *Greek* times met with "fate," Christ's life is impugned "more than is fitting for / A demigod"; if Orientals keep the measure (StA 2: 158; PF 545), here is "one" "That within measures transgresses" (StA 2: 159; PF 547). The status of this "one" in its relation to humans and God determines and conceals itself in the ambiguous construction of the conjunctional clause, "so that the hands of men / Impugn whatever is living." According to this, God's fury flares up on the grounds of human overreach [*Übergriff*]; this overreach is, however, also the consequence of an appearance of God, in which he oversteps his own law and "willfully" turns his son over to the humans by his own "design." In such a way, however, this "one"—which by virtue of its concept alone is related to the "only one"—proves that it is not to be thought in as much isolation from God as the last sentence of the strophe might suggest: "But God hates / The unbound." Rather, the unmediated grasp [*Griff*] for presence, be it a reaction to human overreach [*Übergriff*] or its occasion, is to be regarded as the form of a historical expression of precisely the God who turns, in a Heraclitean manner, as one who is differentiated from himself turns against presence. What is presented in the "one" is the self-identity of God and the desire of men to be immediately one with themselves and not to be dependent on articulation, which introduces something non-identical into the self-relation; at the same time, what is depicted in the "one" is the aporia of identity. That which, in its overstepping, aims at making something that is necessarily posited as different equal to itself; that which, like the grasp of the hand, tries to get hold of the living, realizes its passing/violation [*Vergehen*] in the attempt to appropriate the identical: the "one" is that which "within measures transgresses"—it violates [*sich vergeht*] measure and passes [*vergeht*]. The violence of death is achieved "without resonance" in the movement that oversteps boundaries and in the persistence in the identical: it is achieved in what the Titans banished to Hades represent in Greek myth. They bear each of the attributes that are ascribed to the "evil spirit," the "unbound," and the "one": "hostile to song, without resonance, / That within measures transgresses the violence of the mind." The dominion that the desire for the identical seeks to attain at the end of "happy antiquity" in the complete sensual presence of the demigod—a dominion that, as implied by the ambiguity, is the object of both divinity and humans—must at the same time also be the dominion of an infinite diremption. The presence of divinity, in the way in which it is supposed to take place outside of the boundaries set down by the law—the historical place of this presence being Christ's death—is possible only as one that passes. This dichotomy of identity and decay, of the highest life and destruction, of presence and withdrawal, would have to reproduce itself inextricably and in a self-destructive fashion if no moment of deferral and no instance of putting on hold could become operative in it.

But God hates
The unbound. Yet interceding
//The day of this age holds him back, creating in silence,
Proceeding on its way, the blossom of the years.
And uproar of war and history of heroes holds, stiff-necked destiny,
The sun of Christ, gardens of the penitent, and
The wandering of pilgrims and of the peoples, and the song
Of the watchmen and the writings
Of the bard or the African. (StA 2: 159; PF 547)

Because the "only one" perishes [*untergeht*] through the "one," because with his death the boundedness to the order of measure and thus to the order of history ceases, he would have to disappear without remainder if he were not held back, conversely, by history, which he was unable to determine positively. Because the meaning of the verse "But God hates / The unbound" is controversial—the unbound and God are both the subject and the object of hate—what history holds back is thus both God and the unbound, that which stands opposed to one another as one. The *day* is what lends it a hold, what contains it as its sun ("the sun of Christ"). The spatial-plastic and architectonic moment that emerges in this scene is reinforced even more by the parenthesis "proceeding on its way." Yet it is precisely here where the precision of the image is reminiscent of Greek plasticity—the course walked by the Greek god of the sun, Apollo, in the guise of a king, and that of the sun of Christ, however weakly suggested, come close to one another here—it is precisely here that the significance attached to the metaphor of the way [*Weg*] in the presentation of the Greek positing of measure comes into effect: this way is that of the Greek law of excess and of death: "They do not go the way of death and keep the measure" (StA 2: 158; PF 545) "where / Another goes that way" (StA 2: 159; PF 547). In this manner, that which stands opposed to one another and threatens one another with annihilation is held back by the day as one on the way of death. It is distinct from the Oriental way in that it moves not as one that is "immoderately / Boundless" but rather as "creating in silence." And yet the hold that it grants is achieved not as the negation of excess but in the modification of overstepping—"creating in silence" is still reminiscent of the Titans "without resonance"—and thus on the way of death as its spatial implementation. The injury of the law that occurs with Christ's death and the grasp for identity, the overstepping of the boundary, endures, affirmed, in the movement of the day. History is the affirmation of death, affirmation of a course that breaks everything certain and firm [*Feste*], however delayed it may be.

The appearance that the day of history has a substantial existence is already undone by this movement. On the level of signification, the demise of autonomy, be it of measure or of excess, and the instance of death, whose meaning in contrast to the overreach of the Titans is not determined by identity nor by its negation, assert themselves in the fact that the metaphors for what holds and what is held, what is under and what is above, what is contained and what encloses, are related to one another in such a way that the dichotomous relationship they designate is destroyed. Thus, it is the "blossom of the years" that the day holds, while the day itself is contained in the year; the "sun of Christ" is supported by the "gardens of the penitent" while it is that very sun to which the gardens owe their existence. Just as the linearity of the dichotomous relationships is bent and reversed in the metonymic constellation of their poles, so the identity of the "only one"—and therefore no longer "one"—is subjected to a splitting and a reversal: as the "blossom of the years," the "only one" is dependent on itself as the "sun of Christ," and as that which is held it is dependent on itself as hold; this hold however is itself something held. Through reversal, however, the teleological model of history that could be suggested by an organistic metaphorics is undone: the fact it is a derivation in which the supreme (the sun or God) acquires an indicator [*Anhalt*], that it is something that has already originated on which its condition depends, overthrows the concept of history as the continuum of the subject's self-movement, as it was conceived by Hegel at the height of German Idealism. Such a process, in which the spirit's self-production is to be carried out, would, as a seizure of identity and according to the description in the second version of "The Only One," have to transition into annihilation. To prevent this fate, history for Hölderlin persists, Atlas-like and "stiff-necked," as a history that preserves the difference between the "identical" and the non-identical; not history as something that securely underlies as *hupokeimenon*, *subjectum* but, rather, history as an insecure figure for what originates from a "transcendental subject" and depicts the condition for its preservation without itself being substantial. According to this definition, history is neither something that exists in itself nor something that progresses on its own power, nor is what is preserved by it actually a transcendental subject of history or a subject that produces itself through the process. Like the concept of the subject, the concept of the signified is subverted by the construction of the sentence. God and/or Christ would have to be regarded as that which is designated in song and writing if that to which they are assigned in the nexus of the metonymic complex—as the "blossom of the years" is assigned to the "gardens of the penitent" and the "sun" is assigned to the "day"—were itself not also something that designates. Through the metonymy, the signified is integrated into the position of the signifier; it is a signified not because it stands out autonomously from the domain of meaning but only as a repetition of the signifier in a suspended [*verschoben*] and, here, reversed location. The parenthetical organization of the syntax in which what holds and what is held, the grammatical subject and object, are mixed almost to the point of indistinguishability corresponds to this turn of the structure of signification insofar as it breaches the domain to which the "logically" constructed sentence allocates each of its elements and makes it possible to switch grammatical positions: "history of heroes holds, stiff-necked destiny, / The sun of Christ, gardens of the penitent . . . " (StA 2: 159; PF 547).

The autonomy of the signified gives way to the heteronomy of the signifier, which is not subject to the law of self-preservation or of self-constitution because it is not possible for it to transfer from the position of the signifier to that of the signified. Only the heteronomy that is thereby established is capable of holding up [*aufhalten*] the tendency towards self-annihilating identity, insofar as it alone grounds the possibility of meaning and of self in their distortion and obstruction. The kind of death that meets meaning through this heteronomy is something other than the death that would flow into the "one." This death manifests in the fact that the constitution of the signified is at the same time its deconstitution through the repetition of the signifier in another place, a dissolution of every possible claim to givenness, self-sufficiency, or self-production. Language, which in this strophe of Hölderlin's poem represents a movement of history in which neither it nor what it carries designates mere moments of generation or demise, resembles in its course the course of history. Subjectivity, whose pretension to being something identical determined the first half of the hymn, encounters in Christ, its allegory, both its preservation and its hindrance through history; as the tendency towards a meaning that would otherwise exist autonomously in itself, it encounters through the turn in the structure of meaning the condition of its construction as the condition of its decline.

This progress [*Gang*] of meaning and of history as the affirmation of transience [*Vergängnis*] is also followed by "the wandering of pilgrims and of the peoples"; it is a path that, like the path of the sun, heads towards the evening. "[T]he song / of the watchmen" already no longer belongs to the domain of the light, but rather to a darkness from which the sun has disappeared, but in which the possibility of light is nevertheless preserved. If the hymn had to limit the sun's presence against its Titanic tendency, and erect a border against decay, its function in the night is to limit absence and to retain a trace of the day even where it has declined. In the "writings of the bard or the African" this function, however, reverses once again: it is as the writings of the black man, as black writing, that it bears the light that threatens to decline, by letting the light walk along the path of decline.

> And the destiny
> Of those unfamous holds him, who only now
> Are really having their day, paternal princes, that is. For now that standing
> Is much more godlike than before. For more to men
> Now light belongs, not to youths.
> Our fatherland also. (StA 2: 159; PF 547, mod.)

If one sees "fame," as Hölderlin may well have done, as standing adjacent to the Greek *doxa*,[52] then to be unfamous means to be without luster, to be lightless and hidden. If the destiny of the unfamous holds the day and the sun, then what holds them is what does not belong to the day. In having their day, in emerging, they do not become revealed, but rather they, the unfamous and the paternal princes—who are also assigned to the sphere of darkness by virtue of their context—mark out the dark trace, the African writings, in the brightness of the day. Only insofar as they do not correspond to the law of the light can they maintain a "standing" [*Stand*] that stands fast against being torn away, against the presence of God. "For now that standing / Is much more godlike than before" (StA 2: 159; PF 547). This "before" [*sonst*] takes up again the moment in verse 65 where the "now" refers back to the "this time." In the "boundless" transgression of that which is established as law, proximity to the divine was supposed to be attained "before"; the "standing" is "more godlike" where it introduces difference from positivity as well as from parousia in carrying out the transgression of measure. As standing, standing stands against its own godlikeness; "standing / is much more godlike," standing against its own meaning.

Thus, the sentence "for more to men / Now light belongs" has the meaning that those who are more godlike, who are misunderstood as being radiant, designate the epiphany of God and thus of the fatherland as a realm of light—the parallelism interpreted as a parallel between light and fatherland—subsequently withdrawn from it as the hymn continues:

> . . . not to youths.
> Our fatherland also. For fresh
> // Still unexhausted and full of curls.
> For the Father of Earth is glad of this too,
> That there are children, so that a certainty
> Of goodness remains. (StA 2: 159; PF 547–59, mod.)

Light does not belong to youths because they are still fresh and unexhausted and full of curls; by contrast, grown men possess the attributes of weakness and exhaustion through this formulation *ex negativo*, and therefore also the attribute of light: only through the reduction of their strength do they make possible the remaining of the light in history by producing a difference in it. The economy that determines the exhaustion of light and strength also informs the poetic procedure, insofar as it diminishes the meaning of the sentence "for more to men / Now light belongs," which itself harbors light, in the sentences supplementing it. The domain of its meaning is limited and, in the very sentence that seemed to allow the light to emerge unprotected, the phrase that follows it uncovers what breaks, refracts it. While the light's appearance is bound up with the partial exclusion and exhaustion of light, meaning is bound up with the limitation of its scope. Along with this, Hölderlin's syntax emphasizes the difference in the structure of meaning that is directed against meaning itself, the difference that, just as history and writing hold back God's appearance, hinders the presence of sense and makes possible its articulation in the first place.

Yet it is not only the fact that the limitation is not exercised immediately in the "meaningful" sentence but, rather, occurs through the commentary that shows the disappearance of meaning and its limitation and thus also the diminishment of the power of this limitation. The fact that the same sentence that formulates the limitation will, in a different relation, also affirm the "original" meaning doubles the aforementioned economy of the poetic process by adding its opposite. If, as the order of the sentences suggests, the phrase "For fresh // Still unexhausted and full of curls" refers to the "men," then it is claimed of men, the aged, that they are still unexhausted and still youthful. Light and the fatherland only belong to men as both exhausted and unexhausted, both full of curls and without curls. In being both the limitation and exhaustion of meaning, on the one hand, and its expansion and strengthening, on the other, and in following the economy both of restriction and of excess in *one*, Hölderlinian syntax solves the problem of "the song / Of the watchmen" and of "the writings / Of the bard or the African"; it holds up the difference from the sheer positivity of limited meaning and from the "unboundedness" of meaning that is not "exhausted." It holds both back to the extent that it realizes them both. As the affirmation of both ways, each one of which would have to lead to demise, Hölderlin's poetry preserves meaning only insofar as it cedes it to passing [*Vergängnis*]—"proceeding on its way."

> So too
> He is glad that one remains.
> And some there are, saved, as though
> On beautiful islands. Learned are these,
> For they have been subject to
> Temptations boundlessly.
> Countless fallen. So it went when
> The Father of Earth prepared what is constant
> In storms of the age. But that is ended. (StA 2: 160; PF 549, mod.)

"Countless" are fallen in contrast to the positive finitude of the Greek world when "In youth the Heavenly in plenty / Is numerable" (StA 2: 158; PF 545). "Boundless" are the temptations, just as the design "transgresses beyond / What's divinely ordained" with "immoderate / Boundlessness" (StA 2: 159; PF 547). This overstepping movement that fractures all solid finitude and becomes the fall of the countless—"Countless fallen. So it went . . . "—is the history of the constitution of "what is constant" "in storms of the age." This boundless progress [*Gang*] and this fall of the countless has found an end: the boundlessness is a bound boundlessness, and the countlessness is a finite countlessness. Infinity is interrupted in that in which "the Father of the Earth" rejoices: in the staying of children and of those who have gone through the storms, whether in falling or as saved. "One"—that is, neither "the only one" nor the identical "one—remains; "some" *are*, however, not saved and not on beautiful islands, but rather are saved beings whose being is on beautiful islands, and yet not in the sense of their being—which interprets away the plurality of the "some" and turns "what is constant" into something fixed—but rather in the precise sense of their being plural, their "*are*" [sind] as such, which, phonetically and graphically, is related to the islands [Ins*eln*] in its important, metathetically altered sounds.[53] Not only do the two words have the sounds *s*, *i*, and *n* in common, but the letters *d*  and *el*  also match up with one another in German handwriting. (The prevalence of the graphic figure for the constitution of this text—the writing of the African—also asserts itself in the relation between *auch* 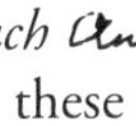 and *auf* 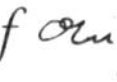.) The rescue formulated in the transition between these two words, *are* and *islands*, in the middle of the final strophe eludes both belonging, be it to solid ground or to the stormy sea, and the choice between finitude and infinity; the rescue also eludes the choice between being and becoming, and of dichotomous opposition as such. The tension thanks to which the "are" leaps over to "saved" also actualizes—against the border established by the comma to preserve the character of the "are" as a main verb—the function that belongs to it as an auxiliary verb.[54] The static character of *being*, supported by the decisively temporal usage of the "are" in the subsequent two verses, is thereby supplemented with the dimension of its infinite becoming. Rather than aiming at any identity between the dichotomously opposed domains of becoming and being, measure and infinity, passing and remaining, the verses "And some there are, saved, as though / On beautiful islands" are aimed at the dissolution of their oppositeness. And they do so in such a way that the graphic, syntactic, and semantic relations that manifest in these verses leap over into a reciprocal supplementation: the "are" supplements "saved" as something that has become and supplements the "islands" as its concretion within something infinite. As such, they are determined as those that leave behind their status, and in leaving it determine that in which they are different. This is the movement of their *modification*, through which alone they convey themselves without synthesizing.

The end of history on islands is not its decline [*Untergang*] nor the reduction of its structure—in contrast to how the Hegelian spirit must have consumed all externality in its "inwardizing re-collection" [*Er-Innerung*][55]—but is, rather, unlike wandering which, as movement, strides through *space*, history's entry into a *place*, into the smallest place. For this place it is significant that it is not reachable by a heroic deed nor through the suffering of a subjectivity, however momentary, but rather as a salvation that is granted to "some." And this place is not reachable through the "Father of *Earth*," but rather "on beautiful islands."

In the second version of the hymn, the poem's second half formulates a philosophy of history that follows neither teleology, nor a monarchic concept of God, nor a synthesizing dialectics as it developed in the aftermath of Platonism. The spatial penetration of what is holding and what is being held in the process of passing away is exposed by this philosophy as the shape that life has to take under the condition of the decay of positivity. While it is this positivity that, as divinely posited, provides a harmless connection of the heavenly with the earthly in the form of the law in the time of the Greeks, it is, however, also this positivity that reduces the divine to its concretion and human ways to the right way. In this regard as well, the "ancient happy shores" are a form of captivity. That which the Greek heroes had to aim at negating—excess, straying [*Irre*], death—is that in whose element the Hesperian, the last of the ancient race, must move. Yet at the same time they must move in it in such a way that a non-reductive boundary [*Grenze*] is inscribed in them, and that they do not fold back into that form of unboundedness that, for its part, returns with an almost dialectical automatism in rigid law. This self-movement of errancy and of the errant [*Irre*] in Greek time is what the strophe concerning Evius tries to formulate for the first time in the third version of the poem. In contrast to the tendency of the earlier version, the power of death is depicted only in a weakened form; Bacchus's deed appears less negatively directed towards excess and death than as a positive positing.

> And boldly I confess, you
> Are the brother also of Evius, who prudently, in ancient times,
> Judged the sullen madwoman [*Irre*],
> The god of the earth, and granted
> A soul to the animal, which roams
> In living from its own hunger and followed the shape of the earth,
> But the right paths he commanded all at One time and places,
> Things, too, he cultivated of each one. (StA 2: 162)

Those who live from their own hunger, those who follow the shape of the earth, which means however one that is not encultured, the errant madwoman [*Irre*]—the command of the god of the earth applies to them as well. For Dionysos is god of "all those astray, the mad" and "the dead," to whom his night, to borrow from the expression from "Bread and Wine," is "sacred" (StA 2: 91; PF 321), as well as the god who, in order to regulate the errant madwoman, begins to command that death be brought to a halt [*Einhalt*]. The unfulfilled subjectivity that lives from its "own hunger" is set an end within its own region: its roaming, which must, in disoriented fashion, always seek out other goals, is given a single goal,[56] which is elevated to the command to keep to [*einzuhalten*] the way that leads toward this goal. The enculturating act of Evius is the act of placing a restriction on the errant madwoman [*Irre*], on unboundedness, and the act of repressing a lack. - If the Hölderlinian hymn undertakes a comparison of Christ with the Greek demigods—and perhaps the second version was discarded because it no longer thematized Christ's kinship with the ancient gods in its historical digression—it must, in the third version, introduce that element of Christ's achievement, of the demigod who is missing from the plastic order of the Greek gods, which corresponds in all transgressions of positive legality to the Greek principle of space, form, and law: that element, therefore, that also makes possible the hymn to him, the moment of its articulation.

A draft of the third version establishes the accord of the heroes in the fact that they all have a "fate." The fact that the father of "worldly men" is the same as that of the "spiritual" ones is disclosed in the following declaration:

> For he has certainly
> Also had One, which tore him away,
> Tall above the head of
> Man. Narrow however it is around him. For each has
> A fate. That is. The world always strives
> Away from this earth. That the earth bares
> Itself. (StA 2: 750)

The sharply interruptive affirmation of fate—"that is"—is, to the same degree as the affirmation of death, also the affirmation of the passing away [*Vergehen*] of that which *remains* in passing away. The affirmation of fate, which tore away, holds firmly in it that which escapes the dichotomy of life and death and falls outside of every concept of death as a beginning or an end, and likewise outside of every concept of life as a form, however it may be constituted, of presence. The dissolution of their dichotomous opposition, and with it also the opposition of law and transgression, is given a more elaborate depiction in the third version.

> . . . For Christ also stood alone
> Beneath the visible heaven and stars, visible
> To those who freely dispose over what's constituted as law, with permission from God,
> And the sins of the world, the incomprehensibility
> Of cognitions, namely, when what persists the industrious overgrows,
> The courage of men and of the stars was above him. For the world always rejoices
> Away from this earth, that it
> Bares the earth; where what is human does not hold the world. There remains, though, a trace
> Yet of a word; this a man perceives. But the place was //
> The desert. So these are equal to each other. (StA 2: 163)

The equation of Christ with his brothers is constructed not where Christ stands [*Stehen*]—that is, where he assumes a Greek stance [*Haltung*], as it were—but where the hymn is concerned with the perception of the trace of a word at the place of the desert. But though the conclusion that these are equal possesses little logical stringency, Christ's standing is also sharply distinguished from the "cultivation" [*Bestelltheit*] (cf. StA 2: 163) of the Greek order. For if the Greek order excludes the errant madwoman, it is the Christian hero who, for one thing, takes on "incomprehensibility" or the "inability to be under*stood*" [*Unver*ständ*lichkeit*], that is the "sins of the world," and, for another, the "courage" of the stars, whose tendency is to go in all too fiery a manner down the way of death. At the place where the earth is bared by the world on its way to death, there was neither a human nor a heavenly being, that is, the "stars," capable of holding the earth back [*aufzuhalten*]. The fact that "a trace/Yet of a word" remains is thanks to the demigod who, formed as both heavenly and human, is capable of using both tendencies in such a way that "industrious" desire and the statics of the spatial order join together in a figure that eludes both.

> There remains, though, a trace
> Yet of a word; this a man perceives. But the place was//
> The desert. So these are equal to each other. (StA 2: 163)

In this scene, which is set in the desert [*Wüste*], the story of Christ's life and death and the history of Christianity come together allegorically. It models itself on the story that, since the Gospel of Matthew, has represented the beginning of Christ's redemptive activity. According to Matthew, Christ experiences three temptations in the desert. The first of these contains the elements that Hölderlin's verses rework: word and citation.

"And when the tempter came to him, he said, If thou be the Son of God, command that these stones be made bread. But he answered and said, It is written, Man shall not live by bread alone, but by every word that proceedeth out of the mouth of God."[57] But Christ is also a word that proceeds out of the mouth of God.[58] Yet Christ does not show himself as *the word itself* to the tempter but rather, insofar as he evades [*ausweicht*] the tempter's command and his own nature as ensouled sound, he presents himself as a word from the written text. Only insofar as Christ denies himself the proof of power demanded by Satan, which would have involved his proving himself as *logos*, and only insofar as he contents himself with citing (himself as) a word from scripture—that is, only where he denies his self and thereby the quintessence of life, and exposes himself to death in the trace [*in der Spur*], does he withstand the temptation to perish in his presence as one who is absent. The testimony that proves him to be the son of God and brother of the demigods is the rigorous reduction of the divine not even to the word, which Christ himself is, but to the remainder of a fleeting word, the trace of a memory of what "is written." Insofar as he passes over into the form of his disappearance, he oversteps the law of persistence [*Beständigkeit*] and lays ruin to the plastic space; insofar as he cedes himself to the form of his disappearance taken as the form of his remaining under the condition of passing away, plastic space also maintains the possibility of living on. Thus, Christ is the word that passes away, and the trace of a word in which the passing word is held fast. At the same time, as he is also the support [*Halt*] of that which is held, which can hardly still be called him, he is also the man who "perceives" the trace of a word, which is to say: captured in the moment also of its flitting away. Yet this man is just as much the one who, like the poet, holds fast to Christ's fate, the disappearing trace of his life, in memory and in his "own" writing. As much as Christ is undone [*aufgelöst*] as the subject of his own salvation in this doubling of the meaning of "man," the poetic subject, too, is undone, once again in the place where it comes closest to what is longed for. It is only preserved as one that remembers that which has almost disappeared; it does not capture the fullness of his form, only drafts [*nachzeichnet*] an elusive trace of him. In this trace, he "remains" as one who is not himself but is, rather, first constituted by the reference [*Verweis*] to a trace. This referential structure [*Verweisungsstruktur*] of traces possesses no referent superordinate to it, no sense to which it could point up; rather, what is signified in it must always refer again and again to something other, since to be identical with what is meant would at the same time be annihilation. According to this, that structure in which the *logos* stays preserved can only be one in which the *logos* has been distorted [*entstellt*] into a trace of a referral [*Verweisung*]: the structure in which subjectivity can realize itself, one in which it becomes the affirmation of its passing away, its overstepping and its disappearance. Through such distortion and referral, history constitutes itself as trace: passing away and at the same time the condition of living on, a third that is not their synthesis.

> . . . But the place was //
> The desert.

Like the trace and its perceiving, the setting is also an allegory for the perseverance of life under the conditions of the presence of the divine or of death. Hölderlin comments on this extensively in his "Notes on the *Antigone*."

> To the soul, working in secret, it is a great aid that, at the highest point of consciousness, it *evades* [*ausweicht*] consciousness; and before the present god overwhelms it, it encounters him with a bold, often even with a blasphemous word, and so preserves the sacred and living possibility of the spirit.
>
> In high consciousness the soul then always *compares itself* with objects which have no consciousness, but which in their fate take on the form of consciousness. Such an object is a land grown barren [*wüst*], which in its original lush fertility has too greatly intensified the effects of the sun and becomes dry for that reason. The fate of Phrygian Niobe; as it is everywhere the fate of innocent nature, which everywhere in its virtuosity passes over into the all-too-organic, to just the degree that man approaches the aorgic, in more heroic circumstances and motions of the affect. And Niobe is then quite properly the image of the early genius. (StA 5: 267; EL 327–28, mod.; emphasis added)

This commentary, which refers to Antigone's "sacred madness" (StA 2: 5: 267; EL 327), is connected with the following passage from the dialogue between Antigone and the chorus:

> *ANTIGONE:*
> I have heard she has become like the desert
> The Phrygian, full of life,
> Whom Tantulus nurtured on his lap, on Sipylus' peak;
> She has become hunched over and, as though in chains of ivy
> Put, contracted into the slow rock;
> And always with her,
> As men say, winter stays;
> And wash her throat do
> Snow-bright tears from under her lids. Just like her
> A spirit brings me to bed.
>
> *CHORUS:*
> But sacred she was called, and sacred she was engendered,
> We however are of earth and earthly engendered.
> Though you perish now [*gleich*], something great is to be heard,
> That you have, like those like God [*Gott gleichen gleich*], received your lot,
> Living and then dead. (StA 5: 239–40)[59]

Under threat of death, Antigone blasphemously compares herself, evading [*ausweichend*] the consciousness of death, with the godlike Niobe, who through her own comparison with the divine had to become infertile, desert, and stone in order to remove from the gods the object of their wrath and, through this evasion [*Ausweichen*], which is just as much a punishment of the gods, preserve "the sacred and living possibility of the spirit." Corresponding to this is the move into the aorgic under heroic circumstances, the move that the world makes when it rejoices away "from this earth," "that it bares the earth." Just as, according to the depiction in the "Notes," the possibility of the heroic in *proximity* to the aorgic, the possibility of consciousness in insanity, is preserved, so the possibility of a relation to God, the possibility of spirit itself, is preserved in the *almost* wholesale extinguishment [*Erlöschen*] of a relation—yet precisely not preserved dialectically in its other, or at most in an other insofar as this other is relation's remainder. In this view, the petrified Phrygian Niobe would be the remainder in which her fertility is preserved; and insanity would be the trace in which consciousness is preserved. Thus, the desert into which Christ withdraws at the outset of his public works is, as the opposite to plastically formed space, its remainder, a place. As much as it is desert, it is also place, just as the reduced word robbed of its liveliness is a trace. The word [*Wort*] that has become trace finds its corresponding place [*Ort*] in the desert. Trace and desert are the places that have been diminished and distorted to the extreme, where spirit *evades* [ausweicht] and where the possibility of life is held fast in the lifeless. It is here alone, at the place that deviates [*abweichend*] from the identity between the highest life and annihilation and where life is not itself and death is not itself, that the spirit perceives the difference in which its possibility, every possible actuality [*Wirklichkeit*], is founded as in spirit's eccentric distance from its own actuality. In this place that is determined by evasion [*Ausweichen*], negation and the condition of staying come to an agreement in an identity that is other than the identity of the self in Hegelian synthesis insofar as it is grounded not in the reduction of the other but precisely in describing the place of the other.

Insofar as space, like the ensouled word, is not only destroyed in the trace and in the desert, but their "sacred and living possibility" is preserved in the trace and the desert, this passage of the poem allows for the construction of an "equality" between the Greek and the Christian demigods.

> . . . So these are equal to each other. Full of joy, plentiful. Gloriously green turns
> A cloverleaf. Shapeless this would be, if for the sake of the spirit one were
> Not allowed to say, as one instructed in the knowledge of bad prayer, that they
> Are like commanders to me, heroes. This the mortals are allowed to do because
> Without hold God is without comprehension. (StA 2: 163)

Metaphors and simile, which seek to depict the demigods, must be inadequate to each of them insofar as each is a spirit, and they must violate the borders of the measure of each and be unfaithful to their "proper" [*eigentliche*] form. Only their distortion in the image, the comparison of the incomparable, does justice to their claim to hold and comprehensibility; only inadequacy and the relinquishment of measure procure a sense for them and for the concept of God: "because / Without hold God is without comprehension." In this way, the comparison with the commanders, like any other, as well as the comparison of the demigods with one another, provides the gods and God with hold in the same way that Christ provides halt as the trace of a word and the desert provides halt. In the "shapeless" comparison, the rejoicing away, the passing away of the spirit, arrives, as the evasion of spirit, at the place that language, as itself inaccurate, lapsing [*sich vergehende*], and deviating [*abweichende*] from its truth, offers to the spirit. In the "shapeless" [*ungestalt*] comparison, just as in caesuras, ambiguities, and inversions, the hymn that oversteps the measure becomes one that leaves behind the dichotomous schema of measure and excess and becomes suspended as a form of the trace and of the desert, just as Niobe, "hunched over," "contracted into the slow rock." The hymn is the figure of the illogical trace that does not correspond to the spirit, and especially not to the spirit of Christ as *logos*: the trace in which the "word" has become distorted and infertile, in which the "word" does not emerge as *logos* or as its emanation—*the* trace, however, in which alone the life of the word is nevertheless rescued in its most deteriorated form, the form most alienated from itself. Thus, it has to be the song that undoes [*auflöst*] the "incomprehensibility of cognitions," insofar as it contracts [*zusammenziehen*], in the "shapelessness" of the comparison, into the trace and the rock. The comparison would fit in with the polarization of "incomprehensibility" and "what persists" if it produced the form of their connection; however, it springs out from this polarization and turns itself in the *shapelessness*[60] into that in which *what persists* and "*incomprehensibility*" collapse. For incomprehensibility and for what persists, the shapelessness has the double character of being their negation and the condition for their preservation. This makes it unmistakably clear that the trace, its place—the desert—and the comparison occupy the same position in relation to the schema of dichotomy. This position is one in which the living presence of plastic spatiality and of the ensouled word evaporates, the law is broken, its transgression arrested, in which meaning itself, insofar as it is bound to, or even constituted by, spatial form or linguistic pronunciation, has to distort itself just to rescue its possibility, which meaning would, as itself, have to annihilate. It is in this position that totality, which was intended by hubristic transgression [*Überschreitung*] as the totality of a closed whole with Greek plastic space, as the totality of an infinity, falls into ruin. Hence, also, the decisive caesura that crosses through the sentence: "But the place was // The desert": at the most exposed, most emphatic position, there appears the emptiest place, which thereby contrasts as decisively as possible with the telos, with the "time and places" with which Evius "commanded the right paths" (StA 2: 163). In the Greek cosmos, place [*Ort*] is posited as a determined goal and as a border, while in Christian history place is the site [*Stätte*] of desertification, the scene of the trace. Yet the hymn's organization does not allow the relation of Greek and Christian history to remain in sheer opposition. In the "trace," the "man," which is also to say the poet who with his comparison provides God with an indicator as a hold [*Anhalt*], perceives what in Greek speech[61] is called "the treasured gem of the house" (StA 2: 162). Accordingly, the "trace" is established in the Greek pantheon, the house of the plastic gods, by the end that this house reaches with the last of its race: it is that sign in which space survives only in a reduced and shattered state. The "trace" of the treasured gem is inscribed into the plastic speech of the Greek gods as their ruination and as figure of their living on. To demonstrate the decisiveness of the difference between the poetology of the "classical" period formulated in the essays of Hölderlin's time in Homburg, on the one hand, and the implicit theory of language of the late lyric poetry, on the other, it may suffice to point to the theory of poetic language set out at the conclusion of the draft "On the Procedure of the Poetic Spirit." Under the subheading "Hint for Presentation and Language" one finds the following passage:

> And if it is the progress and destiny of life as such to fashion itself from the original simplicity into the highest form, where for that very reason the infinite life is present to the human being, and where as the most abstract entity he absorbs everything all the more intimately, to bring back then from this highest opposition and union of the living and spiritual, of the formal and the material subject-object, the life to the spiritual, the shape to the living, the love and the heart to the human being and the thanks to his world again, and finally after fulfilled anticipation, and hope, when namely that highest point of cultivation, the highest form in the highest life was present in the *expression*, and not just in itself as at the beginning of the actual expression,

> nor in the striving, as in the continuation of this expression, where the expression calls forth life from the spirit and the spirit from life, but where it has found the original life in its highest form, where *spirit and life is the same on both sides*, and knows its discovery, the infinite in the infinite, . . . —thus if this seems to be the course and the destiny of mankind as such, then the same is the course and the destiny of all and every poetry, and . . . as the human being only really begins life at this stage of education . . . , so the poet anticipates, at the stage where he also has struggled from an original feeling through opposed essays upwards to the tone, to the highest pure form of the same feeling and sees himself wholly engaged in his whole inner and outer life with that tone, at this stage he anticipates his language, and with that the actual completion for the present and at the same time for all poetry. (StA 4: 261–63; EL 295–96, mod.)

According to the presentation in this passage, poetic language, like life, arrives at its "highest point" in the expression in which the moment of spiritual form, which dissolves the original unity, unites with feeling as the synthetic experience of life; in which, following the Kantian model, the synthesis of synthesis and antithesis takes place in the act of productive reflection. Specifically, it takes place in such a way that, according to the law of reflexivity, goods that were lost in the process of cultivation [*Bildung*] are regained on this higher level of life and language: in the language of "this creative reflection" (StA 4: 263; EL 296–97) "the spiritual" wins back its life and the living its shape, such that the harmonic unity of opposites is attained: *coincidentia oppositorum* just as in all Idealistic systems. The "tone": pure form and pure material, pure spirit and pure life, consummates the reflexive forming-into-one of the antitheses. The fact that language, like life, following the law of perfectibility, only realizes itself in infinite progress, in "infinite beautiful reflection" (StA 4: 265; EL 298), and the fact that synthesis, once again following the Kantian model, is an infinite one, takes nothing away from the paradigmatic synthesis, as it were, that tone achieves, because in tone the activity is determined that yields the condition of possibility for infinite movement. In the theory of language implicit in "The Only One," infinite reflexive synthesis is relinquished. That which was destroyed [*unterging*] in the process of cultivation, self-destructive creaturely identity, is not recovered in the transgression of laws, in the act of which life leaves itself to pass away [*Vergehen*]; rather, shape remains ruined in shapelessness, and an original liveliness does not reproduce itself on a higher level. If one wanted to recognize, in the metonymic reaction depicted by the "cloverleaf" of the three demigods to the scene in the "desert," a refertilization of the desert, it would need to be objected that it is a shapeless fruit that is assembled from the traces of a word and the remainders of a space. Not only is the Idealist theory of reflexivity rejected, synthesis also acquires a new systemic value: it is not the synthesis of simplicity and cultivation, of life and its diremption, but the negative instance at which the condition of its possibility as well as of its impossibility in the trace draw together as an evasion [*Ausweichen*] of synthesis. The synthetic function of this reduced form of the "word," which the trace and the poetic language of the comparison represent, is just as radically distorted as it itself stands as a figure of distortion. Though still very far from drawing these conclusions that "The Only One" and the later theoretical writings will arrive at, the ending of "Hint for Presentation and Language" nevertheless appears to gesture towards a thought that goes in the direction of the graphematic, so to speak, theory of language: "the infinite form assumes a structure," "the infinite subject-matter assumes a euphony," and "both unite negatively in the slowness and rapidity and finally in the cessation of motion" (StA 4: 265; EL 298). Form and matter unite negatively in the cessation of movement thanks to infinite reflection. Infinity is, for the sake of synthesis, relinquished on its own ground and preserves itself where, like form and matter synthesized, its autonomy is lost without having been supplied with a new autonomy by a positive unity. Yet, as problematized as it is, the relation of matter and form is not undermined in principle, and its *negative* unification remains a unification, preserving the idealistic relation of spirit and letter [*Zeichen*] and maintaining the linguistic ontology of idealism as a negative one. If the Homburg essay defines the poet's achievement by his "taking from this world the subject-matter to denote the *tones* of his spirit and *to call forth* from his *mood* the life which underlies it with this related sign" (StA 4: 264; EL 297, emphasis added), and if it defines the poetic act as the construction of a phonological correspondence between the "sign [*Zeichen*]" and that which it designates, which language, as the form of their unification, is at least capable of allowing to be intimated [*ahnen*] in its negative even if it does not realize it—by contrast, the text of "The Only One" suggests that only a sign understood as written sign, in which correspondence with the realm of the spirit must be avoided and inadequacy be striven for, can "fulfill" [*erfüllen*] its function in the infertile, unproductive place of the desert. Its function is to make possible a connection [*Zusammenhang*] insofar as the written sign evades [*ausweicht*] it and enters into a relation with it in which the condition and negation of the possibility of connection suspend the connection in its very constitution. It is decisive that in this process, phonologism, as well as the logic of the reflexive form of the self-present and living word, have to be relinquished. In relation to Christian history, "Patmos" declares, almost programmatically:

> And there's no harm if some of it
> Is lost, and of the speech
> The living sound dies away. (StA 2: 178; PF 561)

Though they are forms of interruption [*Sistierung*], trace, place, and shapelessness are not entirely cleared of the danger of law and presence; the movement that arises from the interaction of law and presence is not concluded:

> . . . But as on chariots
> Humble   with violence
> Of the day or
> With voices God appears as
> Nature from without. Mediately
> In holy writings. The Heavenly
> And men are together on earth the whole time. A great man and similarly a great soul
> If equal in heaven //
> Desires toward one on earth. (StA 2: 163)

This formulation of a connection between the Heavenly and the earthly is followed by a series of sentences that let the diremption of both domains, the dissolution [*Auflösung*] of the connection even between the heroes, appear possible.

> Forever
> This remains, that the world is always wholly chained
> Every day. Often however appears
> A great one not to be altogether fit for
> Great things. But they stand every day, as at an abyss, one
> Next to the other. Those three, however, are
> This, that they are under the sun
> Like hunters are to the hunt, or
> A farmer who, taking a breath from work,
> Bares his head, or a beggar. Beautiful
> And lovely it is to compare. Good does

The earth. To cool. Always however (StA 2: 164)

The connection with the Heavenly, the similarity that can be regarded as a form of decay and reduction, of shapelessness and evasion [*Ausweichen*], leads back to Greek positivity in the chain with which the initial image of captivity is reprised. Yet the difference that, contrary to the tendency of "classical" poetology, remains ineradicable between the spiritual and matter splits humans from God as well as splitting the demigods who stand between them as border and mediators, so much so that the split becomes an abyss. "One next to the other" stand "as at an abyss," insofar as each is an abyss for the other; insofar as they stand "as at an abyss" they put a halt to the danger of death, which is bound up with their and with human beings' proximity to God. This proximity is, due to the abyss, simultaneously the most profound distance. To stand at it means to bear [*ertragen*] proximity as well as distance from one another, the one through the other, without however falling into them—this means, for the function of the demigods, and for the "comparison" and the "together" that take shape in them, that neither incomparability nor equality, neither deadly presence nor distance that kills, but only the place that is "*next* to" it and lies next to both makes rescue [*Rettung*] possible. Thus, accordingly, the enjambment that is positioned before the "one" leaps over to the "next" in this way. Difference of difference and synthesis is what is realized by standing as if at an abyss. The fact that, additionally, each is an abyss for the other permits abyss and adjacency to change their positions from case to case . . .

The problem whose depiction is the common concern of all three versions of "The Only One" and that emerges in a changed form with every turn—how historical contingency is thinkable in view of the epochal break that Christ's death introduces and that separates Greek from Christian history; what language is after the fleetingness of the *logos* and the frailness of form was revealed in Christ; how continuity between the spiritual and the material, between form and life is conceivable if Christ violated [*sich verging gegen*] their binding law: no matter what shape it takes, be it historical-philosophical, language-theoretical, or theological, this problem meets with one and the same solution, structurally speaking. Christ would have been subject to the Gnostically rigorous diremption of the world into a world of death and a world of form, which Greek law equally prescribes for history, language, and the appearance of the gods, if Christ had merely overstepped this law: the one who breaks this law is as rigorously enclosed in the order of the law as the one who obeys it. Christ's deed is double: he breaks the law by surrendering himself to transience [*Vergängnis*], to wordless and shapeless lack [*Fehlen*], and he evades the opposition of the differentiated that is expressed in the law. This evasion [*Ausweichen*] and adjacency [*Nebenstehen*], the topical affirmation of transgression, situates the condition of the law at a place where not only the law itself but also its entire dichotomous order is broken. Be it in history in the form of a memory trace of a cited word, or in the shapelessness of a comparison that evades synthesis—the condition of possibility of remaining [*Bleiben*] is always depicted in the ruination of the life guaranteed in the law by way of its restriction to mere positivity. Not only is the merely positive shape of life undone [*aufgelöst*]; the manner in which it disintegrates, which is consummated in Christ, simultaneously entails a completion by which shape is affirmed in its breakdown. This relation is implicitly depicted in almost all the turns the hymn undergoes; it is explicitly formulated in a draft of its last part, which follows the allegorization of the three demigods as hunter, farmer, and beggar.

> Not so are other heroes,   the conflict is however
> That tempts me
> This, that out of necessity as sons of God
> These have the signs in themselves. For the Thunderer has, advisably,
> Provided still otherwise. Christ however contents himself.
> Like princes is Hercules. Communal spirit is Bacchus. Christ however is
> The end. He is indeed of yet another nature; but fulfills
> What in presence still
> The Heavenly lack in others. This time. (StA 2: 752–53)

The one who fulfills [*erfüllt*] is missing [*fehlt*]. As the one who remained absent [*ausblieb*] in the space of the plastic gods, as the one who passes away and takes on death and the shapeless into itself, and as "end," he completes [*ergänzt*] the "fault" [*Fehl*] of the Greek demigods, who had to deny their own frailty in order to remain [*bleiben*]. This passage makes explicit what previously was only hinted at in an early ambiguity that accompanied the measurelessness of the poetic subject: "That if I serve one I / Must lack the other" (StA 2: 154; PF 545)—that both the Greek demigods and the Christian demigod are "missing" [*fehlen*]. Only where lack [*Fehl*] completes lack [*Fehl*] is the "presence" of the Heavenly realized. The necessity of such completion provides a basis for the legitimation of the hymn's faulty [*fehlerhaft*] progress, too, to which the conclusion of the first version so emphatically confesses. The "this time," which in that earlier version introduces the self-accusation (StA 2: 155; PF 539), here prepares for a sentence to follow the depiction of the "fault" of the old gods, a sentence that probably would have tried to link up the law of history with the law of the hymn: the breaking of law in history and the breaking of law in the hymn. Yet the errors [*Fehler*] hardly complement one another to make up a totality, and the concept of legitimacy, too, seems misplaced in view of the determination with which the hymn laments its excess as fault. Presence finds its fulfillment, through Christ as through the hymn, at the place of illegitimacy, of the breaking of law, and of remaining absent. The transgression and fault of Christian history, however, would have to fall back impotently into the categorial system of Greek positivity and of the ancient fault if they were to fail at the turn with which they *evade* every choice between presence and absence. Through this turn, the break with the law finds a place where it can acquire permanence because the distance from presence and absence has, as their condition, become a figure. It is thus that adjacency [*Neben*], caesura, writing, islands, and trace, among others, stand against the relapse into the order of opposition and of synthesis. Only insofar as transgression realizes them and demonstrates the law as being conditioned and subverted by them will it turn from a step in space that was marked out by the law into a turn, into Hesperian reversal, and into something revolutionary, if you will. To consummate this turn is what this errant [*fehlgehend*] poem attempts. Christ, as the one who realizes the turn, is the demigod who "fulfills / What in presence still / The Heavenly lack in others." He completes presence by subverting its order.

IV. " . . . Almost/Backwards . . . "

The "Notes on the *Antigone*" contain, in decisive contrast to the Fichtean essay on "The Process of Becoming in Passing Away," the outlines of a theory of revolution. The "Notes" describe the structure of Sophocles's play as follows:

> The nature of the action in the *Antigone* is that in a revolt [*Aufruhr*], where, insofar as it is a patriotic matter, everything depends on the fact that everyone, being overwhelmed by the infinite reversal, and thoroughly moved, apprehends himself in the infinite form in which he is moved. For patriotic reversal is the reversal of every mode of understanding and form. But a total reversal in these, like any total reversal without hold, is not allowed of the human being as a cognizing being. And in a patriotic reversal, where the whole shape of things changes, and nature and necessity, which always remain, tend to a new shape, whether going over into wilderness or into a new form, in a change like this, all mere necessities are biased in favour of the change; whence, in the eventuality of such change, even a neutral man (and not only one who is moved *against* the patriotic form), can, by a spiritual violence of the time, be compelled to be patriotic and present in infinite form, in the religious, political and moral form of his fatherland (*prophanēthi theos*). And serious observations of this kind are necessary for an understanding of Greek art, as of all true works of art. Now, the essential mode of procedure in a revolt (which is, of course, only one kind of patriotic reversal, and has an even more definite character) has just been pointed out. (StA 5: 271; EL 331, mod.)

The more determinate character not of this revolt itself, but certainly of patriotic reversal in its Hesperian form, finds expression scattered about in other parts of the "Notes," as the commentary form as well as the political circumstances under which Hölderlin wrote likely forced him to do, having prevented him from laying out a consistent theory of "revolt" [*Aufruhr*]. The reversal in question, for which Antigone's transgression of the law serves as the paradigm, does not lead to relations under which every difference that is presented by limits would be canceled [*aufgehoben*] and a simple adequacy to the law of divinity or of any ideal would be attained. Rather, it can be described, especially in its Hesperian form, as the conscious introduction of a difference that is no longer subject to any form of dominion or monarchic principle—and thus subject neither to the positive law of the state nor to the transcendental law of the spirit, which tears into the "world of the dead" (StA 5: 266; EL 326). The possibility of such a Hesperian reversal is summed up in the shape of Zeus who has come nearer to "our mode of presentation" (StA 5: 268; EL 328, mod.): "In more particular or vaguer contexts one probably has to say Zeus. *In serious* contexts preferably: Father of Time or: Father of the Earth, because it is his character, contrary to the eternal tendency, to reverse *the striving out of this world into the other into a striving out of another world into this one*" (StA 5: 268; EL 328). The reversal of the life process, whose reversal is at the same time a reversal of the ideal and of historical progression, which is to say the return of the gods and of the dead in the "present" world—this reversal has its time and its place in Hesperia, in the evening of history, of the day, and of the artwork. This is elaborated in unmistakable terms in another passage:

> The boldest moment in the course of a day or in a work of art is where the spirit of time and nature, the heavenly by which man is overwhelmed and the object in which he is interested, come to oppose each other most wildly; because the object of sense only extends so far, as a first half, but the *spirit awakens most mightily where the second half begins.* At this moment, a man must *take hold of himself more firmly than ever*, which is why he then stands with his character at its most open.
>
> The tragically mediocre feebleness of the time, whose object does not, after all, really interest the heart, follows the tearing spirit of time most immoderately; the latter then appears wild and does not, like a spirit by day, spare mankind, but on the contrary acts mercilessly, as the spirit of ever-living and unwritten wilderness and of the world of the dead. (StA 5: 266; EL 326)

In contrast to the spirit of the day, which as the plastic spirit of the law may be conceived as the negation of death, it must be the spirit of the night that mercilessly tears over into the world of the dead. The "boldest moment in the course of a day or in a work of art," that moment in which the "second half" begins, must accordingly mark a turn in both as the moment at which the law of its cultivation is smashed to pieces: not midday, as the context to which this remark refers might suggest, but evening. But holding fast to oneself at the utmost in this moment, against the "tragically mediocre feebleness of the time" that the spirit tends to follow, and stopping momentarily at the Hesperian position of works and of history, is the Greek form of resisting the threat of demise. This moment of stopping, of a pause in time, which in the Greek epoch was the only possible movement that could rescue from the "eternal tendency," finds itself spread out into a landscape and its direction reversed in Hesperian time, that is, where an historical place is found for what the tragic gesture of betraying the course of God could only momentarily anticipate: "because we live under the more essential Zeus, who not only *pauses* between this earth and the wild world of the dead, but, on his way into the other world, *more decidedly forces down to earth* the natural process which is eternally hostile to man" (StA 5: 269; EL 330). The earth, towards which the way of death is bent back, is, however, as Hesperian earth, none other than the earth at the edge of death, where the devouring light of day and the chaotic darkness of night come into conflict without, however, either one of them dominating. The earth, which is rigorously distinguished from nature and no less rigorously distinguished from spirit, and the reversal that leads back to it designate the place of difference between the positivity that kills, on the one hand, and the "unwritten wildness and the world of the dead" on the other, between the plasticity of the day and the amorphousness of the night; they thus designate the place at which the festival takes place as in an interlude [*Zwischen*] in the "Evening of Time" (StA 3: 536; PF 529). In its late conception, the festival is, however, less a dreamlike occasion during which gods are made present than it is the human being's sacred betrayal of the gods and of itself. In the "Notes on the *Oedipus*," where "the drama like a trial for heresy" is discussed, Hölderlin writes that "God and man *communicate in the all-forgetting form of unfaithfulness*. This happens so that no gap occurs in the course of the world, and so that *the memory of the heavenly ones does not die out*. Divine unfaithfulness is best to retain. At a moment like this man forgets both himself and the God and, in a sacred manner, of course, turns himself round like a traitor" (StA 5: 202; EL 324, mod.). The "categorical reversal" (StA 5: 202; EL 324) that Oedipus follows in his trial is also the course traveled in *Antigone* by Haemon; this course is, as the note cited above remarks, a course leading "from the Greek to the Hesperian" (StA 5: 267; EL 327). In this, however, the betrayal must be held onto and not turn into the recognition of God as one who is posited, or into a subjection to his tendency, both of which, one like the other, mediately or immediately, lead into the "world of the dead." The reversal of this movement allows it to migrate into a difference, wherein the betrayal of its original goal is affirmed without an unbroken law being restituted.

The collision between law and lawlessness as it is presented in *Antigone* culminates for Hölderlin, who had a conception of the Greek epoch as one that was destroyed by its positivity, in a form whose political equivalent was the republican constitution: "The form of reason which here shapes itself tragically is political, and specifically republican, because the balance between Creon and Antigone, the formal and the anti-formal, is too equal. This becomes especially clear at the end, where Creon is almost mistreated by his servants. Sophocles is right. This is the fate of his age and the form of his fatherland" (StA 5: 272; EL 332, mod.). In this Greek form of revolt against the law, Hölderlin, who knew he belonged to another epoch and "form of fatherland," becomes aware of an error [*Fehler*] that must be avoided in the Hesperian revolution when it comes to pass: the error that "the balance . . . is too equal." It is well known from the fragment "Do you think . . . " that Hölderlin believes Greece had to come to an end because "the patriotic, from them," was "neglected" (StA 2: 228; HSP 279, mod.). The law of plasticity and of the positivity of form, which already in the first letter to Böhlendorff was praised as a special dramatic art of the Greeks, led in terms of political constitution to republicanism as a "kingdom of art," from which fractures within reality, the divergence from the identical that art tries to produce, and especially passion, which oversteps the law, including the law of equality, had to be banned. This law of equality, which was erected in the Greek insurrection, brings equality itself to its fall by virtue of law's positivity. The republicanism in the "kingdom of art," that is the dominion of identity, falls back under the aegis of positive law, to whose transgression republicanism owes its existence. - The Greek state, at whose pinnacle, as at the end of *Antigone*, the republic stood, belongs to the lost forms of historical life. It can be paradigmatic for a Hesperian constitution only insofar as "the infinite, like the spirit of states and of the world, cannot in any case be *grasped* otherwise than from an awkward [*linkisch*] standpoint" (StA 5: 272; EL 332, mod.). Historical or objective justice, that is, *right*ness [*Ge*recht*igkeit*], in the way in which it was also politically established under the Greek principle of identity and of art, is absent from the Hesperian standpoint, which can no longer suppress the "infinite," that is, ineradicable historical difference and the uncontainable passion to diminish it. The oblique perspective that is not subject to a law and that is trained on one's own spiritual and state constitution, however, opens itself up to the Hesperian poet in the Greek works as past works, representations of "the spirit of states and of the world" (StA 5: 272; EL 332) that have become inadequate to the present circumstances. - "The patriotic forms of our poets are nonetheless to be preferred, where there are such, because they do not just exist to explain the spirit of the age, but to hold on to it and to feel it, once it has been understood and learnt" (StA 5: 272; EL 332, mod.). The procedure of Greek art is aimed at understanding, just as the political constitution of its republicanism is aimed at balance and rigorous legality. In Greek art, the "spirit of the age" is compelled to pause and to momentarily stop before it can follow its tendency to pass, by way of the positivity of the understanding and of law, into the "world of the dead." By contrast, Hesperian art—and this is where a Hesperian politics would have to mirror it, though not too much—not only pauses "between this earth and the wild world of the dead" (StA 5: 269; EL 330) but turns "the spirit of time and nature" (StA 5: 266; EL 326) around, compelling it "*more decidedly . . . down to earth*" (StA 5: 269; EL 330). Only this reversal, which is held onto in the "native forms of our poets . . . where there are such" and is itself also consummated, achieves with the historical difference from the political and poetic forms of Greek antiquity the fall of its positive legality and of its tendency towards death, to which positive legality is exposed as to its negation. The reversal turns against one as against the other—and thus is a double reversal. Yet the reversal must endeavor "to hold on to . . . and to feel" both one and the other. The "synthesis"—if one can still speak of one after the reversal of a balance that was too equal, but that itself also bore a synthetic character—that takes place by way of a "patriotic reversal" between law and transgression, between form and death, between equal and unequal, is not a synthesis in which law or equality could be restituted: its connection has been shifted to a place that, as the historical and structural condition of synthetic acts, evades connection, law, and equality. For even Hesperian reversal cannot exempt itself from the validity of the statement that "the infinite . . . cannot in any case be *grasped* otherwise than from an awkward standpoint." In the awkwardness of the Hesperian revolution, in the awkwardness of its poetry, the condition for the connection of the non-identical is localized in its distortion. Structurally, this condition occupies, vis-à-vis the Idealist opposition between equal and unequal, vis-à-vis a dialectically conceived axiomatic relationship, and vis-à-vis a consummated synthesis, the position that is also opened up by the between and the evening of the festival. They are that into which the tendency of time and nature gets bent.

A perhaps earlier form of Hölderlin's theory of reversal as it is fleshed out in the work of his later period can be gleaned from his so-called classical phase for the first time in a passage that invokes the Platonic myth of the *epistrophē* in *The Statesman* ("Politikos").[62] In the final part of the hymn "Celebration of Peace," the anticipation of the festival and the signs announcing it in advance are named; these are not only the fading of the storms that dominated during the time of the gods' absence and the time of history, and not only the idyll of mother and child, but also this:

And few now seem to be dying;
The souls of the oldest even
Held back by a hint, a promise
Conveyed by the golden light. (StA 3: 537; PF 531)

There is no talk of reversal here, but the waiting before death names a moment that has a relevance in terms of content that might only be explicated with reference to Plato's myth. The myth goes as follows: "First, the visible age of each and every creature, whatever it was, stopped increasing, and everything that was mortal ceased moving in the direction of looking older; instead it changed back in the opposite direction, and grew as it were younger, more tender."[63] With this pause in the aging process and its reversal, living beings correspond to the movement of the world that communicates to them God's approach and his renewed dominion over the world's progress. For two courses of the world running in opposite directions determine its life: one is led by God himself, and the other, reversed course deviates more and more from God's course during the time of his absence. For "[t]o turn itself by itself forever is . . . impossible for anything except the one who guides all the things which, unlike him, are in movement; and for him to cause movement now in one way, now in the opposite way is not permitted."[64] It is the world's self-movement that liberates God from the aporia of performing a movement that is in itself contradictory. Yet its autonomy, which is similar to God but only as his negation, needs the highest *autós* and a redirection of its self-movement into the movement of the divine self in order not to become a being that is entirely fallen from it and exempt from its dominion, which is to say from the dominion of similarity with the divine self—and would thus not even be Being [*Sein*] or a being [*Wesen*], since similarity with the most divine, even if on a course that is not directed by it itself, consists in participating in being [*Sein*]. Absolute self-movement, which comprises one of the determinations of the highest being, would, as performed by the world, have to lead either to identity with being or, on the contrary course, to a non-being [*Nichtsein*] that could no longer be regarded as its negative or its reproduction in reverse, and that would have wrested itself from being's dominion. "It is for this reason that now"—when "the condition of its original disharmony . . . as this time ends, comes to full flower"—"the god who ordered it, seeing it in difficulties, and concerned that it should not, storm-tossed as it is, be broken apart in confusion and sink into the boundless sea of unlikeness, takes his position again at its steering-oars, and having turned round what had become diseased and been broken apart in the previous rotation, when the world was left to itself, orders it and by setting it straight renders it immortal and ageless."[65] Just as God, through his alternating proximity to and distance from the world, maintains the possibility of his dominion over the world as a doubly determined, mixed form interwoven from all things contradictory, the kingly art of the statesman lies in unifying the conflicting parts of society in such a way that they "complet[e] the most magnificent and best of all fabrics."[66] Just as for the statesman the twist of the thread in another direction is to contribute to the weaving of a fabric, insofar as the contradictions are interwoven into a unity and thereby secure his dominion,[67] so the cosmic *epistrophē*, in which the courses running counter to one another complete, comparable to the textual movement of politics, a state in the middle between the divine movement and the movement of the world, is the condition of unlimited self-identity of being and the form of its dominion over its negative. As Plato conceived it, cosmic reversal is thus absolutely not an uprising against the reign of being but rather a moment of the double movement that stands under its command, in which the immanent logic that secures for the conception of being its consistency and freedom from contradiction not only fortifies but also makes possible the dominion of being in the first place. In the same way, John's—and probably already the Old Testament's[68]—theory of *metánoia*, of the reversal which this "*poenitentiam agite*"[69] demands, applies to the preparation for the heavenly realm and is the precondition for admission into God's grace and for the restoration of the original connection with the lord and father. Proof of Hölderlin's familiarity with the teaching that Christ's appearance occasioned a reversal can be found in a sermon he wrote on the Letter to the Hebrews, where he writes: "For God saw that the already fallen man would fall ever deeper into blindness and sin if his teaching were not to *call back* his corrupt heart time and again" (StA 4: 171, emphasis added).[70]

There is no doubt that this concept of revolutionary movement as the form of the restitution of original unity or of the negation that is subject to this unity was retained into the "classical" period of Hölderlin's work, namely as the moment of an allegorical depiction of the course of history and the return of the gods. And yet, precisely only as a moment whose significance is determined by its context. In "Celebration of Peace," what follows the depiction of the pause before dying, which is evoked by the myth of the God who approaches and occasions the turnaround, is an allegorization of divine presence, which unsettles the thoughts of an autonomous movement of the divine: for God's appearance, though not only this, is defined as fall, and not as *agens*, but as product.

> Indeed it is travails, designed from
> Above and there carried out,
> That are the spice of life.
> For now all things are *pleasing* [gefällt]
> But most of all the
> *Ingenuous* [*Ein*fältiges], because the long sought,
> The golden fruit,
> In shattering gales *fallen* [*ent*fallen] down from
> An age-old bough
> But then, as the dearest possession, by Fate herself
> Protected with tender weapons,
> The shape of the Heavenly it is. (StA 3: 537; PF 531, emphasis added)

With the fall, the Heavenly enter—in a reversal of that biblical origination scene in which the fall of the human race began with contact with another fruit—into a course on which they abandon their own movement or lack of movement, their origin and their self, and, without autonomy and without power, take up the position of a derivative. In falling, even travails can be pleasing [*Gefallen*] and the "shape of the Heavenly" can be simple [*Einfalt*]. Yet the falling [*Entfallen*] is not absorbed into pleasing [*Gefallen*] as into its negation. The sense of one wants to disappear in the other sense; yet as a modified sense it lingers in this other sense, and only as such, not as its negation but merely as its distortion, can it perish. In this way, the Heavenly enter the evening, as its fruit. The "golden" fruit, as the "Evening of Time" suggests, refers to a Hesperian fruit like those of "the Hesperides, who care for the golden, beautiful apples beyond glorious Ocean and the trees bearing this fruit."[71] According to Hesiod's *Theogony*, the Hesperides live "at the edge towards the night"[72] and "at the limits of the earth,"[73] where Atlas supports the firmament on his head and shoulders. The place where he stands, at the border of the infinite earth, between the day that the gods inhabit and the abyss of the night, the prison of the Titans, is in turn described by one of the most prominent passages from the *Theogony*.

> . . . where Night and Day passing near greet one another as they cross the great bronze threshold. The one is about to go in and the other is going out the door, and never does the house hold them both inside, but always the one goes out from the house and passes over the earth.[74]

It is Hesperia that lies on this border that distinguishes day from night, and forms this space in which they both live, un-united. This place is their connection only insofar as it is the place of their differentiation. In this passage, in which it can be day or night, and in which death reigns and the immortal gods alternately pass through Hades and Elysium—in this passage, which is itself neither of them yet is described only by them, the "golden fruit" and the "shape of the Heavenly" fall: they fall in the place without rule, a place that is exempt from choosing between positive and negative, *and* is determined by these alternatives, and that, conversely, grounds them and dissolves their opposition as the place of their commonality.

The final strophe of "Bread and Wine," and particularly its redrafts, depict, in a thematics closely related to the one above, a "reversal" that, like the fall, takes place un-Platonically as postponement. The distancing from the Platonic and altogether metaphysical model of *epistrophē* can be gleaned from the changes that were made to a late variant by a later one. In the early fair copy, Bacchus, who has to be thought as distinct from the Evius of "The Only One," brings " . . . the trace of the gods now departed / Down to the godless below, into the midst of their gloom" (StA 2: 94; PF 329). By contrast, in the first late correction he " . . . stays while the diseased earth the god holds, / Slowly thundering, and brings pleasure into the midst of the gloom" (StA 2: 607). It is unmistakable how the Platonic myth of the restitution of God's dominion over the earth that has become diseased[75] from his absence takes the place of an allegory of attesting to the divine in the space of the "godless." The very last version once again abandons the allusion to this myth and replaces the earlier correction with the following: " . . . stays. For delighted he is in the wilderness / Too. And sweet slumber stays, and bees and banquet" (StA 2: 607). According to this, however, what delights is what is absolutely removed from the dominion of the gods; what delights, also delights among those for whom there is no god. The divine being does not turn the chaotic wilderness in which being and non-being are mixed back onto its own straight course if it, or even a trace of it, enters together with Bacchus and Christ into that which is turned away from it. Even more important than the renunciation of *metánoia* in the final correction of these verses is, perhaps, the renunciation henceforth of any mention of a redemption or of a gift that human beings are granted by the gods' favor. Corresponding to this demand, the following verses—"Meanwhile, though, to us shadows comes the Son of the Highest, / Come the Syrian and down into our gloom bears his torch" (StA 2: 95; PF 329)—also become verses that virtually contradict them: "Our flowers please and the shadows of our forests / The one dying of thirst.

The one who ensouls would almost have been scorched" (StA 2: 608). Bacchus, Spirit—as he was called in the famous preceding verses about the fatherland that feeds on spirit [*zehren*] and about the colony—enters the wilderness as the only place in which he has the possibility of survival. In the distance from its own, in the other over which its dominion extends no hold, spirit finds its conditio sine qua non. By contrast, its own self would, as immediate self-identity, also be its immediate disappearance. The "externalization" that grants it survival is—unlike that of Hegel's spirit—not the reproduction and production of its *self*, but rather the displacement [*Versetzung*] out of the region of the self and into a heteronomous landscape of self-forgetting. The plant of the Orient, dying of thirst in that landscape and almost scorched, blossoms only as dis-placed and distorted [*ent-stellt*] in Hesperian shadows, its nursery [*Pflanzstätte*]: the "colony."[76] Through the shadows and the wilderness amidst which it is moved, the difference in the self from itself is asserted as constitutive of the self and the self's deconstitution: "Thence has come and back there points the god who's to come" (StA 2: 91; PF 321). In its later reworking and though, like the earlier passage, following upon the changes made to the last strophe, this is turned into a verse in which the Same [*das Selbe*], the devouring Orient of Greek antiquity, is entangled in a virtuoso manner with that Other in which it is rescued, in which the Same is itself something distorted and displaced [*Entstellte*]: "*Thence* [Dorther] has come and *there* [da] laughs the god who *transplants*" (StA 2: 599, emphasis added). Thence he has come as *bacchus nocturnus* in Hesperia: he stands in the glowing embers of the Orient as one who is transplanted to the Hesperian colony, at the place of his beginning as at the place of his end. The trace of something ungodly, the shadow of a displacement and distortion, is thereby implanted in the divine self, the highest being, by virtue of this reversal that is constitutive of it: thereby, however, the divine self, as being, sense, and subject, which would be determined by self-identity or by the capacity to produce them autonomously, is also undone [*aufgelöst*]. Yet the strict border around the night, which makes this element of negativity into a region of its own order, is suspended when, after a long historical process in which such a reversal of history becomes possible, the spirit is rescued from its own self. "For so long it lasts. But the eyes of earth are resting. / The all-knowing, too, sleep, the hounds of the night" (StA 2: 608). These are the hounds that guard the borders of the night and of death.[77] If they who are "all-knowing," which is to say, who are sharply discriminating, sleep, the limit or gate between what is distinct and what is indistinct, between the living form of sense and the deadly chaos of what is not sense, is opened. At this opened border—and Hesperia is nothing other than this—is where the festival of Bacchus takes place, between the "dead" and the "living."

At the borderline of Hesperia, where the absolute dominion of spirit and its living form is set a limit and where the border between spirit and its non-being, between dominion and the impotence of knowing, is situated—this is the place towards which the history of spirit strives as its condition of possibility. Its course does not turn toward its "between," which is both death and life and also neither death nor life, in order to seek out the guarantors of its self-identity in it, as the Platonic god seeks his guarantor in the turn of the cosmos, and to subjugate the condition of its own sense to itself once again; rather, its course turns to its "between" as to that form of its preservation in which whatever it is is also negated. The Hölderlinian utopia has no other goal, and what has been called his eschatological anticipation, being subservient to the sense that subverts Hölderlin's poetry, has no other goal, either. The *metánoia* in Hölderlin's late lyric poetry is not the turning back of human beings towards a lost unity with God but, rather, the turn of God in the difference from the self, the reversal of sense [*Sinn*] in that which makes sense possible while also negating it as a *hupokéimenon* or *télos*. The goal and product of its history is not sense, but what fell from it.

> What of the children of God was foretold in the songs of the ancients,
> Look, we are it, ourselves; fruit of Hesperia it is!
> Strictly it has come true, fulfilled as in men by a marvel. (StA 2: 95; PF 329)

Not God, but the human beings of that borderline are the figure of the "reconciliation" introduced by Bacchus and Christ, the "reconciliation" of day and night, gods and Titans, beautiful form and diseased chaos.

The "song," too, must seek, in its Hesperian turn, to arrive at the place through which the humans are de-fined. Against spirit, the song has to fulfill the task that, in "Bread and Wine," flowers and the shadows attend to—and flowers here are, like *flores rhetoricales*, posited as words.[78] The draft of the hymn "The Titans" defines the task as follows:

> Much does the God reveal.
> For long already the clouds
> Have worked upon what's below them,

And holy wilderness, pregnant with much, has grown roots.
Hot is wealth. For we lack
Song that loosens [*löset*] the spirit.
It would devour
And would make war on itself
For never the heavenly fire
Will suffer captivity. (StA 2: 217–18; PF 629, mod.)

There is nothing less Platonic than depicting God as one who, according to the highest determination of divinity as self-identity without needs, would have to devour his own self, since he has nothing in himself that would protect him against his own devouring powers of fire. Unlike in Plato's *Phaedo*, the body, the non-identical, is not the prison of the soul or of the self-identical, immortal part; rather, self-identity, which must abide with itself, is captivity and self-destruction. But insofar as the divine spirit needs loosening [*Lösung*]—that is, dissolution [*Auflösung*] and redemption [*Erlösung*] through the cooling song—in order to be maintained as spirit, divine spirit can no longer be grasped under the concept of a transcendental subject that would not only be thinkable but also encountered without the slightest modification through something that evades its dominion. Spirit can only remain if it relinquishes its monarchic concept; the subject of revelation must not become the object of the song, that which is signified by its sign—such a relation is never suggested by Hölderlin—but must, rather, become the object of the song's intervention: it *is* only ever such a thing, though not in the privileged sense of a *summum ens*, but rather as something that is negated in each case in its liberation in the other. On no account does this other, the negation of the transcendental subject, take the place of the transcendental subject and hypostasize itself as the transcendental unity of apperception, as Kant's a priori philosophy tried to do in Hölderlin's view, or, materialistically, as the basis for all possible spirit; rather, this other, the song, is the loosening [*Lösung*] of the heavenly fire only insofar as it is its symptom [*Anzeichen*], and it is only as a symptom, as something that is already derivative, that it can resist the danger of itself becoming monarchic force, and it is only as such that it provides hold [*Halt*]. A simple reversal of metaphysically conceived relations of the conditions—whose meaning for the Enlightenment finds an exemplary formulation in Lichtenberg's statement that if "God created man in his own image," this would mean that man has created God in his own[79]—this simple reversal remains tied to the thought of the *hupokéimenon*, of that which lies securely at the basis, and to the idea of primacy and priority and thus of dominion, and so affirms liberation only in wordplay—for in wordplay, the sentence proves itself to be constitutive of meaning and at the same time the medium of its distortion [*Entstellung*], with the weakness of being subject to the dominion of meaning, but also gifted with the sovereign capacity to usurp meaning's dominion. If nevertheless even the force of the gods and of God is not entirely relieved of the necessity of protection and indication [*Anhalt*], this force must proceed to the place of what it needs, of the other as its sign, and to the place of the song, in order to find itself there in the sign. One of the latest hymns, which is not preserved in its entirety and to which the editor gave the name "The Ister," describes this movement and this place.

> Now come, fire!
> We are impatient
> To look upon Day,
> And when the trial
> Has passed through the knees
> One may perceive the cries in the wood.
> But, as for us, we sing from the Indus,
> Arrived from afar, and
> From the Alpheus. (StA 2: 190; PF 581)

The beginning of the poem is located at the end of the historical movement that began with the Indus and the Alpheus, from another Alpha of history, and ends up in the shadows of the woods of the Danube and in Hesperia. The actual "now," the desire for fire and for the beginning from which the hymn itself began historically, is thus first uttered at the place where the fire's dominion is in decline, where the domain of the day meets its limit, and where history has contracted into the punctual "now." The desire at this historical place is no longer the desire for presence or for extinguishment in the identity of pure light; it is, rather, a desire that is directed at a "day" that, far removed from its "original" place, can only arrive after a long detour:

> . . . long we
> Have sought what is fitting,
> Not without wings may one
> Reach out for that which is nearest
> Directly
> And get to the other side. (StA 2: 190; PF 581)

This "that which is nearest," which can be reached "directly" only "*with wings*" [Schwingen] that carry over long stretches, and via detours that pass along "the *more curved* route" [*die* geschwungnere *Bahn*] (StA 2: 50) can be seen precisely in this hymn, in the fire and the desire. After a long search, they can be grasped as Hesperian on the "other side," though only "with wings." And it is not they themselves that, in Hegelian manner, would grasp themselves in their Other, but rather, with a little postponement, only "that which is nearest." Just as hymn and desire arrive at their own possibility only in their historically acquired Other, just as the fire only experiences the condition of its remaining in the shadows—so the Greek hero, too, must enter the Occident in order to rescue the Oriental. The landscape into which he wanders is that of the Ister:

> Beautifully he dwells. The pillars' foliage burns,
> And stirs. Wildly they stand,
> Upright, amongst one another; above,
> A second measure, juts out
> The roof of rocks. (StA 2: 190; PF 581, mod.)

The burning here is no longer of a devouring kind, but rather one that is protected against itself, the burning of a color. The Titanic trait that appears in this landscape in proximity to Hades as wildness—as the first measure—is juxtaposed to a second measure: protection, which the roof of rocks provides against the hubristic and upright movement of the trees. This standing upright "amongst one another" is modified by the second measure, not actually negated: the trees are the pillars of the roof without their movement dissipating into art. This modification of Titanism into the Hesperian house is the living space of the Ister. The Ister seems to have invited the Greek hero into this living space as its guest:

> No wonder, therefore,
> I say, this river
> Invited Hercules,
> Distantly gleaming, down by Olympus,
> When he, to look for shadows,
> Came up from the sultry isthmus,
> For full of courage they were
> In that place, but, because of the spirits,
> There's need of coolness too. That is why that hero
> Preferred to come here to the well-springs and yellow banks (StA 2: 190–91; PF 581–83)

The earlier draft of verses 33 and 34 marks, more clearly than what has been passed down as their final version, the danger that would threaten spirits without coolness: "There's need however of coolness too, / So that, unbound, to the dead / The burning breast does not go" (StA 2: 809). Thus, just as the spirit needs the song in order not to devour itself in its captivity; just as Bacchus's transplantation to the Hesperian colony rescues him from dying of thirst in the Oriental heat—so Hercules must establish the material element of the shadow in the spirits in order to hinder and protect them from the danger of their disappearing. The fact that only the land made arable by the Ister represents the terrain in which the spirits can discover this condition of their survival, however, concerns in principle the possibility of their *being*, the possibility for what could appear, as pure beginning and as autonomous essence and identity, to be a *self*. However, it is not by looking at the myth, which Hölderlin learned from Pindar, nor by looking at the thematic connection into which he brings the myth, but only by describing the *texture* through which the thematic complex of the myth is articulated that the poem's problematization of both the Oriental spirit and that which is inscribed in it—the Is [*Ist*]—can be presented. For, just as the naming of the Greek name for the Danube is followed by the appearance of its elements, scattered across the subsequent lines—in "*wohn*t er" [he dwells] and "re*g*et si*ch*" [stirs]—in order not to expose the name immediately to its own "sense," so, too, the Greek landscape is presented in its relation to an Is [*Ist*] and to a Self [*Selbst*], both still unquestionably appearing in it, as "*ist*hmus" and an "in that place" [*Da*selbst]. The constant opposition of *i* and *r* in the verses

> . . . Darum zog *j*ener l*ie*b*er*
> An d*ie* Wass*er*quellen h*ie*h*er* und gelben Uf*er*
> [That is why that hero
> Preferred to come here to the well-springs and yellow banks] (StA 2: 190; PF 583)

also allows the "spirits" [*Geist*er] to be read along the lines of this oppositional model; moreover, though, it allows one to see the *-ist-er* in them, to see them shortened by the shadow thrown by the texture of the Hesperian and the Hölderlinian hymn, even at the place where the Is [*Ist*] of the spirit still apparently exists in itself unproblematically. The Hesperian shadow, which the woods of the Ister provides, grants the spirits the obstruction they need by inserting in them a border to their self; the progress of history and the progress of Hercules lead from the "Ist*hmos*"—a pure affirmation, as it were, of being—into a "*h*ie*h*er" in which the question of the Ister poses itself, the question of whether he [*er*] or it is [*ist*] it; the Hesperian hymn shows, however, that in the "spirits themselves" the question of whether they are it must have been inscribed in them, as their shadow, in order that they may come to "be" at all.

At the end of this strophe, the opposition between *i* and *r* is superseded by the other opposition between *s* and *t*, which together with the first forms the "name" of the Ister:

Hoch duftend oben, und schwarz
Vom Fichtenwald, wo in den Tiefen
Ein Jäger gern lu*st*wandelt
Mi*tt*ag*s*, und Wach*st*um hörbar i*st*
An harzigen Bäumen des I*st*ers.[80]
[Highly fragrant on top, and black
With fir woods, in whose depths
A huntsman loves to amble
At noon, and growth is audible
In resinous trees of the Ister.] (StA 2: 191; PF 583)

It is not so much the *mundus sensibilis* opening up in the woods of the Danube—fragrance, colors, movement, sound, as depicted, content-wise, in these verses—but, rather, its determination through those elements that express a relation in it to the Ister: the secret conditionality of sensibility, as evident in whatever, like the Ister, limits the pure presence of spirit, suspends Being, and turns away from its self. It is this determination that is realized through the texture of the poem. The mode of this turning, of reversal, as carried out by the Ister, and thus also the reversal of the condition of possibility of Being, is expressed in the first verses of the third strophe, in which Beissner (StA 2: 815) and also already Pigenot[81] recognized the "nucleus" of the poem.

Der scheinet aber fa*st*
Rükwär*ts* zu gehen und
Ich mein, er müsse kommen
Von O*st*en.
Vieles wäre
Zu sagen davon. . . .
[Yet this river seems almost
Backwards to travel and

I think it must come from
The East.
Much could
Be said about this.] (StA 2: 191; PF 583, mod.)

It is the *ritardando* of the Ister, the leisureliness of the progress towards the *East* [Ost*en*], and the delay before the *Is* [Ist] through which it [*er*] appears to "almost [travel] backwards." The interpretation by the I—of which it may perhaps be supposed that, far from the self of the East, it is in German script that its kinship with the graphic form of the Ister is announced: *Ich* / *Ister* 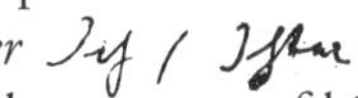—locates its second origin in the East and lets it follow the progress of history and the travels of the Oriental hero, out of the identity of the Is [*Ist*] and into the Hesperian shadow. By not naming the "actual" movement, the poem depicts this almost reversed movement, which displaces the origin and situates the goal where it "is" not, that is, the almost backwards running of the Ister, as the movement with which the Ister's gives its "real" goal and its "real" direction the shadowy woods in which they encounter, as a condition for their being, that being's obstruction or inhibition [*Hemmung*]. In this way, the second movement proves itself to be the condition and the premise of the first movement. With this movement, however, it not only turns away from the Orient and from the general origin; if it appears to come from the East, the origin in the West is also negated. Thus, in each instance the Ister turns one origin against the other, one goal against the other, and brings about the disappearance of the possibility that one of the two would, as the actual one, hypostasize. But it can do this only through the semblance that it invokes, not through its actual course; thus, not by the fact that it travels backwards, but "almost . . . backwards." The "almost" calls the statement into question as much as the Ister calls being into question.

The Ister's movement, a decided retardation, and its interpretation in the hymn, that it travels almost backwards, describe the spatio-temporal and interpretive form of movement taken by the distancing from goal and origin: that is, they describe Hesperian reversal. By appearing to flow "almost backwards," the Ister does not negate Oriental being, but turns it toward a question, and in this question, in which the affirmation of being is undone and traversed by the possibility of non-being, Oriental being discovers its condition as being in the element in which its dominion passes away. In their Hesperian turn, the spirits must, for the sake of their own preservation, immerse themselves in the element that diminishes and distorts them as spirits. Yet the Ister is unable to be this element unless it poses the question, into which it draws the Is, to (its Self) itself and (is) it: is it [*Ist er*]? If it turns in its return flow from the East, toward which it flows, and away from pure being, it only "almost" does so and not as one that itself is [*seiender*], but as one that appears to do so [*scheinender*]. Almost as an echo of the last words of the second strophe, "of the Ister," the first line of the third strophe reads: "Yet almost this river seems." Thus, it is not through the interpretation of the "I" [*Ich*] but through the fact that the Ister (itself) draws the figure of interpretation that the delay of the movement towards the East is linked with appearance and reversal.

There is another form of withdrawing from the tendency towards the East, the Self, and being. While the Ister travels "straight," but "almost backwards," the Rhine turns away from the "line" that leads immediately from West to East and goes "sideways" away from it.

> And why does
> It cling to the mountains, straight? The other,
> The Rhine, has gone away
> Sideways. Not for nothing rivers flow
> Through dry land. But how? A sign is needed,
> Nothing else, plain and honest, so that
> Sun and moon it may bear in mind, inseparable,
> And go away, day and night no less, and
> The Heavenly feel warm one beside the other.
> That also is why these are
> The joy of the Highest. (StA 2: 191; PF 583)

The sign that presents the courses of the Ister and the Rhine, however different they may be, makes it possible—just as history can, "with wings," get to "the other side"—for the gods in *their* beyond to descend to earth. However, the sign is neither the language of gods—the first draft formulation, "For they should / Become language" (StA 2: 810) is explicitly rejected—nor is it a designation whose object is the heavenly beings. According to the function ascribed to it by the poem, the sign is to be determined as the element that, independently of the change in the time of day, will synthesize the heavenly beings that are distinct from one another, the "sun and moon," which are not in a position to annul their separation of their own accord. Only the plain and honest sign, as the element that is one with itself, could bring about the synthesis of synthesis and the opposite, and in such a way—that is, in strict contrast to the differential function of the mortals in "The Rhine"—lend heavenly beings the capacity to "feel" themselves: each itself and one another. In an epistemological context, the sign would occupy the systematic place that transcendental consciousness and the categories grounded in it occupy in Kant's *Critique of Pure Reason*. The functions it fulfills are comparable to the synthesis of apprehension, the reproductive synthesis of the imagination, and the synthesis of recognition in the concept, all of which belong to the "transcendental actions of the mind" (A 102). In Kant, however, the synthesis of the a posteriori manifold is carried out in a pure, original "standing or abiding self" (A 107); among its determinations is "the original and necessary consciousness of the identity of oneself" (A 108); and, furthermore, "the mind could not possibly think of the identity of itself in the manifoldness of its representations, and indeed think this *a priori*, if it did not have before its eyes the identity of its action, which subjects all synthesis of apprehension (which is empirical) to a transcendental unity, and first makes possible their connection in accordance with *a priori* rules" (A 108). The demand that Hölderlin's poem places on the sign—"A sign is needed . . . "—corresponds to what Kant sees as being realized in the transcendental consciousness. Yet the reality of the sign that the Ister presents adds to Kant's demand, thereby also, however, causing significant distortions to the composition of the condition of possibility of all experience and cognition. The Ister does not inscribe itself into "dry land" as a self that exists and remains in itself but as a river, to which the statement that it is not even possible to ascend into the *same* can apply because its determination, on the contrary, is the dissolution of selfness. The figure of the Ister is not original, but turned away from the origin, and it conditions the origin as non-original; it is not identical, but identity, like that of being and of the spirits as they turn away from themselves; as such, the figure of the Ister subverts the condition of possibility for experience as was still conceived by speculative Idealism. In its reversal and its turn away from original and produced identity, the sign relinquishes the possibility of having a synthesizing effect; it relinquishes itself as sign. The Ister introduces the heavenly beings into this reversal and turn away from the self towards an other that represents not the negative of the self but its suspension; and, insofar as it diminishes the unity that it was tasked to establish, it does what the shadow does to the spirits and what Hesperia does to fire and desire. Therefore, it can also be that "Not for nothing rivers flow / Through dry land," and "That also is why these are / The joy of the Highest" (StA 2: 191; PF 583). These verses would be misunderstood if one were to find in them the assurance that the Ister is satisfied with the demands raised in the concept of the sign. The first as well as the last lines of this strophe address this clearly enough:

> That also is why these are
> The joy of the Highest. For how
> Would he get down? And like Hertha green
> They are the children of Heaven. But all too patient
> He seems to me, not
> More free, and nearly derisive. (StA 2: 191; PF 583)

The claim that "like Hertha green / They are the children of Heaven" sets up an equation between the color of the earth and the color of the river is forced, as one can judge from the context. Any such simplicity of meaning for the sentence's second half is annulled by the fact that it answers the question of how the highest comes "down": by reproducing itself in the rivers. The fact that the rivers reflect the blue of heaven lets them appear as its children. In this way, the "how" has no less an adversative meaning than a comparative one: the sign, which is a child begotten by heaven with earth, has to display aspects of both in equal measure; the blue, the child of heaven, must also be green. Yet even this synthesizing, which is carried out in reproduction and reflection, is resisted by the Ister: " . . . But all too patient / He seems to me . . . " The semblance that attests to the father and in which the father, Being, reproduces itself, is held back by the Ister, just as it holds back the progress towards the East.[82] Thus, not only does it seem to travel "almost backwards," but its appearing goes almost backwards as well. This double turning away from both the "East" and the "Highest" is articulated in the single phrase, "But all too patient / He seems to me." He does not seem, as the sign should seem, in such a way that that which refers to his reproduction in the sign and to the continuity between East and West as the condition of his self-experience would be able to rediscover itself in him as his Other; the semblance of the Ister refuses (itself) the formation of a semblance of a highest being to which it would be subject and of which it would be a mere moment of its self-appropriation. The double turning is also preserved in the phrase " . . . and almost derisively," which follows. It is easiest to see that this is a double turning from an earlier version of the phrase, which reads "and almost apingly" (StA 2: 811). In aping, imitation turns away from the binding character of the original image and only *seems* to make itself equal to it. The derision, which is not reduced to the mirroring relation, turns away both from the reproduction of a highest and from the progress towards origin and goal: almost. Were this small limitation on the movement of its reversal and on its derision not to apply, the Ister would succumb to a determinate tendency, from which it could be construed that this tendency exists, whereas, modified in this way, the Ister's course removes itself from every determination that could lay a claim to truth. And together with the Ister's turn away from self, being, reproduction, and synthesis, together with the turn away from a true and not just a seemingly true relationship to these entities, a subversion of the possibility of a "cognition" of this turning away is carried out: "Yet what that one does, the river, / No one knows" (StA 2: 192; PF 585). What is not known is not only how the river flows, what it is, or how it appears; it is also not known *whether* it is: whether it makes "incisions" in the rock or digs "furrows" in the earth and therefore does what rivers, of which it is one, do, according to what the poem establishes in its first strophe: "For rivers make arable / The land" (StA 2: 190; PF 581). In contrast, the lines of its final strophe suggest, without drawing the conclusion that is hinted at:

> But the rock needs incisions
> And the earth needs furrows,
> Would be desolate else, unabiding;
> Yet what that one does, the river,
> No one knows. (StA 2: 192; PF 585)

Just as the Ister, through its all too patient seeming and its near derision, suspends the reproduction and production of the father as one that experiences itself, just as it almost refuses to be the father's fruit, as it were, and thereby hinders the cognizability of God in the sign—the Ister is (itself) perhaps infertile, which is to say neither fertile nor infertile, and imprints (itself) as little in the knowledge of human beings as it leaves behind incisions and furrows in the rock and earth; or rather, barely. For it is not negation, whose position would have to be defined according to the requirement that it strive to undo itself, which distinguishes the manner in which "reversal" proceeds as depicted in the figure of the Ister; rather, reversal proceeds by hesitation and by holding back vis-à-vis the positions of self, being, highest, and reproduction, a holding back that also protects itself against that which might appear as its negative, such as sign, semblance, and infertility: the

Ister only fulfills the function of the sign by exempting itself from its law; its appearing is neither false semblance nor the reflection of a highest, but its deferral; it is infertile, undecidably, and perhaps also not. The argument against skepticism that might be levied against the hymn, namely that the hymn presupposes with its form the cognizability of that which it calls uncognizable, since non-cognizability has been cognized, does not hold up because the Ister as well as the hymn about it only want to suspend and put into question its self and its fertility, not claim to be their negative. Insofar as the "overstepping" carried out by the Ister is not a "step over" but is rather a hesitation and a restraining of the step, insofar as this transgression denies itself the claim to mediation, which is raised implicitly by the domains diverging towards the East and West, before and after, above and below, and defers the law of dichotomy already mediating between them, the Ister's transgression grounds the possibility of the synthesis of that which is opposite to one another and, at the same time, withdraws from it all ground; if it depicts the condition for the spirit's and the highest's self-experience and self-reproduction, it also depicts the condition of their impossibility; it abandons the constitutive form of being and cognition while at the same time it carries out its deconstruction.

By contrast, the Hegelian philosopheme of the self-identity of Absolute Spirit seems practically antipodal, as can be seen in an example from the Jena natural philosophy, which was composed around the same time as Hölderlin's very last hymns. In a section under the heading "Solar System," Hegel writes: "Absolute Spirit must recognize itself as Absolute Spirit; it must, in order that he be living God, itself as Absolute Spirit become an Other and find itself in this Other, or it is only living God insofar as it is, as the Other to its self, just as absolutely equal to itself."[83] A few years later, in the final chapter of the *Phenomenology of Spirit*, Hegel reformulates this in a much more differentiated manner, this time taking spirit to be the historical process that determines its own genesis: "However, this substance, which is spirit, is its *coming-to-be* what it, the substance, is *in itself*; and it is as this coming-to-be which is taking a reflective turn into itself that spirit is truly in itself *spirit*. Spirit is in itself the movement which is cognition—the transformation of that former *in-itself* into *for-itself*, of *substance* into *subject*, of the object of *consciousness* into the object of *self-consciousness*, i.e., into an object that is just as much sublated, or into the *concept*."[84] This self-production in the medium of reflection, by means of which the spirit becomes capable of assuming absolute dominion over itself as over its own Other, has to be subverted by the Hölderlinian figure of the condition of cognition, because in the concept of the autochthonous self, spirit has recognized the aporia that its unification with the Other has only succeeded thanks to the restriction of its otherness, and thus thanks to ap*propriation* [*An*eignung]. This aporia, from which Hölderlin's drafts from the Homburg period are also not wholly free, insofar as they place so much emphasis on the free unity of the different and the united, includes in it the other aporia, namely that the subject remains a monarchic principle[85] and the principle of dominion, so long as it remains itself or produces itself; and, furthermore, it includes the aporia that spirit, as that which conceives itself, only seems to escape from its objectlessness and either stays timidly in its self, or, without the possibility of synthesizing under the concept of the subject, passes away upon encountering what it is incapable of conceiving. This Other, which is withdrawn from the grip of a transcendental subject, extends itself outward as the scene that the work of late Hölderlin describes. In the "Notes on the *Antigone*," this Other is called the "unthinkable": "This is the proper language of Sophocles, since Aeschylus and Euripides know more how to objectify suffering and anger than human understanding passing through the midst of the unthinkable" (StA 5: 266; EL 327, mod.). This statement serves as the commentary to a short dialogue between Creon and Antigone:

> CREON: Yet, like good the bad should not be taken.
> ANTIGONE: Who knows, below there may well be a different rite. (StA 5: 266; EL 326)

It is as the violence of death that the "unthinkable" spreads to the condition of possibility of understanding and law, and at the same time, as the condition of their impossibility, undoes their validity. The violence of death (is) that which is at work in the suspension of reflection and reproduction in the Ister; it is that in whose medium the process of self-production has to be at the same time the discontinuous act of a destruction of the self. In the *Phenomenology of Spirit*, by contrast, the power of death stands not as perverting [*verkehrende*] but as reversible [*umkehrbare*]; insofar as spirit "look[s] the negative in the face and linger[s] with it," it acquires "the magical power that converts [*umkehrt*] it into being."[86] Yet death can be for spirit the element of its reflection only as already reversed death, that is, only as a death that turns a "countenance" to spirit; more precisely, death is an element of reflection, one that, being fertile, receives and conceives [*empfängt*] the projection of spirit's countenance, authenticating it to the producer as spirit's own reproduction. What remains unthought, because the status of thinking as self-production disintegrates in death, is the blindness of spirit, the infertility of the other and of itself. Even of death under the Reign of Terror during the French Revolution, and even of "the coldest, emptiest death of all," it was said that it was "without any more meaning than chopping off a head of cabbage or swallowing a mouthful of water."[87] Metaphorically, though not only metaphorically, this almost meaningless death must therefore also be brought into connection with acts of reproduction, of drinking and eating, in order to keep the domains of the self and of its meaning unscathed. What remains unthinkable, thereby evading the claim to dominion that spirit directs at universality, is an other that would not be the other "of it" and be bound possessively to it; what remains unthinkable is an expropriated and expropriating other. The repression of blindness, infertility, expropriation, and perversity [*Verkehrtheit*] in the philosophy of reflection drives speculative dialectics into the bourgeois phantasm of the self-production of the subject. The subject discovers its apotheosis in a revolution conceived as the concrete reflection of its absolute truth. "Never since the sun had stood in the firmament and the planets revolved around him had it been perceived that man's existence centres in his head, *i.e.*, in Thought, inspired by which he builds up the world of reality . . . . This was accordingly a glorious dawn."[88] During the French Revolution, the bourgeois *epistrophē*, the chopped-off head of cabbage, celebrates its resurrection as the sun. Following strictly metaphysical custom, whatever is digressive [*Abwegige*] and perverted [*Verkehrte*] in a historical epoch is led back by what it grounds, through the negation of negation, to the correct path of its "proper" form. Hegel's innovation: it is the process itself that, in its negativity, carries out the revolution, carries itself out as revolution.[89] Hölderlin's "laying out" and thus "interpretation" of the metaphysical tradition is that its constructs—Being, self, and process—must enter into the element of their impossibility to become even thinkable and actual. Only where they have entered the scene of a death that "is" not "theirs" and for that very reason meets them as break, limitation, transgression, infertility, interlude [*Zwischen*], postponement, or deferral; only where spirit and history accept their impotence as the uncertain and unknowable condition for their efficacy; can there take place that which could only still provisionally be called a revolution. Hölderlin's attempt to sketch out a non-metaphysical "concept" of revolution that does not begin with self-production and self-appropriation designates a *point de suspension* that resists bourgeois idealism and its politics, a point from which a line, though certainly not a straight one, could be drawn to point out the work that could be done to dissolve present systems of coercion, be they economic, political, or philosophical.

V. Dissemination, Mourning

The "fatherland [*Vaterland*]," that is, the land that no longer stands under the rule of a feudal lord[90] or of a bourgeois monarch,[91] was conceived by Hölderlin as the product of lengthy historical movements, that is, as a fruit; he conceived of his human beings as a "fruit of Hesperia" (StA 2: 95; PF 329) and the Hesperian form of the gods as "golden fruit" (StA 3: 537; PF 531). According to the draft of a very late hymn entitled "At one time I questioned the Muse . . . ," the fatherland is a forbidden fruit.

> At one time I questioned the Muse, and she
> Replied to me,
> In the end you will find it.
> No mortal can grasp it.
> About the Highest I will not speak.
> But, like the laurel, forbidden fruit
> The fatherland is, above all. To be tasted last
> By any man. (StA 2: 220; PF 635, mod.)

With this, everything that the fatherland seemed to encompass as mature plenitude, life held in support [*gehaltenes*], and presence of the highest, is lost. Only "last," though now not even devoured, but as fruit that has merely been tasted, is the fatherland itself left to the end, where "Beginning and end / Greatly deceive us" (StA 2: 220; PF 635). The fruit that is only found at the end, the forbidden fruit that may only be tasted "last," itself goes missing thanks to the deception of the end. It is impossible that it ever proffers itself in its "true" form. For the "end" and the "last," the condition of its being found, designate a death that will not be able to be experienced as what it "is" because it abandons itself to something that possesses no being, no reality of its own, and no truth. Thus, neither fruit nor end can be interpreted as determinations that could simply be predicated by being. In life, they designate what does not belong to it as its boundary;[92] in life, they (are) neither life nor an Other that *is* dominated by life; and like the end, so, too, the beginning; like the fruit, so, too, its production: deception. The border of history, which the fatherland marks out, is not only infinitely deferred by the character of deception that is constitutive of it—for it was never the "true" border—history itself, whose domain is defined by this border, is in this way also de-bordered [*entgrenzt*], traversed by a deception against which it can never itself hypostasize as an autonomous time period [*Zeitraum*] or as processual subject. It cedes an element to deception in which it, like the fruit, does not rediscover itself or its own other but, rather, the illusion of what it is not. This illusion cannot be a medium of reflexive synthesis, since what was given to it cannot be recovered.

> And never now will he
> Give away what's dearest to him
> To those unfruitful, from now on
> The holy is fit for use. (StA 2: 221; PF 637)

The "dearest"—whose place was previously occupied by the "holy"—whatever it might be, be it the work of the artist, the fruit of history, or the fatherland, is given away to those through whom it cannot regenerate itself. Whatever combines the productivity of life and the intention of its acts goes away empty-handed. This dispersion of life and its reproductive possibilities—a dispersion that, however, has to be conceived as the *conditio* of history—points to a baroque trait in Hölderlin's late texts. This trait manifests most obviously in the correspondence between these lines of the hymn fragment and a verse that Walter Benjamin cites in a prominent passage of the *Origin of the German Mourning Play*: "Weeping, we scattered the seed on the fallow lands / And mournfully we went away."[93] Just as such relinquishment of the seed, as well as of *logos spermatikos*, lets go not only of a product but also of the possibility of its self-reproduction, the Hölderlinian fatherland, even if without any *ponderación misteriosa*, gives itself over to a sphere in which it is lost as substance or as an autonomous subject whose criterion is the capacity for self-preservation: to Hades, to Thanatos. The between, in which Hesperia is located, belongs as end and as a mode of deception to the abode of the infertile *kat' exochen*, that is, the abode of the dead—to which nothing belongs; in the domain of history, which is defined and undone by the Hesperian end, Thanatos "asserts" himself as the subversion of the self's lordship, as withdrawal from fulfillment and compliance [*Erfüllung*], as the loss of the product, as non-productivity, and as deception, which suspends its truth. Unusability is invoked not for the sake of exchange, but as gift: "And never now, from now on / The holy is fit for use."

Like the fruit of the Occident, the seed of the Hesperian song must also be shaken out and dispersed in such a way that no fruit are borne, and must, just as it makes itself impotent, also make impotent those to whom the song's element is supposed to bear witness and breed interpretation.

> Yet one thing remains
> To be said. For almost
> Too suddenly
> This happiness would have been granted,
> This lonely happiness: that, lacking comprehension
> Of what is mine
> To the shadows I would have turned,
> For because you gave
> To mortals
> The tentative shape of gods,
> Why waste a word? So then I thought, for he hates speech
> Who husbands the light of life that spares that which nourishes the heart.
> In ancient times
> The heavenly beings themselves interpreted
> How they had taken away the strength of the gods. (StA 2: 216; PF 627)

The process of articulation presents itself as loss, as the deferral of "happiness," as the separation of that which, spared, would have to lead to the "lack of comprehension" and loneliness, and as dissociation that must rescue from dissociation. It is the *logos* that, in accordance with the metaphorics of the prologue to the Gospel of John, is, first as word and speech, but then also as the "light of life"—"And the life was the light of men"[94]—set in opposition to, and introduced into, the darkness of "what is mine." It is as an interior *logos* that *logos* is the "light of life" that nourishes the heart in the "shape of gods." Its externalization in speech and as word, which alone can rescue the "comprehension" [*Verständigkeit*], the comprehensibility and the continuing existence of the *logos*, must be hated because in giving itself out, overspending [*Verausgabung*] itself in speech, this shape is deprived of its nourishment and also of its continuing existence. The shape of gods must be broken up by the *logos*, just as the plastic space of the Greek gods must be broken up by

Christ, and nourishment, the light of life, must be extinguished; *logos*, which is essentially a self-relation, must shatter itself and disappear in speech, not in order to reproduce itself dialectically in its disappearance as a free *logos* no longer bound to the shape of gods, but to rescue the smallest modicum of "comprehension," of shape, and of the word; for *logos* only "almost" escapes the lack of comprehension, "happiness" would "almost" have come too suddenly. The Hölderlinian "almost," the "barely" and the "nearly," contrary to the tendency of the Hegelian dialectic that rests at every one of its positions at the zenith of a self-certainty that incorporates and devours time itself, mark a non-conceptual moment of time that distances itself from the self-sublatory process of the *logos* by a minute difference, diminishing its acuteness. In this difference, which is opened up by the "almost," and with the trace of comprehension left behind by the self-negation of the *logos*, such that as the spared light of life *logos* is lacking in comprehension and unlogical, the poetic subject speaks: ("Yet one thing remains / To be said.") The wastage [*Verausgabung*] of light, life, nourishment, and continuing existence through the articulation of the *logos* thus takes place where the *logos* is no longer the inner word, has not yet become the externalized word, and is in difference with itself. This wastage, *logos*'s giving itself out, is thus not the form of an externalization or of an expression, thanks to which *logos* might be able to reappropriate itself in another form; rather, it is the affirmation of the difference between two forms of its impossibility. Its process is depicted by a mythological paradigm:

> In ancient times
> The heavenly beings for themselves, by themselves, interpreted
> How they had taken away the strength of the gods. (StA 2: 216; PF 627, mod.)

These verses do not name an isolated fact but, rather, allude to the structure of an entire mythological syndrome. The strength of the gods, which is an equivalent to the light of life, is not only taken away as *logos* and as Christ from the earth; it is robbed in the act by which Uranus is castrated by Cronus, and Cronus in turn by Zeus, the ruler of the new race of heavenly gods. The death of *logos* and the castration of the old gods is set up as the self-interpretation of the heavenly beings in opposition to the articulation that they encounter in the poet's speech. Yet castration and wastage are self-interpretation only insofar as they interpret "by themselves" [*von selbst*].

The comma that separates the "by themselves" from the movement of the sentence—they interpreted "for themselves, by themselves, . . . how they" [*sich, von selbst, wie sie*]—not only marks the opposition to the interpretation of the gods in the hymn; the comma exposes the extractive sense of the "by" [*von*] in such a way that the self [*Selbst*] becomes that which, as the actual "strength of the gods," is removed in the act of its interpretation.[95]

The witnessing [*Bezeugung*] on which the gods are dependent as on the condition of their self-experience as well as of their survival, if it now occurs by virtue of its own act or through the speech of humans, realizes itself as the deprivation of the power of procreation [*Zeugungskraft*] and of that which is procreated [*Gezeugten*], the fruit. The wastage of the *logos spermatikos* in a speech that does not collect it again in another form as comprehending [*verständigen*] *logos* presents, as interpretation, the condition of possibility of a highest authority [*Instanz*], of sense [*Sinn*], and of meaning [*Bedeutung*] conceived on the model of the *logos* or of the spirit; it presents, as castration, which interpretation is at the same time, the condition of impossibility of a self-sufficient subject, of a sense that produces itself or reproduces itself processually through its Other, of an "actual," but not always already expropriated meaning. Jacques Derrida, who, in an interpretation of texts by Mallarmé that are related in the most astonishing way to Hölderlin's, introduced the "concept" of dissemination for the scattering of meaning and the de-interpretation [*Entdeutung*] of sense, can for the same reason emphatically insist that castration is just as little a category of origin as is dissemination: "No more than can castration, dissemination—which entails . . . castration—can never become an originary, central, or ultimate signified . . . . On the contrary, dissemination represents the affirmation of this nonorigin . . . . "[96] For in the same act by which interpretation and articulation generate sense, they separate the generative root that they represent from itself and abandon it to the fall. Through its interpretation, *logos* is bestowed upon those among whom it is not itself, that is, upon the infertile.

It is not only sense that goes astray on this path, but also what signifies it: that which remembers its downfall with mourning. If the first strophe of "Mnemosyne" demands that "And much / As on the shoulders a / Load of logs must be / Retained" (StA 2: 197; PF 587), like a load of logs [*Holzscheiten*] and like the failure [*Scheitern*][97] in the form of which history must be borne, the conclusion of its final strophe knows of a different fate for memory and for fidelity, and another fate for mourning, the mourning for that which failed, in which even the mourners lose themselves.

> But by Cithaeron there stood
> Eleutherae, Mnemosyne's town. From her also
> When God laid down his festive cloak, soon after did
> The powers of Evening sever a lock of hair. For the Heavenly, when
> Someone has failed to collect his soul, to spare it,
> Are angry, for still he must; like him/it
> Here mourning is at fault. (StA 2: 198; PF 589)

The excess of mournful remembrance allegorizes itself in Mnemosyne's town. Just as God lays down his cloak, so Mnemosyne, dead, has to part with her locks and make of them a gift to the gods of death; in the excess of meaning, which she grants to the fallen and the failed, signification [*das Bedeuten*] must exhaust itself for her. Because her concern, like that of those who are retained in her, was not to get a grip on herself, but rather to give herself out to those with whom it cannot be sublated—the mourner must, therefore, follow those who mournfully go to their death. The surplus of their meaning over the self is syntactically realized in the ambiguity of the phrase "for still he must": the one who commemorates a loss must, in order to preserve himself, get a grip on himself, but he cannot do so by virtue of the same compulsion of memory. Similarly, the subsequent overdetermination is also a result of a diminishment and an abbreviation: "like him/it / Here mourning is at fault" [*dem / Gleich fehlet die Trauer*]. The meaning of the fault [*Fehlen*] is not, as commentators argue,[98] absolute: rather, its determination is relative to whatever is linked with the "him/it" [*dem*]—which leads to a line break. If the him/it refers to the one who, in mourning, is not in control of himself, it also refers to the entire context of this and the preceding lines: that is, to the fact that the mourning subject and the one who was preserved in his memory have been taken away; correspondingly, "fault" [*fehlet*] means in one instance the misconduct [*Verfehlung*] of a mourning that oversteps the measure of the self and of life, but in another instance, with the death of Mnemosyne's town, the failure of mourning to appear [*Ausbleiben*]: "like him/it / Here mourning is at fault." The "like" [*Gleich*] is unlike [*ungleich*]. Just as the one meaning abandons itself to that which it is not, so memory abandons itself to the disappeared one that it tries to retain. The one movement of Mnemosyne to repeat a loss in remembering it turns against Mnemosyne herself: loss repeats itself in the ruination of its own form. Yet form is destroyed and laid out in interpretation only when it goes too far. Mourning—and meaning, which is also a "strength of the gods"—ends where it follows loss in lamenting it. The situation of the failure that sought to catch one that was vanishing. Where the vanishing "faults" [*fehlt*].

SEPTEMBER–NOVEMBER 1971
Translated by Julia Ng

II Parousia, Stone-Walls

Mediacy and Temporality, Late Hölderlin[1]

On the 9th of November, 1795, Hölderlin writes to Johann Gottfried Ebel, explaining his reason for wishing to "communicate" to him "something more specific" of his "literary works and other things that your spirit occupies itself with and takes a share in":

> You know, spirits must commune, must share of themselves wherever a living breath stirs; unite themselves with everything that must not be expelled, so that out of this union, out of this invisible church militant, may arise the great child of time, the day of all days, which the man of my soul (an apostle, whom those now parroting his words understand as little as they understand themselves) names *the advent* [Zukunft] *of the lord.* I must stop, otherwise I'll never stop. (StA 6: 184–85)[2]

Writing to his brother three years later, on the 28th of November, 1798, Hölderlin offers a similar politico-theological clarification of epistolary communication: "So we must still bring a sacrifice from time to time for the deity that exists between you and me; namely, the easy, pure sacrifice of speaking to one another about it; of celebrating the eternal being that unites us in these dear letters—letters that have only become so rare between us because they come from the heart, and not, like so much, from the pen" (StA 6: 293). Communicating, sharing with one another: this may be a profane act of brokering a position, of friendly instruction, or of loyalty and fond inclination among relatives. Yet for Hölderlin it is always a sacral act of conjoining in a unity or of attesting to a connection that, while already existing, needs to be clarified, extended, and intensified. The communication of that which "your spirit occupies itself with and takes a share in" follows a movement toward ever greater unities and toward a burgeoning whole which, in every part—every communication [*Mitteilung*] and every participation [*Teilnahme*]—is already in effect and, in the accomplishment of its telos, should arise—go forth—as all-comprehensive gathering, as *ekklesia*, and, beyond this, as fruit of the union, as "great child of time," as "day of all days" and "*advent of the Lord.*" Hölderlin joins the thought of communication, whether it be intimately epistolary or openly literary, with the thought not only of a religious, Christian-Messianic community, which, with a view to his own and to Ebel's revolutionary-republican inclinations, he characterizes as an "invisible church militant," but also of a time that comes to an end and that, ending, should become the "*advent of the Lord.*" The apostle from whom he borrows this trope—"the man of my soul," as he refers to him with great emphasis—indeed remains unnamed. Yet a letter to Hegel dating from the same month as the letter to Ebel lets one suspect that this apostle is Paul. "I had already thought," Hölderlin writes to his former Tübingen classmate, that "paraphrasing the Pauline letter in accordance with your idea must be well worth the effort" (StA 6: 186). In the first letter to the Thessalonians, Paul uses the trope *parousia tou kyriou*, translated by Luther as *advent of the Lord*, several times in order to characterize the *plēroma* of fellowship binding all the faithful together in love. "May the Lord make you increase [*pleonasai*] and let love become full among all and toward each, . . . that your hearts should be strengthened, irreproachable in holiness before God our Father, upon the advent of the Lord Jesus Christ" (1 Thess. 3:12–13). A corresponding formulation in the same Pauline epistle speaks of the day of the Lord, which will come like a thief in the night (1 Thess. 5:2). Hölderlin understands the *parousia* of the Messiah Christ as his "advent"—a "future-to-come" that, as the letter to Ebel puts it, first "arises" out of the communing union of spirits. This "*advent of the Lord*" is conceived as going forth from a communication present in each instant; it does not arrive—does not ad-vent—from outside of this communicative act as heterogeneous time. Thus it is not a *futural ad-vent* [*zukünftige* Zukunft] in the emphatic sense, but the result, consequence, and fruit of both past and present tendencies of unification. The language of correspondence among friends speaks and is spoken, or indeed speaks itself, *toward* the future [*Zukunft*] brought forth *by* it and *from out of* it and first finds therein the horizon of its movement of fulfillment and union. As communication between speakers and hearers, it can only succeed by turning itself toward its more fulfilled future and hence its own *parousia* as pervasive and unrestricted context. The *parousia* of language, of the "living breath," must therefore be at once [*in eins*] the *parousia* of historical—linguistically mediated—time, since, in Hölderlin's letter, otherwise than in Paul's, the advent of the Lord is called "the great child of time," and thereby names a time *out of* time that at once is *all* time. "The day of all days" is not only the *summum* and the sum, comprehended therein, of all days—it is the time of all times: that time therefore which contains the destination [*Bestimmung*]—the goal, the end, and the determination—of every time. The union of all communications that is expected to come from this time must be thought as a communication of all communication, in which the structure of communication as such exhibits itself. Every communication—whether in letters or in other expressive forms—accomplishes itself in the movement toward an eschatological time; every time-movement proceeds within the horizon of an eschatological language, at whose end—the advent of the Christian Messiah—both language and time as such, the *parousia* of the messianic language-time, appears.

Hölderlin wrote the letter to Ebel after his return from Jena, where he had attended Fichte's lectures, and, as he reported to Hegel in a letter dated January 26, 1795, had read "Fichte's speculative pages—*Foundations of the Entire Science of Knowledge* [*Wissenschaftslehre*]" (StA 6: 155). It is during this same time that he would have studied Schiller's *Letters on Aesthetic Education*, which, according to his February 1796 letter to Niethammer, he planned on continuing and surpassing with his own "philosophical letters" under the title "New Letters on the Aesthetic Education of the Human Being" (StA 6: 203). These philosophical letters—Hölderlin allows no doubt about this—were to have been the theoretical complement to the poetic letters of *Hyperion*, which he was working on at the time. Indeed, as one can conjecture from the allusion to Hegel's idea of a "paraphrase of the Pauline letters," they were to have been a renewal of the Schillerian letters in a Pauline spirit. Regarding his conversation with Schelling, he reports that they are of one mind that "new ideas can be represented most clearly in the form of letters" (StA 6: 203)—that, hence, the precise and pithy communication of what is new, of what has never yet existed, reaches its apex in the specific form of communication that is the letter. Written perhaps as a partial draft of the never-realized project of the "New Letters on the Aesthetic Education of the Human Being," where Hölderlin wanted to "proceed from philosophy to poetry and religion," the draft "On Religion" ends with the conclusion: "Thus all religion would be in its essence poetic."

Hölderlin entrusts "the union of a multitude into one religion" to those sorts of "poetic representations" in which each "mythically celebrates . . . his own god, . . . his own higher life," while all "mythically celebrate . . . a common god, a common higher life" (StA 4: 281). Religion is, according to the argument of this fragment, essentially poetic; poetry [*Poesie*] is the essence of religion, because it is alone "poetic representations" that sublate [*aufheben*] the distinctions between the moral and the mechanical, the intellectual and the physical world in the unity of concept and experience—a unity that can be attained in no other form of representation. In poetry, as the substance of religion, "self-subsistence" [*Selbstständigkeit*] and "intimate connectedness," "facts" and "ideas," "parts" and "inseparability in its parts" are correlated with one another in such a way that the singular characteristic of both—of the parts and of their indivisibility—is not properly retained, but rather is generated for the first time, and ever anew for the first time. Poetry, "poetic representation," the essence of religion, is the generative procedure in which the partial regions of experience and thinking, having fallen to pieces, can be brought together for sensation—beyond the mechanism of nature and thus also beyond the special competences of thought and memory—in a living representation, united in an all-in-all of thought, memory, and feeling.

Since every unity includes the danger of a "standstill of *actual* life"—even if only "momentary"—(StA 4: 275) in the form of a rule, a duty, or a fixed corpus of assertions, poetic-religious "representation" must not only be a progressive synthesis of thinking and feeling but must also realize the "activity" constituting it in a procedure or "procedural mode" that exhibits the entire course of the generation of the sum total (StA 4: 277). It is not as an isolated product that a representation—even a religious one—is poetic, but only as the continual active result of its coming into being. It is not only a process of bringing about a result but is, in its result, still a process. The demand that Hölderlin joins with the idea of a religion and of a religion constituted from religions in the medium of poetic representation is the demand for a representation that must itself be the movement of representation, in order that, even where it touches what is most extrinsic and most rigid for it, it may thereby remain with it as its own [*Ihren*] and hence entirely at home with itself. Therefore, Hölderlin's doctrine of poetry cannot be a theory of imitation or even merely of the mimesis of something given, of something already posited, or something positive; it must be a theory of poetry as the generation of a "figure" (StA 4: 275), in which every presupposition proves to be its own positing, every prefiguration its own figuring, and even its self-reflection proves to be "creative reflection" (StA 4: 263). To reproduce itself in itself and in the other: this law of poetic procedure makes every instance of poetry into an originary self-generation. It makes every poem into a self-creation even in its other as that which, while indeed not created by it, nevertheless, insofar as it is freely chosen, has been released to itself. Poetry—only on this account can it be an infinite and universal process of cultural formation—must be, in its *summum*, the generation even of the conditions of generation. It must be absolute auto-genesis, and only thus can it be its own telos. Hence no poem can represent autobiographical material without at the same time making its own activity into its theme, and in turn this theme into the act of its presentation. Poetry of poetry, it exhibits itself as the generative process—going forth from out of itself, forth beyond itself, retreating into itself—of a linguistic and historical totality that is in each case singular. It itself *is* only by being the exhibition of its exhibiting, *poiēsis* of the *poiēsis*, making of the making. Since it figures anew all prefigurings from out of itself, it is, in each of its shapes, a figure *ab initio*, underivable *novum*, absolute inception. Since it pursues no goal external to itself, it is something final, irreplaceable, and unsurpassable. And since it brings into relation to one another in every possible manner all the communications that it contains, together with its partitions and its unpartibilities, it is the always-actual accomplishment of the *religio* of all religions and of religion itself. In poetry Hölderlin finds not only the substance but the occurrence of that "invisible church militant." And as the essence—the *ousia*—of religion he finds therein the Pauline *parousia tou kyriou*, the future-to-come as the presence of God, of which his letter to Ebel speaks. Poetic *parousia*, *parousia* of the poetic—not as one time among others but as the one time of the temporalization of all time—is that occurrence in which the human being becomes human and thereby becomes divine, the poetic occurrence of an anthropo- and theogony. This is precisely what would have had to be addressed by the Pauline-inspired "New Letters on the Aesthetic Education of the Human Being." His brouillon "On the Procedure of the Poetic Spirit"—like the draft "On Religion," this could have been intended as a preparation for the "New Letters"—offers a clear statement of the relation between the coming into being of the human being and the coming into being of poetry, between anthropo-theogony and poetology: "thus if this seems to be the course and the destiny of mankind as such, then the same is the course and the destiny of all and every poetry [*Poësie*]" (StA 4: 263).

Hölderlin was not able to develop his dynamic theory of the poetic—and only because it is poetic is it also religious, social, historical—self-generation of linguistic universality without turning his attention to the fundamental structure of generation. If the self must become representable to itself in order to satisfy its self-determination, then it has no choice but to pass over into another, in whom it must not lose itself and yet whom it must also not overpower. Hence, it must traverse a movement toward that which can neither be dominated by it nor is entirely alien to it. If it is to be a free connection, yielding a sum total of reciprocal determinations, the connection between it and the other must not be subject to either's dictate. Yet a pervasive reciprocal determination between the elements of a sum total is only possible if these elements do not start out by resting in themselves as essentialities closed off in themselves and indifferent to one another, only first passing over outside of themselves and toward the other through a heteronomous impulse. It is only possible insofar as each one of these elements always already passes beyond itself to the other, and thus is essentially a transition [*Übergang*]. Each one is itself only insofar as it is out beyond itself and toward the other. Being-one is being-to-the-other, and indeed to an other that, for its part, is being-to-the-other and hence one with being-one. It is only in the transition to the other of itself that every being-one goes back into itself; only in this manner is it its path to itself. In his fragment on religion and its poetic essence, Hölderlin takes account of this movement of self-generation from original self-transcendence by tying the "recital of myth"—hence poetry—to a double condition. On the one hand: "through their pervasive bilateral expedient [*durchgängige gegenseitige schikliche*] restriction neither [of the parts] juts out *too* much and in just this way each retains a certain degree of self-subsistence." On the other hand: "Every part goes somewhat further than is needed" (StA 4: 281) in order in this way to retain its inseparability. The inseparability of the parts is thus preserved through a paradoxical double-movement: of restriction in opposition to one another and at the same time of the transgression of their strictures. While the restriction of the self-subsistence [*Selbständigkeit*] of the parts as well as the unity concretized in them offers security, this self-subsistence only maintains itself by going "somewhat further than is needed." Namely, it is first this modicum of excess that discloses to the self its free connection with the Other, and, with this, its equally free connection with itself. These two movements interpenetrate one another, without relinquishing their oppositionality, in the one moment that Hölderlin, in the text on religion and even more insistently in other drafts from the same period, characterizes with the concept of "degree." "Degree" means in each case at the same time both "stage"—self-subsistence and detachment [*Abgetrenntheit*]—and a step out beyond itself to the other—the free movement of unification. A degree is not a fixed unit-measure, but is—as the tension, tendency, or striving of an element of experience, thought, or exhibition out beyond its own measure to an over-measure [*Übermaß*] in that which is different from itself—the originating moment of every possible unification.[3] Because the degree is the determination of the transition between two different moments, and thus is essentially their reciprocal determination, it must also contain that determination on which is based all further determinations of the context and its parts.

In the highly abstract and eminently political—and, in turn, political-theological—draft "The Perishing Fatherland . . . ," which Beißner published under the title "Becoming in Passing Away," Hölderlin identifies the "degree" with the "moment" in the sense not only of a *movens* but also of an irreducible element of time, an instant [*Augenblick*], characterizing both of these as phenomena at once of dissolution and of origination. "[T]he perishing or transition of the fatherland . . . feels itself," he writes, "in the limbs of the existing world, such that, in precisely the moment and degree to which what exists dissolves, the newly-entering, the youthful, the possible also feels itself" (StA 4: 282). The perishing of what exists, being felt, must at the same time be a transition to the new. Indeed, this new thing, in the moment or degree of perishing, is not in the first instance actual but possible. Yet it is a possible thing that reveals the possibility of an all-ness [*Allheit*] of future relations and connections, of a totality [*Totalität*] of actualities and necessities, and hence of a sum total of the categorial determinations of a world that had not only been concealed but indeed restricted and curtailed in what has perished—the fatherland that has in each case perished. Hölderlin thus conceives of the moment in which the "existing world" disappears as precisely the moment in which the possibility of a world as such dawns. The eschatological instant is the instant of world-genesis. In the last thing a first thing emerges: namely a first both of the world—even of the world of worlds—and of its time and the language in which it articulates itself. "For the world of all worlds," Hölderlin writes, "the all-in-all-things, which always is, *exhibits itself* only in all time—or in perishing or in the moment, or more genetically in the coming into being of the moment and the inception of time and world, and this perishing or inception is, like language, expression sign exhibition of a living yet particular whole, which in turn becomes present in its effects" (StA 4: 282). If the "inception of time and world" is at once its linguistic exhibition, then there is time as well as world only as linguistic; there is language—in the very general sense of exhibition—only as temporal and worldly, and they exist, more precisely, solely as the language of an incipient world that incepts out of its perishing; as the language of an incipient time that incepts out of its passing away; and finally as the language of a language that incepts out of its falling silent. As Hölderlin's emphatic "*is*" conveys, world, time, and language *are* only—they only have Being—in passing away, perishing into their mere possibility. They *are* only in their potentiality and as still incepting this potentiality, thus as expressions, exhibitions, and out-puts, ex-positions of world, time, and language that themselves first make their possibility possible and disclose the moment of inception: possibilizations of the possibility of a world, temporalizations of time, bespeakings [*Ersprechungen*] of a language that grants the possibility of speaking. Hölderlin's meticulously tentative formulations, in which the "or"—"in all time—*or* in perishing *or* in the moment, *or* more genetically in the coming into being of the moment"—regularly has the meaning of a more precisely stated correction, grasps the determination "in all time" more precisely with "in [the] perishing" (of time), even more precisely with "in the moment," and most precisely, in other words "more genetically," with "in the coming into being of the moment and the inception of time and world." In this sequence of more and more precise formulations, "the inception of time and world" and, furthermore, the inception of language and the exhibition of this time and this world, shows itself as the "coming into being of the moment" and hence as the coming into being of the inception of time. It shows itself neither as the sort of moment that could appear [*vorkommen*] in some already-given time, nor as the atemporal coming into being of time, but as a moment resting in nothing but its coming into being, in nothing but its inception and its going-beyond-out-of-itself. Since the genesis of the moment of time follows the same logic as the genesis of the world and of language, this genesis can only be thought as a retreat into the *possibility* of a moment of a language-world-time as such, and hence as a transcendental genesis—in itself unitary—of time, world, and language.

Hölderlin speaks, in the same connection, of a "(transcendental) creative act," so as to characterize the "transition" from a seemingly "real nothing" into a new reality (StA 4: 285–86). Since, however, the coming into being of the moment proceeds from the passing away of a world and its time, it can only thus arise because it passes through the mere *possibility* of an abiding relation. A world may perish together with its time and its language, yet the logical as well as the empirical possibility of its perishing is bound to the possibility that this is able itself to be experienced—which is to say, thought and felt—as perishing *for* someone and *a limine for* this world itself. It is only the transcendental-modal structure of perishing—the fact that it is a retreat into possibilities—that allows it to be at once transition and inception of a new world and its time. Because the possible, and in the perishing of a world the possible alone, is the last residuum of actualization, Hölderlin can emphasize the rank of the possible and of the "(transcendental) creative act" that is accomplished, at a structural level, in it. "But *the possible*, which enters into *actuality* when *actuality dissolves*, takes effect, and it effectuates both the sensation of dissolution and the remembrance of what has been dissolved" (StA 4: 283). Unlike possibility in the transcendental philosophy of Kant, the *possible*, regarding which Hölderlin insists here that it takes effect and effectuates both sensation and remembrance, is not one of the root concepts of the understanding. It is not a logical category but the movement of generation from which categories, concepts, and linkages between concepts first arise, together with the sensations intertwined with them. It is the pre-categorial act of inception that, from the possible *as* possible, effects the coming into being of the historical language-world in its entirety.

Converging with the sequence of thoughts contained in this passage from "The Perishing Fatherland . . . "—a passage that is itself of decisive significance for Hölderlin's way of thinking time and language—is the observation made later in "Notes on Oedipus": "In the outermost limit of suffering there exists nothing more than the conditions of time or space" (StA 5: 202). Just as here the tragic process displaces all its elements into passivity and, as the process of a transcendental and ultra-transcendental reduction, takes effect on the "outermost limits" of experienceability as such, the poetic process that Hölderlin describes as "the perishing of the fatherland" lays bare in the course of this reduction the structural limits of possible experience and hence the transcendental form of the determination of time, world, and language. Leading to the perishing of one world and the possibility of a new one, both processes are tragic and both are theological-political, and both run along, or—as Hölderlin more precisely formulates it—*in*, "the outermost limit" of what can be experienced. Because, in this superlative extreme of experience, nothing more "exists" than "the conditions of time or of space," these processes of the reduction of experience are at the same time processes of the reduction to the fundamental structure of linguistic generation. Since the "coming into being of the moment," and hence "of all time," in the perishing and transition to another moment must be simultaneously the genesis of language from its passing away, Hölderlin, following the formal analysis of the structure of transition, can conclude: "Hence the thoroughly original [quality] of every authentically tragic language, the perpetually creative . . . the emergence of the individual from the infinite, . . . the conceiving, animating . . . of the inconceivable, of the wretchedness [*Unseeligen*] of dissolution, and of the strife of death itself, through the harmonious, comprehensible, animate" (StA 4: 283). Tragic language is original because it conceives its own dissolution, and hence something linguistically incomprehensible: the tragic paradox of every language lies in being an *origo* of a new language in its very loss of language, and hence the creation of language out of the annihilation of language. Language is original only when it is still the language of language loss. It is able to do this, however, not through the capricious replacement of an antiquated or obsolete language with a new one, since that would merely continue the temporal succession that, with the perishing of world-time, has been broken off. It can only become the language of the language-less, the conceiving of the unconceivable, the life even of death, by retreating into the mere being-possible of a language between life and death and thus on this side of both, and by speaking as language *in potentia*—as the mere possibility of language as such. Original language—and this is the language of poetry in its entirety and in a drastic sense, the language of tragedy—is language "in the outermost limit" of its mere possibilization [*Ermöglichung*], in that irreducible residue that preserves itself as transcendental, as the language of language.

The concept of a poetry articulating the transcendental genesis of language and its time contains two mutually linked implications that work towards a critical transformation of the formalism of Kantian transcendental philosophy. On the one hand, a language of the generation of language cannot be a pure transcendental language without at the same time being individual, material, and historical. Hölderlin drew this conclusion, once again in "The

Perishing Fatherland . . . ," with the observation that the transcendental "spirit" of transition must form a unitary nexus in harmonic opposition with its linguistic "sign" as a "material of transition" that has itself been isolated from it. The transcendental language of poetry, and again primarily of tragedy, is thus not a metalanguage describing the formal structures of a subordinate language but is in every single instance the only language that it itself speaks. It is always a singular, "isolated," and "newly-individual" language (StA 4: 286), even where it seeks to comprehend in itself the totality of all languages or to actualize their universal law. The language of linguistic genesis is, in each case, a singular transcendental. It is not only finite, but the finalization of all the infinite possibilities intertwined with it; not only historical, but the becoming-historical prevailing in each case of the formal possibilities of language as such. It is not merely actual but the condition of every actualization; not only singular, but the transcendental of every singularization. It is in this sense that Hölderlin was able, regarding one of his latest hymnic fragments, to jot down the following formulation, which at once surpasses and breaks with every transcendental formalism: "The *apriority* of the individual / over the whole" (StA 2: 339). Therewith it is also said that this singular-transcendental language is not only finite but the language of finalization, and that it is only as this finalizing language that it is infinite; again and again, for the first time, something "infinitely-new." (StA 4: 287). And that, "over"—and beyond—"the whole," it is in each case more than the whole and more than the *totum* of an individuality. The unity in the opposition of "transcendental" spirit and the "isolated" singular "sign" is not to be thought as a unity subsumed under a concept, but as the movement, unitary in itself, of the transgression of every conceptual, willed, and felt unity. It is to be thought as the fundamental structure of a transition that goes essentially beyond every whole and its unity, and that, as this going-beyond—as more, surplus, and excess—determines the *moment*, which, as possible, discloses every actuality of the language-world. It is transcendental unity only as unity of transcending in the *dynamis* of a moment that is, in each case, singular.

The transition, which comes to pass in the transcendental language of poetry as the genesis, in each case singular, of a language as such—and therein, on the other hand, lies the second implication of its "creative act" (StA 4: 286)—must be, *in extremis*, the transition "between being and not-being" (StA 4: 283). Thus it must be the transition between the sorts of things between which a transition is not thinkable in logical concepts but is at best able to be felt. Such a transition can be accomplished only in degrees of feeling and the capacity for feeling [*Fühlbarkeit*], without any of these degrees ever being able to attain a maximum or minimum. Even the extremes of the movement of transition, being, and not-being come under consideration for Hölderlin only as degrees. Contradicting the thought from which the "Oldest System-Program" takes its departure—the thought of a creation out of nothing—he thus writes: "out of nothing comes to be nothing, and this, taken in a gradual sense, amounts to saying: that which is going toward negation, and insofar as it proceeds out of actuality, and is not yet something possible, cannot take effect." The positive implication of this is the following: only in the degree to which something moves [*rückt*] nearer to the nothing does it also move nearer to its possibility and hence at the same time to its effectivity. Out of nothing, to be sure, comes nothing, but out of the approximation to nothing emerges at once, together with its possibility, the actuality of a something. Since with every degree, so far as it is the transition between one thing and another, and, *in extremis*, "between being and not-being," the moment of a movement of the generation of the possible and, further, of the actual must be traversed, "the coming to be of the moment"—the inception of the generation of a time, a world, and its language—accomplishes itself in every moment. The movement of temporalization as well as of language- and world-genesis is the movement of the degrees of intensity "between being and not-being," between the times passing away and the times to come, between the languages passing away and the languages to come. These degrees of intensity in each case transgress their "own" measure—be it even only "somewhat further . . . than is necessary" (StA 4: 281)—making a transition from over-measure to over-measure. Every moment is, as a degree of time or a degree of language, a moment of transition. This is because it is the momentum of the over-measure and of the exaggeration—*Über-treibung* ("the over-drive")—of itself to another that is different from it. It is because it is, to use the rhetorical concept that appears in Hölderlin's draft "On the Procedure of the Poetic Spirit," the "hyperbole" (StA 4: 252) of a movement in which what is different is kept apart as something in each case singular and at the same time is referred to a freely-chosen "point of union." Time, like language and its world, originates in this "hyperbole" and "hyperbole of all hyperboles" (ibid.), which each moment is whenever, in the perishing of the one thing, it discloses the transition into a possible new thing and, in the "now" that prevails in each case, achieves an effect and determination that "is to be held firm with freedom."

For Hölderlin, the moment is, as transition, not only possibilization but the dynamic partition of the measure that has been in each case attained; its division, distribution, and virtual conjunction into a new actuality. And it is solely as this differential movement, hyberbolically transcending every measure, solely as a transcendence beyond every mechanical transition—even if the mechanism in question is merely the mechanism of thought—that the moment is the coming into being of time. To retain time—which is to say, historical time—in this procedure of its hyperbolic and hyper-hyperbolic generation and therein to disclose a time that is new in each case is for Hölderlin the *officium* of poetry. Kant had rejected "intellectual intuition" as the non-sensible source for the generation of time (B 68); Hölderlin adopts it, though indeed with reservations, yet drives its hypertrophic unity apart by recognizing that it is in need of exhibition, and hence of partitioning and imparting: "The unicity present in intellectual intuition makes itself sensible to the very measure to which it goes forth from out of itself; to which the division of its parts takes place, which only ever divide because they feel themselves to be united" (StA 4: 269). Every unity, and in particular the unity of sensibility and understanding, must therefore be *too much* unity. For it can only be the moment of an infinite—and, more precisely, *more* infinite—occurrence of possibilization and differentiation by driving forth out of itself and driving toward further unities. No unity is unity enough to give space to the infinity of the possible that holds sway in it. There is no infinity that is not surpassed by a further infinity; no determination—be it unity or infinity—that would not have to be rendered over-determinate and in-determinate through another determination. And so Hölderlin continues his characterization of the tragic process in the draft "On the Difference of Poetic Kinds": "And here, in the over-measure of the spirit in unicity, and its striving after materiality, in the striving of the divisible, the more infinite, the more aorgic . . . , because everything that is more determinately and more necessarily present makes necessary something more indeterminate, something unnecessarily present, in this striving of the divisible, of the more infinite, after division . . . , in this necessary *arbitrariness of Zeus* lies what is properly the ideal inception of the actual division" (StA 4: 269). If "Zeus" designates the immediate relation of the self to itself in the "intellectual intuition," then the "over-measure" of its unicity attests to the necessitation of stepping forth from out of itself and, in a free choice, conjoining itself with the contingency of a material that is alien to it.

More powerful than unity is its divisibility [*Teilbarkeit*], since unity implies a lack of partition that sets limits to its unity—limits that its drive to unity must set aside [*sich hinwegsetzen*]. Since unicity is a lack—a lack of separateness, a lack of relation to what is external, and a lack of contingency—it must immediately be super-unicity; it must immediately be mediation and transition to itself as that which is in each case other. It is first as a transitive and transitory moment—as a moment of its necessary self-alteration—that unity is the "inception of the actual division" and generation of a time that exhibits itself not as the unneeded emanation of a self-sufficient substance but as necessitated de-completion *within* [*in*] the substance. Time originates in the "over-measure of spirit in unicity"—in its immanent externality and hence as its immediate hetero-affection through something "isolated" in each case, something singular, that, being material and corporeal in a manner that is always different—for, insofar as it occurs each time in a transcendentally non-prefigurable way, it is always indeterminable—must be contingent and linguistic. Time is the linguistico-material interruption and ex-position [*Aus-setzung*] of the unity of self-positing in its necessary self-dissamblance [*Selbstveranderung*]. It is the partitioning and imparting of "Zeus": his "necessary" division, turning his need of unity, turning this need toward the earth; the interruption of his self-relatedness and deformation of his transcendental formalism in an element of irreducible materiality. The "divine moment"—the draft "On the Procedure of the Poetic Spirit" speaks of this as the "making present of the infinite" (StA 4: 251)—can be none other than the moment of its profanation. It must be the moment of absolute finalization, of the atheologization and alogicization of the One God. The trace of something non-living must draw itself into his own life for the sake of this life. The momentum of the "divine moment" lies in its own self-disowning dissociation. It is a fulfilled instant merely because it is the over-fulfilled instant—failing to meet up with itself, vacating itself—which turns into a content-less, purely formal [*formell*] transition, in order to affix itself onto a wholly heterogeneous material and an alien language. As the moment of its rupture and interruption, the "divine moment" therefore must not only be the originating moment of temporalization but must at the same time be the moment of the generation of a finite, contingent, and irreducibly manifold language. This language refuses to be subsumed under the measure of unity in the intellectual intuition. As speechless—not fit, that is, for the language of the transcendental safeguarding of meaning—it withdraws from every function of mediation. It belongs to the *dynamis* of the unity in God that this unity de-divinizes itself; that its world and its time de-deifies itself, with the language in which it should exhibit itself falling *a limine* silent. Yet the "divine" must be every moment of the genesis of time, and every moment must display the structure of a *poiēsis*, of a genesis from out of the hyperbole of an over-measure, in order to preserve the mere possibility of an instant, the possibility of a world, its time, and its language. In this possibility of the moment is always also preserved the possibility of its expiration. To articulate ever anew the precarious conjunction between these possibilities is the matter of language at its outermost limit: the matter of poetry.

That which is possible feels itself "in just the moment and degree wherein what exists dissolves," Hölderlin writes in "Becoming in Passing Away." (StA 4: 282) Moments are degrees, and degrees are parts of a continuum, of which each single one is determined through those that surround it. Hence, they can be grasped as elements of a reciprocal determination both under the category of relation and under the narrower category of limitation. In this way, Fichte characterizes the concept of degree in his *Foundations of the Entire Science of Knowledge* (F 1: 129–30; 122), which Hölderlin, in his letter to Hegel dated January 26, 1795, designates as "speculative pages." It is possible that Hölderlin—whose reflections on "Becoming in Passing Away" could have taken their point of departure from Fichte's theorem of a "becoming through disappearing," and whose poetology of tonal alternation likewise links up with Fichte's doctrine of transition as "alternation" (F 1: 179)—also obtained his arguments for the generation of time out of the "striving of the divisible . . . toward separation" from his critical reception of Fichte's decisive analyses of the structure of the "moment" and the "degree." For Fichte's doctrine of positing rests on the "*mediacy* of position" as the "law of consciousness" (F 1: 183): this mediacy alone, so he writes, "grounds the essential opposition of the I and the not-I, and thereby all reality of the not-I as well as the I" (F 1: 183). In other words: the I, in positing itself and therewith its Being, at the same time posits, by virtue of its not-positing, a not-I, whose reality comes into effect as the limit of the reality of the I. The "mediacy of positing" thus grounds both the "essential opposition" of I and not-I, the antithesis of activity and passivity [*Leiden*], and—*uno actu, una passione*—their synthesis in the union of both: it is immediate mediacy, and hence a partition, which is a decisive structural element of the unity of the accomplishment of the I itself (F 1: 182–84).

Hence, as Fichte stresses again and again, there can be no "hiatus" and no "gap" in the continuum of divisions (F 1: 152, 167, 170, 208). Hence, every division must remain a *co*-division, every parting a communicative imparting, within a coherent whole of reciprocal determinations, and their rigorous relation to one another can maintain itself through all alterations with the gradual shifting that takes place between the effectuating I and the not-I that, opposed to its effect, restricts it. For Fichte, however, the immediate mediacy of the process that, in itself unicity, arises out of the positing of the I and the not-positing of the not-I is not only the "law of consciousness." It is, for this very reason, also the law of the time constituted along with consciousness. Time is that form in which the positing of the I finds itself restricted through the not-positing of something different, material, contingent, and thus determined as a "moment" (F 1: 179). Both the positing and the non-posited determination, in the conflict brought about between them, are, through the power of imagination, held for a "moment of *time*," as Fichte puts it, in "abeyance." Thus they form [*bilden*] the original time, whose synthesis can be unfolded into a succession of moments (F 1: 217).

As closely related as Hölderlin's ideas may be to this Fichtean explanation of the genesis of time, Hölderlin exposes the law of mediacy, which he borrowed from it, to an idiosyncratic radicalization, which unsettles its function as "law of consciousness" no less than the structure of mediacy in its entirely. The nature of this radicalization can be most clearly deduced from a short remark that attempts to comprehend "The Meaning of Tragedies" from out of its paradox. In this note Hölderlin clarifies that "everything original, because all capacity is parceled out justly and equally . . . does not" appear "in its original strength but properly in its weakness," and that therefore "the light of life and the appearance" belongs "to the weakness of every whole" (StA 4: 274). This implies that the phenomenon, indication, or sign, whatever it may be, can only signal something and bring something to light that is more powerful than its phenomenal or linguistic appearance. The sign is, as derivate of the original matter—the "nature" or the "whole"—weaker than this itself, and hence only allows the matter to come to appearance weakened. Yet if the weakness is driven to the extreme and the appearance is annulled, then the matter—the "nature," the essence or the ground—can exhibit itself, uninhibited and unveiled, in its entire sway. This occurs in every tragic process. "In the tragic," Hölderlin can thus continue, "the sign in itself is insignificant, without effect, but the original is straight out [*gerade heraus*]. Properly speaking, therefore, the original can appear only in its weakness, yet insofar as the sign in itself is itself posited as insignificant = 0, then the original, the concealed ground of every nature can exhibit itself" (StA 4: 274). The paradox of a strength that exhibits itself in its appearance only as weakness can easily be regarded as a variation of the paradox of an I that becomes able to feel itself only with the resistance of a not-I that has not been posited by it. And yet, though in the Fichtean conception every not-I indeed takes effect as a negation of the I, because of the incessant reciprocal effect in the degrees of determination it always acts as a divisible non-I on a divisible I. With the "insignificant" and "effect-less" sign = 0, Hölderlin introduces an element that puts an absolute limit on every partition and hence also on every imparting and reciprocal determination. On the scale of intensive magnitudes to which Fichte's quantitative realism of mediation refers, there is neither a maximum nor a minimum that could not still be increased to an infinite degree. There is no null, but only values approximating it. If Hölderlin assumes a null-sign and characterizes it as "in itself insignificant, without effect," then, with this sign that is no sign, nothing can enter into appearance, neither a "ground" nor a "nature," neither something "original" nor its "strength": nothing appears, and yet the hitherto "concealed" ground "is straight out" and must "exhibit" itself without semblance [*scheinlos*].

It is possible that in this passage, Hölderlin committed an error of argumentation into which Schiller's *On Aesthetic Education* seduced him. Openly drawing on Fichte's *Wissenschaftslehre* and the paragraphs on the anticipations of perception in Kant's first *Critique*, the thirteenth letter speaks of the flawed anticipations of the drive to matter and drive to form, of extensity and intensity, both of which come to "nothing," to a null (S 4: 230). In the twenty-first and twenty-second letters, the human being in the "aesthetic condition" is defined as being in one regard "null" and in another regard "highest reality" (S 4: 256). For Kant, by contrast, following the Leibniz-Wolffian tradition, intensive magnitudes were represented as unities in which a "multiplicity" is apprehended "only through approximation to negation = 0" and which, when construed in this manner, are able to exhibit in each case a degree, a moment [*ein Moment*], or a moment [*einen Moment*] of reality: an instant (A 169). For Kant as for Fichte, the null is thus only a *limes* that can never be reached without interrupting the continuum of intensive magnitudes. But even if Hölderlin may have been taken in by a misleading Schillerian metaphor, his employment of the "sign = 0" attests to his interest in a semiotics of extremes, in which the continuum between matter [*Sache*] and appearance is driven to the outermost limit and broken off. If "the concealed ground of every nature" can exhibit itself in something meaningless, in a null-sign, then it is only as a nothing that refuses every appearance—every meaning and interpretation—and ruptures every organic, arithmetic, or semiotic relation. The exhibition in a null-sign is the annulment of every phenomenality of nature and its "concealed ground"; yet for this very reason, it is the exposition of the ground in its concealment. It is not that the proximally concealed ground is revealed by means of a sign but, rather, that the sign, which does not signify and in this fashion immediately erases its own character, itself has the structure of the "concealed ground": it is that very sign that does not show something else and does not show itself and that in this manner—as the ground of every exhibition—conceals itself. The sign = 0 is itself the "concealed ground," and its exhibition is, by virtue of the annulling of the sign, the very thing exhibiting itself therein. The concealment shown in the null-sign does not cover over the "ground" of nature after the fact, say, through an external wrapping, but itself belongs to its structure as ground. If concealment is constitutive of the ground of nature, if a riddling character is constitutive of what is original—if, according to Heraclitus's saying, *physis kryptesthai philei* (fragment 123)—then exhibition participates in what is exhibited only insofar as it, paradoxically, has no part in it, and then the law of mediacy is alone valid insofar as, rupturing on contact with something absolutely immediate and unmediatable, it leaps over into lawlessness. *Parousia*, the emergence of the "concealed ground of every nature," can only fulfill itself in the disappearance of the phenomenal world and in the "future" or arrival of concealment *as* concealment, thus in the absolute restraint of the coming itself. With this it is said of time that it first results from its withdrawal—the withdrawal of the "future" and the present and past consigned to it. With this it is said of language that it results from its absence of meaning and effect—from its annulling in asemia and its imperformance. What speaks, speaks in each case *with* its muteness and *out* of it; what comes, whether future, present, or past, comes *as* coming only *with* and *out* of its infinite non-adventuality, as something that is just as distinct as it is discrete. For this *parousia* there is no longer any synthesis that would not have to be interrupted and exposed [*ent-setzt*] by its absolute dysthesis.

His later work was not the first time that Hölderlin touched on the limit of the principle of mediacy in dissociation. The gnomic utterance from the Rhine hymn, "a riddle is purely originated,"[4] still seems, together with the "hardly" in the following sentence, "Even / Song may hardly unveil it" (StA 2: 143), to follow rigorously the theorem of the infinitesimal approximation of degrees of intensity to an origo. Yet the poem's central stanza, the eighth of fifteen, speaking of the participation that the gods need and that "another" must grant to them, makes it doubtful whether such participation is possible without its destruction. "For since / The most Blessed in themselves feel nothing / Another, if to say such a thing is / Permitted, must, I suppose / Feel, by participating, in the name of the gods, / And him they need." (StA 2: 145, mod.) Participation [*Teilnahme*] happens not only *in* the name [*Namen*] of the gods, but also as a participation in their name—and indeed of the name "Rhine" in the immortal ones, who are called "pure" [*rein*] and even the "purest" [*Reinesten*]—moreover, though, it happens as a participation in the name itself, in the name "name" and literally in such a way that a part of this name is taken [*genommen*]. The introductory sentence of this central stanza explains: "But their own immortality / Suffices the gods, and if / The Heavenly have need of one thing, / It is of heroes and human beings / And other mortals" (StA 2: 145; PF 505). Sensibility—the capacity for feeling—can only come to immortals through a diminution of their immortality and thus through a taking [*Nahme*], through a taking of a part, through a partaking, which is not *methexis* or mystical participation but withdrawal and predation. "Another" can hence partake in the name of the gods only by taking from them a part of their name, a part of their divinity, of their immortality and incapacity for feeling; only by partly depredating the pure ones, as the demigod Rhine, of their name. In the middle of the fifteen-stanza hymn, between the eighth and ninth line of the central stanza, in the enjambment belonging to what is formally the most striking passage of the entire composition, the alternation from *Nahmen* in the sense of "name" to *nehmend* in the sense of "taking" occurs in the transition—or the turn, the *strophe*—from "in the name [*Nahmen*] of the gods" to "participating another [must] feel" [*Theilnehmend fühlen ein Andrer*]. This alternation not only becomes the linguistic accomplishment of the therein-named process of dissamblance [*Veranderung*] and finalization but is itself also grounded in the "name," and hence the "taking," and "name-taking," of the name: the "name" [*Nahme*] of the gods is the taking [*Nahme*] of the gods, with which they partake of the mortals just as the mortals partake of them. The equality of immortals and mortals thereby made possible is avenged with destruction as soon as the participation goes so far as to tolerate nothing "unequal":

> . . . but their verdict is that
> He shall demolish his
> Own house and curse like an enemy
> Those dearest to him and under the rubble
> Shall bury his father and child,
> When one aspires to be like them, refusing
> To tolerate anything unequal, the fantast. (StA 2: 145; PF 505, mod.)

No imparting, no participation, and no name can escape the danger of equality with what is named, taken, or imparted in at least one infinitesimal point—may it be as insignificant and contingent as the homophony of *Rhein* (the river) and *rein* ("pure"). And hence, as here in the middle of the poem, even the partition of the minimal "with" of their correspondence is shattered. The participation in the name—in the name and commission of the gods—is annulled by the gods themselves, and the name, in which alone they can come to speech and feel, is fractured. The pure ones purify themselves from the "Rhine"; the father buries himself with his child under the ruins of his house. What this outermost paradox—that the infinite ones manifest themselves by erasing their finite manifestation—opens, in the transition of mediations, is not only a vacancy in which finite and infinite only relate to each through their divorce. In the shattering of their "name/takings" [*Nahmen*] the infinite ones at once also become those who for the first time make everything finite—"heroes and humans / and other mortals"—into what is finite by putting an end to their lives. What is taken from those who participate in the name, and who themselves take a part from the name of the name, is not only their language, their house, and their life but also their relation to the other mortals as well as the immortals. What is also taken is "being" [*seyn*]—for the verses "When one aspires to be like them, refusing / To tolerate anything unequal, the fantast" speak not only of the mortal who wants to be *like* the immortals, but of the one who, like them, wants *to be*; who aspires not only to divine equality but, together with this, to *Being* as such—eternal, timeless, and changeless Being—instead of contenting himself with "what is unequal," the Being-otherwise and otherwise-than-Being that is his "share," his fate, and his destiny.

That the prohibition on equality is not only a prohibition on imitation and images but a prohibition on Being is also expressed with dramatic acuity in "Patmos," where there is talk of the wish that "a servant may copy / the image of God": "Not that I should be something, but rather / to learn" (StA 2: 170; PF 239, mod.). The disjunctive particle *sondern*, which sets "being" in relief to "learning"—and which moreover is itself detached from the latter by the line break as though by a caesura—here, at the same time, when understood as an infinite verb, designates that which is to be learned: the sundering as what is different from Being and differing from Being must be learned, and this learning itself, insofar as it happens with respect for the unattainable doctrine of Being, is for its part not only a tendential diminution of difference but rather the conscious, differential comprehension of differentiation. "[B]ut rather / to learn" not only designates an occurrence both of sundering and of learning but, in the facture of Hölderlin's verse, is itself an occurrence of intralinguistic differentiation, in which even the designations "sunder" and "learn" shimmer with change, sundering themselves from their syntactic function and their semantic content and accomplishing—*in* themselves, out of their vicinity, their distance to themselves—what it means not to be something "but rather / to learn." It is, as Hölderlin's dramatic accumulation of disjunctions and sunderings of sunderings demonstrates, in a gesture that is almost entirely technical, a training in the caesura. Its iso- and iconoclastic imperative results from the anontological law: that Being is only possible out of the distance that it entertains with itself. Being is alone feelable, thinkable, sayable from the *distantia* to Being, and thus alone by virtue of that which itself *is* not and can never *be* itself, nor can it be a self. That whereof Being is asserted can only ever be the very fact that it is not capable of being—it *is* alone in its absolute incapacity to be. Wherever this paradoxical, parontological clause is disrespected, Being—together with saying, feeling, speaking, and acting—falls without resistance into a dull nothing, precisely what it should not be. Hence, it follows from Hölderlin's insight that all fundamental propositions of Being and the sum total of poetic procedures subject to their dictate disembogue in an ontological (and hence also political, historical, and psychic) catastrophe: in the catastrophe of the onto-logy that itself means to say Being and, in its saying, means to inhabit [*innehaben*] its Being, and yet for which, on precisely these grounds, Being as well as language must become unaccomplishable, nugatory; must become chatter. For Hölderlin, the proof that this catastrophe is possible and that, under certain social, psychic, and in the final instance linguistic conditions, it had become actual was to be found as much in the Parmenidean vision of the identity [*Selbigkeit*] of Being and knowledge and the Empedoclean plunge into an all-encompassing unity with nature and spirit as in Fichte's doctrine of the positing of Being and the first philosophy of his younger friend Schelling. It is the consequence of what Kant and the philosophers of the Enlightenment considered to be the "extravagant" use of reason, which they in turn attributed, as would Hölderlin in the central stanza of "The Rhine," to the "fantasts." As a structural possibility of speaking, the panicked identification with the other, which leaves one stunned and speechless, cannot be denied but must be clarified, analyzed. Again and again, at the critically drawn limits of language, it must be dissolved in the differential use of language and the dispositions of feeling—each time anew and each time differently. It is even necessary to participate in the obsession with unification and mediation in such a way that this participation does not itself succumb to the obsession against which it must offer a support. For Fichte the "law of mediacy," being immediately identical with the positing of the I as positing of Being, decrees a fundamental unity—internally differentiated, yet to be unsettled by nothing—of the participating moments. Now, however, the "law of mediacy" must still be exposed to the law of ontic distance. For Fichte, mediacy is the structure of Being; for Hölderlin, imparting and participation are that occurrence in which Being is diminished, altered, finalized, and distanced from Being: an occurrence that does not take place in the horizon of ontology but rather first discloses this horizon through distancing. The "but rather" in Patmos and the "participating" in "The Rhine" designate and stage a process without which Being could not be experienced, and yet, experienced in this process, it "is" always Being out of difference.

Hölderlin's poetics of participation is a poetics not of assimilation, let alone identification, but of in-equation. The participation of the mortals in the immortals—a participation that turns out to be needed [*notwendig*], since it turns around the need of the immortals [*die Not der Unsterblichen wendende Teilnahme*]—results in the destruction both of the part and of those doing the taking. And what remains is not a part in which the harmony of those who are opposed, the mortals and immortals, could gain a concrete shape, but only shards of this part, fitting together into no whole and not forming the elements of a dialectical integration. That in which a part participates is itself not a whole but something infinite, whose single moments are, for their part, infinitely divisible and hence never able to be encompassed as closed magnitudes. That in which a part participates therefore withdraws from every partaking, every apprehension, and every concept, and itself demolishes the principle of mediation.

If there is mediation, then only with the unmediatable. If what follows the participation stanza of "The Rhine" reads: "So happy he who found / a well-allotted fate / where the remembrance of wanderings / and, sweetly, of sufferings still / rushes up on banks that are secure!" (StA 2: 145; PF 505, mod.)—then this "remembrance" is not only [directed] *at* sufferings that have been withstood but is a remembrance *of* the sufferings themselves; it is "the remembrance of sufferings" directed at the limits of remembrance and thus the continued experience of the traumatic difference between finite and infinite, between the longing to feel the infinite and its abrupt frustration; in extremis the irreconcilable paradoxical experience of the impossibility of experiencing that which is called finitude. Remembrance would be, as it is still characterized in "Becoming in Passing Away," the reservoir of what, bygone and thus past, feeds on the possibility of another future, another to-come. "The remembrance of sufferings" is only a remembrance directed at the shattering of temporal coherence, at the breach of the time-series, at the defluvium of the possibility of reminiscence and remembrance. It does not belong to time and is not already subject to temporal conditions. It is, as Hölderlin stages it in "The Rhine," not a memorializing thought occurring within a time that is still coursing away, and, unlike the "remembrance of dissolution" in the earlier theoretical sketch (StA 4: 284), it is not the manner in which time is generated from out of the possible as the transcendental ground of world-experience. It exhibits a unique and extreme mode of temporalization in which remembrance hits upon precisely that which allows no remembrance, whereby limits are set to the integration of the infinite into a totality, and memorializing thought needs to take upon itself something unthinkable as its heteronomous condition.

If remembrance is to encompass and reproduce from itself the sum total of bygone time, it must also still comprehend from the beginning the time of its own accomplishment, and it must always therefore be the remembrance of something unrememberable. This unrememberable thing, which remains unforgettable because it resists remembrance, must be at work as the constant accompaniment of the time-stream Rhine, as it rushes up against its limits "on banks that are secure." Yet, since it is not activated by the capacity of a unitary constitutive subject but is, rather, a continued "suffering" from what is incompatible with it, it must actualize itself in the tense manifold of multiple limits—"So that this way, that way with pleasure / He looks as far as the boundaries / Which God at birth assigned / To him for his term and site" (StA 2: 146; PF 203, mod.). The limits that are assigned to the river "for his term and site" are no more posited by the river itself in an act of autonomy than "the remembrance of sufferings" can originate from an autonomous action of temporal generation. In Hölderlin's verses, remembrance is thought as itself passive, a passion and a suffering, and hence also, with regard to time, as neither constituting, nor productive, nor even merely capable of production. The law to which the time-river Rhine is entrusted is not the positing of an I nor the transcendental act of a subject or of one of its foundational faculties, but is posited for it, and can only be felt as the suffering of a remembrance: the remembrance of the shattering failure of a participation that should have made it into a transcendental subject. Unlike the unifying horizon of ontology, the horizon of time is that of a divorce suffered as passion and pain: time is not a deed [*Tat*]; it is done in [*angetan*]; it is not synthesis but diathesis, not empiric but empathic [*nicht Erfahrung, sondern Erleidnis*]. The infinitude that the Rhine, as finite, sought to mediate in feeling only becomes sensible in the pain of taking leave from the infinite and its mediation—not as remembrance of a bygone yet objectively existing world but as the remembrance of the fact that, with the generation of a world and its time, remembrance fails [*versagt*]. Remembrance does not generate time but attests to the shattering failure of this generation; for this reason, however, it is not the merely deficient organon of world- and time-constitution but that process that, in becoming aware of its incapacity, opens itself up to something other than a world, to another time and something other than time. Hence "The Rhine," in its penultimate triad, following the stanza that speaks of contentment, is able to turn to a "demigod," Rousseau, who "foolishly, divinely / And lawlessly gives it away, the language of the purest" (StA 2: 146; PF 203, 205, mod.). Yet Rousseau can give language only because he does not generate it out of remembrance but learns it in forgottenness: "[a]lmost wholly forgotten there," "[l]ike beginners." Only on this account can the hymn end with the thought of the primeval foretime—unrememberable, ordered through no temporal structure of any kind: the "night, when all is mingled / Orderlessly and back again comes / Primordial confusion." (StA 2: 148; PF 209, mod.). Primordially old, older than old and older than time, the "confusion" does not return by virtue of the constitutive accomplishment of a remembrance, which in its reproduction could only bring forth the order of time. Nor does it return according to the cyclic order of a more powerful time. Rather, it returns in such a way that even this return succumbs "orderlessly" to the confusion of fore- and un-time. At the outermost limit between time and un-time, order and un-order, speech and speechlessness that is designated by the last word of Hölderlin's hymn, remembrance maintains itself only as remembrance of a wholly heteronomous "confusion," a "confusion" not made by it and not in its capacity. That the "smile of the ruler"—one may suspect: of the ruler of time—is "never . . . / concealed" under or in this remembrance attests to a sovereignty *over* time, which is free from its positings and oppositions, its mixture and its confusion, yet is not indifferent toward it. This smile, in which the ruler is out beyond himself, his reign, and his time, remains—whether painfully, benevolently, or ironically—something other than time and its provenance, such a thing as only lets them do as they will without belonging to them.

In "Becoming in Passing Away" Hölderlin still credited remembrance, as the conjunction of perishing and inception, with the power of exhibiting in time and in language the "world of all worlds, the all-in-all-things, which always is" (StA 4: 282). Through his critical revision of the Fichtean doctrine of mediation as well as the Kantian theory of auto-affection, remembrance was able to be, for him, the originating moment of the generation of time, language, and world because it alone offered the possibility of laying the ground for a transcendental poetics of a time that is not merely the mechanical time of the understanding—not the time of mere succession and also not the time of the self. Hölderlin's annexation of his conception of time to Kant's, whose philosophy is, in the ambiguous words of his extraordinary 1799 New Year's letter to his brother, "the philosophy *of time*, the sole possible time," is still subject to a reservation: it cleaves "too one-sidedly to the great self-activity of human nature" (StA 6: 304). For Kant time is in fact pure self-activity of the mind; it is, according to the definition given in the general remark on the transcendental aesthetic, the positing of representation, and more precisely: "the way in which the mind is affected by its own activity, namely this positing of its representation, thus the way it is affected through itself" (B 67–68). If Hölderlin undertakes to correct this one-sidedness, it is not by dogmatically opposing it to another side, but in such a way that he displays in its own dynamic its conjunction with a time other than that of self-activity. The "reproductive act" of remembrance—the act, corresponding to the "synthesis of reproduction" in Kant's transcendental deduction, in which the "(transcendental) creative act" not only of the poetic spirit but of every spirit accomplishes itself—is characterized by Hölderlin as an action "through which life traverses all its points, and, in order to gain the entire sum, tarries at none of them, dissolves itself at each, so as to bring itself forth in the next" (StA 4: 284). Yet it follows from Hölderlin's supposition that life—or the feeling of life—can only bring itself forth integrally in this "reproductive act," can only produce itself integrally in its reproduction, if, in "free artistic imitation" (StA 4: 283), the "start- and endpoint" have already been "posited, found, secured": "Thus, in the remembrance of dissolution, because both its ends stand firm, this becomes wholly the secure unstoppable bold act that it properly is" (StA 4: 284). It is only under the ideal conditions of art and, furthermore, of the technical procedure of understanding that remembrance ultimately still allows that which was "solely excluded, incipiently dissolved" (ibid.) to arise from the sum of all sensations of emerging and passing away. There must be such an "incipiently" excluded and dissolved something—something not thought by Kant—because time can constitute itself as succession only when the mind attends solely to its own acts of representation and secures these in accompanying actions of reproduction and recognition, while keeping at a distance whatever is not its own activity. The constitution of the temporal order therefore rests on the exclusion of every experience not originating in the pre-sentation of the mind and its return to past presentation—every experience not originating in auto-affection but in a hetero-affection by which every self is infinitely transcended. If Hölderlin trusts in the fact that this transcendence of the other—another time or something other than time—having been excluded from and by the transcendental representational time, "arises," at the end of passing through all the stations of remembrance, in "a whole feeling of life," then it is only because he thinks this end at once as the closure of totality and as an opening toward an infinity. The poetological drafts that Hölderlin worked on until 1800 seek to construct the conjunction between *totum* and *infinitum*—which, according to Kant, no cognition can attain and is alone accessible in the idea of reason—in a "tragic style" that results neither from certain subjective or objective aspects of the whole nor from this whole itself, but from its infinite divisibility: "if it [the intellectual intuition] takes its departure from the highest divisible [thing], as from Zeus in the case of Oedipus, then it [the style] is tragic" (StA 4: 270). Yet the conjunction attained in "tragic style" between the whole and the infinite can be actualized only in the feeling of its infinite division; can become capable of being felt only in the scission of the "reproductive act" of time-constitution, in the opening of the autonomous action of temporalization toward a time or untime fully heterogeneous to it. The "start- and endpoint" of remembrance, insofar as each may be "posited, found, secured," must be divided, parted, isolated, scattered. On the one hand, remembrance must open itself up to something that is absolutely external to it, absolutely unrememberable; on the other hand, it must turn into something strangely disconcerting to itself. With the firmness of the limit-points of time and of the act of reproduction that posits these points, representational time as such—time as transcendental form of intuition—has proven to be the merely passing [*passager*] moment of a trans-subjective and trans-formal, hence at once ultra-transcendental and in each case singular, occurrence of temporalization.

Hölderlin intensified his reflections on the structure of time in the poems from 1800 on, yet it is not until 1803 that, with his "Notes" on his translations of Sophocles and with the "Pindar Commentaries," he once again gave these reflections a theoretical form. Without remaining tied to the temporal-poetological conceptions sketched out in the brouillon on "Empedocles" and the preparatory notes for the philosophical letters, he nevertheless has recourse to their fundamental reflections, even if often under a drastically altered perspective. At the end of the "Notes on Oedipus," he resumes the thought of the start- and endpoints of remembrance from "Becoming in Passing Away." Directly after characterizing the dramatic peripeteia of "Oedipus," he writes:

> In the outermost limit of suffering there exists, namely, nothing more than the conditions of time or of space.
>
> In this [limit] the human being forgets himself, because he is entirely in the moment; God [forgets himself], because he is nothing but time; and both of these are unfaithful: time, because in such a moment it categorically turns, and beginning and end absolutely do not let themselves rhyme in it; the human, because, in this moment, he must follow the categorical reversal, [and] hence in the following can in no way equal the inceptive [*Anfänglichen*] (StA 5: 202)

"Categorical," as Hölderlin applies it here, presumably not only has the meaning of "structurally necessary, in contrast to merely hypothetical," but at the same time the meaning of the Greek *katēgoreō*, that is, on the one hand, to "speak against someone" or "accuse" and, on the other, to "make recognizable" [*zu erkennen zu geben*], "indicate," or "betray." It is in this sense that, immediately before the above-cited passage, Hölderlin says of the human being that he "turns . . . himself round like a traitor." If time winds around, this is because it turns from the point that it once had reached, in accordance with a movement that Aristotle calls *peripeteia* or *metabolē*, back again to the points that lie ahead, and thereby follows the path of recognition, of remembrance, or of the "reproductive act." Aristotle explains that *anagnorisis* is technically best situated when it enters at the same time as *peripeteia*, which is the case in "Oedipus" (*Poetics* 1452a). Yet in Oedipus's turn back to his own prehistory, he proves himself to have been something that he is not, and to have done something that he did not know. The time of presentation is referred to a "pre-" that is not thanks to any positing of consciousness and does not attest to the "self-activity" or self-affection of the mind. The "categorical" turn of time, in which Oedipus turns himself around "like a traitor," indeed betrays something about him to himself, but at the same time it is a betrayal of what he is in the time of his turning-back, a betrayal of his function as law-giver and preserver of his city, a betrayal of the time of presence and of steady progress, destroying, together with him and the stability of his city, time itself as the consistent order of the course of the world. "Recognition" cognizes nothing that has ever been known and thus transgresses the limits of what is cognizable. Remembrance meets with nothing of which Oedipus had ever been aware and dissolves on contact with [*an*] something un-rememberable. The "reproductive act," in which alone time can arise as the regulated sequence of that which is present, apprehends what was never present and, going beyond the limit of time, leads to the perishing of everything that could be called time. And just as Oedipus's turning-back into a beyond of reproducibility dissolves the possibility of the back to which he would turn and hence the possibility of time itself, so too does the turning of the god, whether it be Apollo or Zeus. By making it possible for Oedipus, through the Delphic oracle, to engage in "the depressing, almost shameless, striving to gain power over himself, the foolishly wild search for a consciousness" (StA 5: 199) and hence the destruction of the time of consciousness, this god—who is "nothing but time" (StA 5: 202), that is, the quiescent order of presence in its firmly circumscribed dimensions—also turns himself "categorically" against himself, turns himself as time against time, becomes "unfaithful" to himself, a "traitor," and does the very thing that absolutely destroys the possibilization of a time through "self-activity": he "forgets himself." The turn of time, which, for Kant, under the form of the synthesis of reproduction and recognition, is the condition of time itself, becomes in Hölderlin's reading of Sophoclean drama the forgetting of time. It becomes its self-forgetting and hence the end of the time-form as such. The fact that "beginning and end absolutely do not let themselves rhyme in it" and that the human being "cannot in the following in any way equal the inceptive" (StA 5: 202) is the catastrophic consequence of the constitution of time through anagnorisis and reproduction: its remembrance must become the remembrance of something without consciousness [*Bewußtloses*], bringing about its expiration in forgetting. Its constitution must immediately whip around into destruction, its genesis turn into the erasure of time. With the insight that tragic time brings about a tragedy of time itself, Hölderlin has taken leave of the image of a time with secured limits, a constantly reproducible linear course, and an immovable origo in the representational activity of consciousness.

With the discovery of the fundamental paradox of remembrance and of the representational time that originates with remembrance, Hölderlin likewise discovers that such time has its time; that it is not "unchangeable and abiding," as Kant would have it (A 144) but, rather, transient and finite. Time is a chronocide, and if God is "nothing but time," then he turns himself, his own "betrayer," as "antitheos" against himself (StA 5: 268) and is in himself theocidal. Nevertheless, the fact that representational time itself has its time does not merely mean that it is finite. Above all it means that its form of temporalization is not a transcendentally guaranteed invariant but that, as the transcendental, pure form of generation, wherein the "self-activity" of consciousness blazes its course for itself, it must first be brought forth and brought about by a different instance than consciousness and in a different manner than through its "self-activity." The "categorical" turn betrays that time, at the precise place where it seeks to assure itself of its provenance, transgresses its own precinct, and tears itself away from itself. Time, still pursuing its work of destruction in the reproductive time-constitution, is raptus [*Raptus*]. Hölderlin characterizes it as "the natural power that tragically removes man from his sphere of life, from the middle point of his inner life, into another world and rips him off [*entrükt*] into the eccentric sphere of the dead" (StA 5: 197). If he speaks of its "eccentric rapidity" (StA 5: 196), it is entirely in the sense of the *rapidum tempus* of Seneca's "Ad Marciam de consolatione" (16, 8), and presumably in connection with formulations from the eleventh letter of Schiller's *Letters on Aesthetic Education*, where it is said of the human being under the influence of the drive to matter that he is a fulfilled moment of time, which "time tears away with itself." The "tearing time" [*reißende Zeit*] (StA 5: 198; StA 2: 224) that Hölderlin thinks is certainly not the Schillerian time of sensibility but the time of a pure form: moving out beyond itself, it tears itself away. The fact that time, as the raptus even of the raptus, does not wholly disappear is solely thanks to the circumstance that, unlike how it has been thought within the entire philosophical tradition, time is conceived not monologically, not mono-chronologically, but in such a way that, in the strife between the tearing-away and its form, some third thing holds up its disappearance: its "categorical" turn, that is, proceeds in such a way that "god and the human being, in order for the course of the world to have no gap and for the *memory of the heavenly ones not to die out, impart themselves in the all-forgetting form of unfaithfulness*, since divine unfaithfulness is best to retain" (StA 5: 202). Accordingly, what is retained of the "categorical" turn of time (though not in the form of a "reproductive act" of consciousness but in the manner of the objectifying holding-back, holding-on-firmly-to, and keeping-within-strict-bounds—which is to say, in the manner of the *katechon*) is only this: that it does not hold. As the rip into the "eccentric sphere of the dead," time must not only have a deathly—"deathly-factical," as the "Notes on Antigone" put it (StA 5: 270)—effect on the human being and god; but it must, as "all-forgetting . . . unfaithfulness," annihilate itself. It must bring itself, and thereby everything, to be forgotten. This disappearing, which is not *in* time, but of time itself; this "faithless" diversion and division of time from time, its partition from itself, is the only thing that "imparts itself," and, imparting itself in this way, can be "retained" as the "form of unfaithfulness."

Communication or imparting [*Mitteilung*], understood in this way, is anything but the common participation in a substance or a substantial activity of the subject, be it positing or opposition; it is the form of being exposed to the pure insubstantiality of a deathly movement of rapture [*Hingerissenheit*] and forgetting. Exposed to forgetting, yet also by forgetting, it imparts of itself in imparting only exposure itself as the pure form of impart*abil*ity or communicability. This is what Hölderlin calls the "outermost limit of suffering"—of which, he says, in it "exists . . . nothing else than the conditions of time or space" (StA 5: 202). It is not time and space as conditions of experience that exist, but rather "the conditions" for time and space, and they exist alone as leftover and residue, as mark of the factical impossibility of remaining. What is retained of time and space are, "in the outermost limits of suffering," only the limits of time and space without any contents, only the "conditions" without something conditioned, and these limits and conditions remain not as that which has been posited by the "self-activity" of a transcendental subject, but merely as what has been left over by their disappearing. If Hölderlin says that "divine unfaithfulness is best to retain," this is because the retaining of a lethal time is not the solid ground of temporalization, whether it be transcendentally or theologically secured, but a relic of *de*temporalization, a residue of the transcendental form of intuition and the trace of a god who has had his time. The fact that god, who is "nothing but time," is a bygone god of a bygone time—a time that is past, and past as time: precisely this is "best to retain." A god who was still a god, a time that was still there: having not arrived at their "outermost limit," these would not be "to retain." Yet the past of the bygone-ness [*Vergängnis*] that god and time were does not let itself be retained in an unqualified sense, but only retained "best"—thus only in such a way that even it has not been secured in memory for the duration but, rather, only in such a way that the trace of its erasure can still be erased. The outermost, ultimate foothold against the chrono-theological raptus, the atranscendental relic of the rip of transcendental time, the minimum of its insubstantial impartability is not itself secured against disappearance but is only the form in which its own disappearance attests to itself.

Hölderlin names this retaining and holding-back of the raptus of time using a term taken from the discourse of metrics that he extends to the composition of tragedy and the structure of time: "*caesura*." In *Oedipus* and *Antigone* the caesura is marked by the speeches of Tiresias, the third party, who, in attempting to resolve the strife between the hero and the time-god, holds up the course of the action. Stressing that the sum total of the composition encompasses not only the faculty of understanding but also "representation and sensation and reasoning," Hölderlin determines its temporal order in its entirety as consisting in "successions" to which, in the case of a tragic composition, he attaches the name "*transport*": "The tragic *transport*, namely, is properly empty, and the most unbound" (StA 5: 196). Here "*transport*" means not only, in accordance with "Becoming in Passing Away" and hence Fichte, "transition," and it means not only, in accordance with the draft "On the Procedure of the Poetic Spirit," "metaphor" (StA

4: 243) or, in other words, transference. Brought into sharper focus, it also takes on the sense of two further concepts named in the latter text—"hyperbole" and "hyperbole of all hyperboles" (StA 4: 252)—by evoking the French expression "le transport" in the sense of "manic rapture," "exaltation," "seizure," "raptus." Such *transport*, the fundamental structure of tragic succession, finds no content that would inhibit it, and is not bound to any plot; rather, it tears plot and content away with itself. It is thus called "properly empty." If the succession is in itself "empty," this means that, as mere form of appearance, it lacks what Kant, in the chapter on the schematism, names the "transcendental material"—a "something insofar as it fulfills time," hence, thinghood [*Sachheit*], reality. For Kant, reality and its negation stand opposed to one another as "fulfilled" and "empty time." Kant quantifies this "empty time" with "= 0," just as Hölderlin, in "The Meaning of Tragedies," utilizes a "non-signifying sign" (StA 4: 274). Where time, as the mere form of succession, is empty, it not only lacks the sensation of reality but also that thing whose "concept in itself indicates a being (in time)" (A 143). For Kant, it was possible to think—but not to represent—an evacuation from time of all sensation and the material corresponding to it, inasmuch as the form of the intuition of time would be annihilated together with the category of reality; Hölderlin, by contrast, for whom time as raptus tears even itself away, must determine the outermost limit of time—and, with this, its proper definition—as its emptiness. Time is the evacuation of those contents that could have indicated a being in time. And for this very reason, it is also the evacuation of the representation "time," hence fulfilled alone by its emptiness. Only where it contains no more representations, and where the very representation of time is lacking in it, thus only where its "*transport*" is "properly empty, and the most unbound," can the structure of time itself, as mere presenting, emerge—and must emerge as mere presenting, if it is at all possible therein to hold firmly onto the structure of finite existence "in its outermost limits."

"Hence"—because the time-*transport* is empty—Hölderlin writes, as he continues in his characterization of tragic time:

> *the rhythmic succession of representations wherein the* transport *exhibits itself makes necessary a counter-rhythmic interruption, a pure word*, that which in metrics is called a caesura, *in order to encounter the tearing alternation of representations at its climax [auf seinem Summum], so that not the alternation of representations, but the representation itself appears* (StA 5: 196; EL 318, mod.)

In this sentence, consistently regarded as decisive for Hölderlin's late poetology of time, what was previously known as succession and *transport* is now called "rhythmic succession of representations," "tearing alternation of representations," and "alternation of representations." If the caesura, as "counter-rhythmic interruption," "encounters" the *transport*, then it is not in order to isolate one of the alternating representations therein and oppose this to the entire series of successions. First of all, there is, for Hölderlin, no single representation that would not be, as such, submitted to alternation. Secondly, he explicitly calls this alternation—the *transport*— "empty" and excludes, throughout the entire course of the tragic process, its attachment to a specific content-dependent representation. Thirdly, a determinate single representation would indeed be able to "encounter" another single representation. But it would not be able to "encounter" the *transport* as such—and indeed, as is explicitly stated, encounter it "at its summum" [*auf seinem Summum*], in its *peripeteia*, that is, in the moment of the time that is not only tearing but tearing itself away. When it is said that, by virtue of the intervention of the caesura, it is "no longer the alternation of representation, but representation itself [that] appears," then this must mean that the alternation and loss of representations originate in the accomplishment of a re-*pre*-sentation [*Vor-stellung*]. The *transport* of the original presentation and the series of representations following from this can be grasped in a single fundamental representation. Hence the time of succession, tearing all representations away with it, has its standing reserve [*Bestand*] in re-*pre*-sentation, and, in the representation of this re-*pre*-sentation, comes to stand and to appearance.

"The representation itself," the "caesura," is time itself.

It is time without any content, and it is not itself the content—a limited period or phase of another time—but the holding-in or pausing of presenting in its explicit accomplishment. In the pause that the caesura opens in the succession of representations, time does not stop, representation does not stop; neither of them is set aside, and thus neither of them stops or remits [*setzt aus*]; rather, in the pause, representation [*Vorstellen*], as a placing [*Stellen*] and stabilizing [*Zum-Stehen-Bringen*] of a sheer pre- [*Vor*], sets in and holds itself out in this re-*pre*-sentation. Without the alternation of representations in it, time is the placing in relation to a mere out-ahead [*Voraus*], the there-ahead [*hin*] to a there-behind [*da*], which holds itself in its aheadness, a holding out of what has no hold over itself and remains uncontrollably different from it. In order that the transport can become understandable in its emptiness and lack of footholds, it is necessary, as Hölderlin says, without naming a subject, to "encounter" the *transport*--to hit upon it as well as upon that which it is, its essence, but also to come up against its raptus—and to let it come to light and come into language in this encounter. Yet the only language that can correspond to it is not a language that relates itself to representations that are given and always merely fleeting; rather, it is only that language that gives to itself the representation of an "ahead" that withdraws itself from it. This language must likewise have the character of *transport*; it must be empty, without representational contents, and related to something that is rigorously differentiated from it. It is the language in which pure time appears only by itself being pure language and the form of appearing that is stripped of all appearances.

The blind seer Tiresias, whose speeches insert the caesura into the tragedy, is thus also designated as a "supervisor" over time (StA 5: 197)—in other words, as what the Greeks called an *episkopos* or *epistatēs*. He does not see the visible representations in their changing and disappearing; rather, he sees this changing and disappearing as itself arising from the representational structure that grounds them. And he does not see this structure with his eyes as an empirical object, but brings it to representation with a speech. This speech can, therefore, be called the "pure word," since it is a word that fixes its untenable "ahead" *as* untenable, thereby bringing its *transport*—its hyperbolic fundamental-movement—to a stand. Hence, the "counter-rhythmic interruption" that comes to intuition-less appearance in the "pure word" of Tiresias is nothing else than the sheer time of temporalization itself as it enters into the time that is coursing away as detainer, into "categorical" time as *katechon*. Insofar as time is displayed in its emergence, it shows itself as standing out in that which does not persist, holding out and retaining what is absolutely without standing: by withstanding what has no stance, it is the dividing that is divided from itself; it is Being from out of the distance and in the distance to itself. Hölderlin understands this structure of temporality as the form of the tragic process, and by taking his point of departure from it, he offers a new interpretation of the Aristotelian doctrine of catharsis—an interpretation that is able to disregard all humoral-pathological and psychological intuitions. "The exhibition of the tragic," so he writes, "rests primarily on this: that the uncanny enormity of how god and the human being unite . . . thereby comprehends itself in that the boundless unification purifies itself through boundless divorce" (StA 5: 201; EL 323, mod.) This divorce happens in the caesura as the "pure word" and the pure time-space—not insofar as another, less uncanny or less monstrous word enters, but insofar as the uncanny thing, time and the word itself, "conceives itself" as "limitless divorcing" and, in its divorce, "purifies itself." Only in this catharsis, which speech-time [*Sprachzeit*] accomplishes with itself in the divorcing, is such speech-time preserved as the finite possibility of finitude. The "caesura" in the "successions" "retains" this divorcing, that is, the "divine unfaithfulness," but it only retains it "best" and not for an eternal duration if it stays the disappearance of the time-form in the representation of this disappearance. This—about which Hölderlin writes—is what is realized in the caesura: "god and the human being . . . *communicate in the all-forgetting form of unfaithfulness*" (StA 5: 202). The caesura is the communication, vacated of all contents, of mere divisibility—the imparting of mere divisibility.

The fact that the caesura brings about a representation of the time that tears away all representations; that it lets the disappearing, as disappearing, pause; and that, as the "pure word" of the bygone-ness of all words, it interrupts the passage of its passing away: all this makes the caesura into a thoroughly ambiguous figure. It allows passing away to pause by bringing about its exhibition as that which it is; it exposes the law of finitude and thereby itself consigns the law to finitude. It is the infinite finitude, and hence itself neither finite nor infinite, suspended between mortals and immortals. In it time is saved, "sheltered," as Hölderlin's text twice puts it (StA 5: 196); but it is only sheltered as finitude, not as trans-finite perseverance. There is time, but only for a time. Insofar as, in the Attic tragedy, Tiresias "no longer pronounces the alternation of the representation, but representation itself" in "the pure word," he conducts himself like the philosopher Kant, who defines time as the mere form of representation (B 67–68), yet characterizes it as "the pure image . . . of all objects of sense" (B 182, mod.), thereby conceiving the schema of substance "as of a substrate of the empirical time-determination as such, which thus remains while everything else changes" (B 183). Yet Tiresias is only Kant insofar as he opposes the Kantian one-sidedness noted by Hölderlin. His caesura corresponds to "critique" only by turning against the Kantian notion of representational time originating from "self-activity" of the subject and exposing a time that is other than merely subjective, even if again under the concept of "representation." "The representation itself" opened up by the caesura indicates—and this is different from Kant—not "a being (in time)," but the aporetic Being of time itself; it shows this not as a mere form of relation that could correspond to a sensation and fulfill a concept.

It is not subject to the category of substance, since it is not the perseverance of subjective activity—be it of a human being or of a god—but alone pronounces its disappearance. With Kant against Kant, the caesura expounds "the representation itself" as the kind of representation that does not "remain while everything else alternates" but only remains in such a way that it itself continues to alternate. Hölderlin writes to his brother, in his letter of January 1, 1799: "Kant is the Moses of our nation, who leads them out of Egyptian torpor into the free solitary desert of his speculation and brings the vigorous law down from the sacred mountain" (StA 6: 304). Yet this law is only a law of universality and of the universalization of the activity of the self. For Hölderlin, the law did not have to do only with this; at the same time it also had to do with the possibility of historical singularity and with the not merely formal but also corporeal structure of the particular—with the different times of time and the in-each-case-singular manners of its "representation."

For Hölderlin, the law of representational time exposed by Kant and Tiresias thus contains not the whole truth, but only the "transcendental truth" (A 146) of time, and hence it can only have validity for him as an element in the dramaturgy of a general occurrence of temporality. Because it is one among several elements of the time-movement, the caesura, the law of time-representation, is only able to exercise a determinate, not merely epistemic effect in this dramaturgy insofar as it delays, holds up, stays the "tearing time." It can inhibit the time-raptus and can "shelter" it against itself, yet it cannot prevent it from continuing beyond this statutory caesura and pulling the clarification and structure of the time-tear into this tear. The caesura lays down a law of time—a law that is indeed "necessary" (StA 5: 196) but is itself exposed to time. "Calculated and taught," the *epochē* of time brought about in the caesura can hence be applied as instrument in a "statutory calculus" and can "be always reliably repeated" (StA 5: 195) in the exercise of poetic handiwork. Yet as calculable, applicable, and repeatable as the caesura may be as a means, it is so not as an act of subjective spirit, which establishes its law as the law of time-consciousness, but solely as something occurring *in* consciousness, something that is itself calculated and applied by another consciousness or by something other than consciousness. The poetic-dramaturgical procedure to which the caesura together with time is submitted follows a calculus of historical time—essentially a calculus of shifting and hence of the disclosure and vicissitude of a space and of wandering in a space. Not only are the place and function of the caesura thereby transformed, but the temporal structure of the caesura is itself altered in the historical space-movement. That Hölderlin thinks temporality together with spatiality, that he thinks space as time and thinks a spatial determination in time, explains the ponderous "or" in the sentence: "In the outermost limit of suffering there exists nothing more than the conditions of time or space" (StA 5: 202).

The caesura, as "the representation itself," is already a word of spatialization: the forward or out-ahead and in-a-pre-senting [*des Nach-vorn- oder Voraus- und In-ein-Vor-Stellens*]; and Hölderlin stresses with conspicuous emphasis that the entire calculus according to which the caesura is placed is "in tragedy more equilibrium than it is pure succession" (StA 5: 196). This spatialization of tragic succession under the sign of equilibrium may take its bearings not only from the image of justice as a balance, which is associated with the image of the scale, but also from Schiller's employment of this image in the twentieth letter of his *Letters on Aesthetic Education*. Here the production of the properly aesthetic condition of "mere determinability" is described as being attainable insofar as the condition of sensibility is posited as "fully empty in content" and is balanced through an opposed condition of the drive to form. Only in this way, Schiller writes, is it possible "to at once annihilate and retain the determination of the condition": "The bowls of a scale stand at an equal height when they are empty; but they also stand at an equal height when they contain equal weights" (S 4: 152–53). The caesura, which should preserve this equilibrium—for Hölderlin, it is always relative and always "slanted"—of "mere determinability," wanders, however. According to the account of the notes on Sophocles, it has a different position in *Oedipus* than in *Antigone*, and it would not be a caesura if it did not itself first come about, independent from its respective context, through a shifting. If, for Hölderlin, the decisive movement of the caesura rests in the fact that it "encounters" the alternation of representations (StA 5: 196) and thus first "retains" time as bygone-ness (StA 5: 202), then it is not only the speech of Tiresias that constitutes this caesura, but also Antigone's speech in *Antigone*. Of her, Hölderlin writes:

> To the secretly-laboring soul it is a great aid that, at the highest point of consciousness, it evades consciousness; and before the present [*gegenwärtigen*] god actually apprehends it, it encounters him with a bold, often even with a blasphemous word, and so retains the sacred and living possibility of the spirit. (StA 5: 267; EL 327–28, mod.)

Like the elucidation of the caesura, this clarification also has to do with the "encounter" with the raptus of succession and with the "retention" of its possibility. Both can succeed only through evasion—a sideways movement leading from consciousness into a space over which it has no power.

The encounter between Antigone and the "present god"—Hölderlin names him the "spirit of time and nature" and the "tearing time-spirit" (StA 5: 266)—cannot be frontal; this encounter in the caesura can only be lateral. The "secretly laboring soul" must "evade" consciousness at its zenith, displacing itself into another location, taking on the shape of a spatial unconscious or counter-consciousness. Only from the side, distorted and unshapely, can it withstand the confrontation with the time-tear. The encounter in the caesura is not a relation that consciousness has to itself but is always such a thing that another entertains with it. Language is no more a process of self-affection than time is; in order to be what they are they must have been diverted from the straight line of the succession of consciousness. Hölderlin praises this diversion, which constitutes the decisive trait of the constitution of time in the caesura, in Antigone's taunt:

> I have heard she has become like the desert
> The Phrygian, full of life,
> Whom Tantalus nurtured on his lap, on
> Sipylus' peak;
> She has become hunched over and, as though
> In chains of ivy
> Put, contracted into the slow rock,
> And always with her,
> As men say, winter stays,
> And wash her throat do
> Snow-bright tears from under her lids.
> Just like her
> A spirit brings me to bed. (StA 5: 239–40, 852–61; HS 96, mod.)

"Indeed, the highest trait of Antigone," Hölderlin adds, "[the] highest human appearance," rests "on the superlative of human spirit and heroic virtuosity" (StA 5: 267). Yet this quiescent summum, the "bearing" [*Haltung*] of Antigone in the superlative of human spirit, can only be "bearing" and the maintenance of the "possibility of spirit" because the soul (and not consciousness), "laboring secretly," compares and makes itself equal to that which is absolutely unequal to it: a spatial object without spirit or life, a crag in winter, an empty space, the desert. Hölderlin continues commenting on the movement of evasion:

> In high consciousness the soul then always compares itself with objects that have no consciousness, but which in their fate take on the form of consciousness. Such an object is a land grown waste, which in its original lush fertility has too greatly intensified the effects of the sun and becomes dry for that reason. (StA 5: 267)

Halt, *Haltung*, *Erhaltung*—support, bearing, maintenance—are gained by evasion: by a lateral movement of likening and transition, by a diversion that displaces consciousness, soul, and spirit *next* to themselves and into the field of crude externality, thus making possible their encounter with themselves in this sideways way. The encounter with time only lies *in* time because it lies *next* to the path of its linear course. The re*pre*sentation [Vor*stellung*] called "time" can alone be gained through *para*sentation [Neben*stellung*]—through a parataxis, therefore, in the literal sense, which can be a syntactic principle of order only because the disarrangement accomplished in it offers the ground for every temporal synthesis. The caesura is not the location of the *in*version of the time-movement, but of its *de*version into space and, more precisely, into its outermost limit, a space-rudiment, that is, the desert; only in this way can time appear in it *as* time and, in its pausing at a spatial residue, *appear*. Yet it is not only that time first *appears* as bygone-ness in empty space: diverted into it, paralyzed, and as an *epochē* of time, its structure of exteriorization [*Veräußerlichungsstruktur*] and therewith its principle of generation, its mere "possibility," maintains itself. In contrast to the earlier time-related poetological drafts, the "Notes on Antigone" finds this "sacred living possibility" neither in consciousness nor in spirit, neither in a "(transcendental) creative" nor in a "reproductive act" (StA 4: 286, 284) and thus not in the transcendental productive power of imagination, as Kant had thought, but in the entirely passive, rigid material of an objectified space-time. This possibility is not the possibility of a future actuality but that possibility for which it is impossible otherwise than as its own actuality: only in its dry facticity is it "sacred," the detached and "living" possibility. What had once been the productive and constantly self-reproducing matrix of existence is here an infertile, dead mother, robbed of her children.

If Hölderlin says of the "sublime taunt" in Antigone's Niobe simile that it is "more soul than language" (StA 5: 267), this is presumably because it is not the language of the consciousness of consciousness but, rather, the language of the pathos of something without consciousness [*einem Bewußtlosen*]. The way into the desert, into a crag, into the abiding winter is not the way of sense [*Sinn*] but of a "sacred madness [*heiligen Wahnsinns*]," yet this "madness"—a "dementia" against the dementia of consciousness—along with its aberrance from the straight path of time-consciousness, is necessary for every possibility of sense, since it alone obtains the conditions of consciousness and time, by being and doing what it is and does: "sacred," it insists on differentiation; as dementia, it displaces itself into the residuum of space, which is nothing other than the testimony of the raptus, the seizure, of time. Hence it is said that time, consciousness, and language can alone be understood from out of that which evades, or is left over from, their movement. Only the deviation from time maintains their possibility; only the aberrance from consciousness gives a tenacity to consciousness; the residue of the raptus of language first makes speaking possible. Parachrony is the structure of time and of finite life. All consciousness refers to the manic time [*Wahnzeit*] of evasion in the face of itself as the condition of its maintenance and possibility. The transcendental grounding of language in the self-activity of the subject is incomplete without the ad-transcendental—and atranscendental—disarrangement into a realm over which language, as activity of a subject, has no power, because it is in this realm that it can first find a hold.

The lines of verse that Hölderlin jots down in the fragment "Home" follow this evasion—a bending, a bowing, an inclination sideways: " . . . at noon, when in the yellowish cornfield / There is a whisper of growth, by the straight stalk, / And the ear inclines its neck sideways / Like autumn . . . " (StA 2: 206; PF 267, mod.). And in the late stages of "Whatever Is Nearest": " . . . Not for nothing / Did someone bend sideways from the mountains of youth / The range and turned it to face / Towards home . . . " (StA 2: 238; PF 303). And in the draft "You securely built Alps . . . ": " . . . where / A momentary one I might be allowed / To lie buried, at the place / Where the road / Bends . . . " (StA 2: 232; PF 299). In "The Ister" the Rhine is described in this way: " . . . The other, / The Rhine, has gone away / Sideways . . . " in comparison with the Donau, here called by its Greek name, the Ister. The Ister, indeed, proceeds "straight" and yet, "all too patient"—almost taunting its course to the East—flows so slowly that this will be said of it:

"Yet this river seems almost / Backwards to travel and / I think it must come from / The East . . . " (StA 2: 191; PF 257, mod.). The delay of the path to the goal is hence characterized as an alternative to lateral bending. In both, the movement of the time-river does not follow its destiny [*Bestimmung*] to the end but, rather, holds itself back, turns itself around or turns itself away, in order to thus leave space for time and a path for language. When Hölderlin stresses "Yet what that one does, the river, / No one knows" (StA 2: 192; PF 257), he also indicates that the *rallentamento*—the slackening pace—scarcely different from digression, belongs not to the time of the knowing consciousness but to its delay and diversion—just as the name "Ister," though one can't really know this, can also pose the very question, "Is it [*Ist er*]?" which consciousness poses wherever it encounters something that seems incompatible. The movement of time is most starkly designated in an aside that can be found in the first verses of the late ode "Chiron," which was the first of Hölderlin's "Night Songs." Here it is written: "Where are you, thoughtful one! That must always / Go to the side, at times, where are you, light?" (StA 2: 56; PF 91, mod.). The assonance between "Zur Seite" ("to the side") and "zu Zeiten" ("at times") suggests that "at times" be understood not only as "occasionally" and "once in a while," but also as a semantic parallel to "to the side." If light goes to the side, declines, and expires in the night, then it goes "to the time" [*zur Zeit*] or "to the times" [*zu den Zeiten*], and in fact in such a way that it enters into its time and into that time as a space, in which it has its abode. Chiron, who lives as a blind man in this night, the side, awaits time [*Zeit*] going to the side [*zur Seite*], time coming at the time.[5] The difference between time and side, that is, time and lateralness, in which it would for the first time become what it is, the difference between the S of *Seite* and the Z of *Zeit*, remains, to be sure, ineluctable [*unaufhebbar*], for, as with light, time too would have to expire on the side. Where it becomes entirely one with the side, it would no longer be time; and it is not time where it has not yet entered into its place, the side. Thus, it can only be on the side of the side; it can only remain siding [*Seitigung*], untimely, un-tidy, spatial, unapproachably lateral; and it can appear "by you yourself // Locally, the day's errant star" (StA 2: 57) only as in the errancy of its place, not as itself, only "by" itself. The *parousia*, the time of time, must wait in its para-.

Delay [*Verzug*] and evasion—both of which are modalities of the caesura—join together in the trace that is left over from, and in, the raptus of time. This was not only a subject matter within Hölderlin's poetological discussions regarding a "statutory calculus" of the art of poetry; in his poems—the late ones especially—he also thought about and dramatized ever anew the trace as the minimal structure of language. A draft of [the third version of] "The Only One" speaks as follows of the trace as the residue and condition of *logos*: "For the world always rejoices / Away from this earth, that it / Bares the earth; where what is human does not hold the world. There remains, though, a trace / Yet of a word; this a man perceives. But the place was // The desert . . . " (StA 2: 163). This man is the Christian Messiah; he "perceives" or "catches" [*erhaschet*] the trace of a word, for even this trace is not something substantially abiding but a fleeting moment—just as erasable as the word of whose erasure it is the residue. This Messiah is *logos* only in the measure in which he catches the trace of his own disappearance. He is *logos* only as writing in the critical moment of its passing away, which the caesura holds firm. The caesura is not *Christos logos*, it is *Christos graphē*; and this caesura, the condition caught by the time "rejoiced away," is Christian-Messianic time. It is essentially writing, insofar as in it God appears not as himself but in a means [*Mittel*] that holds him firm and shelters him as much as it holds him at a distance and upholds the space, differentiated from him, of mere finitude as distance. God appears, so "The Only One" continues, "Mediately / In holy writings" (StA 2: 163). In the same sense, the "Notes on Antigone" parenthetically note that the "god of an apostle"—hence the god who only speaks in the word of his emissary, in his speeches and letters—is "mediately" the "highest understanding in the highest spirit," not "entirely one with man" (StA 5: 269). The Christian god, the "god of an apostle," is the only one who, by means of his appearance, the script, the captured trace of a word, keeps to the law of mediacy to which not only human beings but also gods—and each is "nothing but time"—are likewise subject. In the Pindar fragment translated by Hölderlin under the title "The Highest" it is called "The law, / King of all, both mortals and / Immortals. . . . " And Hölderlin comments: "Rigorous mediacy is, however, the law" (StA 5: 285; EL 336, mod.). Hölderlin's "statutory calculus" of the caesura is a doctrine of the remanence [*Bleiben*] not of the *logos*, but of the remanence of its fleeting residue. It is theology, and messianic, only by grace of a cenography, a hollow, vain writing. The thought of and hope for *parousia* are only possible in this doctrine because it is blocked by mediacy, which insists on differentiation and thus the impossibility of mediation.

In the word that is "pure" because it is far from words, the possibility of the word—and thus the possibility of spirit and time—maintains and preserves itself, just as in "Patmos" the decapitated head of the prophet and baptizer of Christ is so maintained and preserved: "inedible and like an unwilting writing / Was visible on the dry bowl" (StA 2: 185). No longer, therefore, as even still in the first version of "Bread and Wine," do there "originate" [*entstehen*] "words, like flowers," which is to say, wiltingly (StA 2: 93). In a distant and unexpressed remembrance of flowers, words have died off, yet they preserve themselves by virtue of their death, "like unwilting writing," as a writing that, inassimilable to organism as well as to consciousness, is inedible, but first becomes enduring in its deadness: it, too, is a trace of a word in the desert, "on the dry bowl." In the last extant letter to his mother, Hölderlin writes of the time of these words, which is the time of his poems: "Time is letter-precise [*buchstabengenau*] and all-merciful" (StA 6: 467).

In his late theoretical and poetic texts Hölderlin's labor focuses on traces and steps, on letters of the alphabet, on curvatures and digressions, on asides, relics, and on everything that remains left over and stands to the side. This is because he recognized in them both the formal and the material, both the transcendental and the singular conditions of possibility of a language and a world, conditions that cannot be derived from anything else. The caesura and its "pure word" have such an eminent weight for his late poetology and his late poetry above all because they expose the condition of the possibility of a finite world of language and sense—and expose this condition as finite, in each case particular and necessarily peculiar in the facticity of its contingency. His discoveries concerning the structure of time include not only the discovery that, as standing out ahead in something that has no hold over itself, something untenable, it must itself come to a halt; and not only the discovery that its process occurs thanks to deviations and lateral shifts onto spatial residues; but also the discovery that these shifts disclose a time of historical space-movement and that this time, at its end—this, too, is Hölderlin's discovery—strikes upon an irreducible, unshakeable, undissolvable fact. This fact may still be called "representation" and may still be associated with the entire complex of standing and understanding; but it is not a representation in which an I and its language could still find themselves again, and not a representation that would still contain the possibility of speaking.

Immediately after his translation of and commentary on the Sophoclean dramas, Hölderlin turns to working on the new poems that will later appear in the *Pocketbook for the Year 1805. Devoted to Love and Friendship*. This we know from the letter to his publisher, Friedrich Wilmans, dated December 8, 1803. Among these poems, it is "Half of Life" ("Hälfte des Lebens") that takes up, already in its very title, the great motif of the "Remarks": the motif of the "middle"—the "half"—of time (StA 5: 267), hence, the "categorical reversal" and the "caesura." This poem begins with the idyllic image of the mirror-symmetrical correspondence, subtly developed around the apostrophe "You lovely swans" in the pivotal verse of the first stanza. Breaking up this image of an autumnally fertile land and the lake in which it is reflected—of enthused, "drunken" swans and "sacred-sober water"—the elegiac question of the I arrives in the second stanza of this poem. How is such a correspondence to be achieved in another season and at a different historical time, in "winter," and in another place, a place that lacks pears and roses, swans, water, sun, and shadows (StA 2: 117)? Given that "lovely swans" are allegories of the poet in the Platonic and Horatian tradition and that "flowers" are the traditional metaphor for the poetic word, the question posed in the poem—"Woe is me, where will I take, / When it's winter, the flowers, and where / The sunshine / And shadows of the earth?"—concerns not only the possibility of the correspondence between the landscape and its image in the lake but also the possibility of poetry as such. The second stanza does not stand in a symmetrical relation to the first; rather, it begins by plaintively establishing the threat and then proceeds coldly to declare the loss of the symmetrical correspondence evoked by the first stanza. The loss of symmetry is also the loss of the conditions of a poetic speaking that would impart itself to a world that corresponds to and appears reflected in it. Whereas in the first stanza the swans, dipping their heads "into sacred-sober water," designate the union of speakers and language, poetry and world, the second stanza harshly presents the impenetrable resistance of a world that does not mirror, does not respond, and does not itself speak. The elegiac question "where will I take . . . " remains without an answer and without the echo that the schema of correspondence in the first stanza would have led one to expect. No echo in the second stanza responds to the narcissistically tinted mirroring in the first stanza. After the question has come to a close, what follows is not an answer but an explanation in a tone that is no longer elegiac but, rather, dryly constative—clarifying that an answer will not follow: "The stone-walls stand / Speechless and cold, in the wind / The weathervanes clang." The succession of images and of their reproduction in the plaint has been broken off; of the I and its woe—a woe still firmly holding on to the remembrance of the world of art that is passing away—there is no longer any talk. There is talk only of the fact that there is no longer any talk that could still mediate between past, present, and future, between world and language, between language and itself. In the pause after the question— "where will I take / When it's winter"—time, with the rhythm of representations and tones, turns to winter, and this pause thus marks precisely that which Hölderlin calls the "counter-rhythmic interruption," "*caesura*." And in the verses, "The stone-walls stand / Speechless and cold, in the wind / The weathervanes clang," the winter of this caesura stands still: the stone-walls "stand" therein as a crude fact of time and language standing and standing still. In them nothing else is said than that only a cold wind remains of the "living breath" of communication (StA 6: 184). Of the pronoun *you* in "you lovely swans" and "you dip" only a *clanging* remains; of the poetic *swan* and its doubling in the lake only *vanes*, a "*nefas*" (StA 5: 197; StA 4: 150)—not echoes, still less remembrances, only shrill relics, traces, distorted residues. "Half of Life" ends on a voice break [*Sprachpause*]. The last verses do not proceed beyond this pause with a novel succession of representations; instead, they only elucidate the mere standing in the exposure and suspension [*Aussetzen*] of language. These last verses are the explicit fermata of the caesura.

While the poem turns from the first to the second stanzas and, furthermore, from the elegiac question to the unanswered pause, the time of poetry, together with the time of the year, turns. Yet it does not turn to the time of another poetry but to verses pronouncing the rigidification of time in its turning, the "winter," the "wind," and the walls [*Wänden*]—and the rigidification of language in "stone-walls" that stands without language [*sprachlos*]. It is tempting to discover in "Half of Life" a reprise of the gesture with which Antigone "at the highest point of consciousness . . . evades consciousness," thereby preserving her capacity for speaking, as she likens herself to a "desert," a "slow crag," and abiding winter. Yet language in the half, the midpoint, of life—in the caesura and its elucidation—does not maintain itself by evasively turning to speechless stone-walls. These stone-walls are not a metaphor of language, not an allegory of its living on in something unliving, not an emblem of secret linguistic capacity. They stand speechless, without echo, and therefore they stand there as precisely the mute location in which no word reproduces itself in another, no language turns back upon itself, no consciousness can become aware of itself. They are metaphor-resistant instances of a facticity that does not let itself be occupied by any meaning, and if they can still be named rhetorical tropes, then only as tropes of the atropy of rhetoric. Nothing winds along these walls [*Nichts wendet sich an diesen Wänden*].

Neither representational contents nor representational forms let themselves be translated into these stone-walls, since whatever is translated into them therein becomes mute and stops [*hört auf*].[6] If the poetic world that is invoked in the first stanza of the poem, with the evocation of the "sacred-sober," the "swans" of Apollo, and a drunkenness that can only be enthusiasm—the immanence of God in the word—exhibits itself as correspondence between the world and its gods, the second stanza, accomplishing the diversion from this poetry, falls back evasively in the "stone-walls" upon something wholly ungodly, something starkly unspiritual, a marginal phenomenon to which nothing corresponds and in which nothing more, and least of all a deity, appears. These stone-walls may be related to the building [*Gesetztem*] with which the stone-walls in "Vulcan," another one of the "Night Songs," are associated: "our city walls and . . . fence / That in long toil we built . . . " (StA 2: 60; PF 99)—a building that also, significantly, appears in an earlier volcano image from a draft of "The Archipelago" with the "patriotic walls" (StA 2: 638). The stone-walls are, no doubt, intimately related to the "wall of law" [*des Rechtes Mauer*], regarding whose connection with the "crooked deception" of the stone-walls, according to the commentary on Pindar's "The Infinite," a decision must be "ascribed" to "a third," namely the I (StA 5: 287). They stand, finally, in the vicinity of that "rigorous mediacy" (StA 5: 285), which, according to the commentary on the Pindaric fragment "The Highest," is the "law" [*Gesez*] that rules over gods as well as men. The speechless stone-walls of "Half of Life" distinguish themselves from all these walls, buildings, positings, and laws by this above all: because they resist every attempt at a "reproductive act" (StA 4: 284) that could ground knowledge, they are not instances of a sundering that could be cognized and recognized *as such*. No remembrance can find a foothold in them. If Antigone's elegiac hyperbole anticipates her own death and is, in this respect, still the representation of a subject, the lapidary verse of the stone-walls standing speechless speaks not of subjective re-*pre*-sentation but of a standing in which no subject is ahead of itself and from which no subject returns to itself. The "sacred living possibility of spirit" (StA 5: 267) is not retained in this verse; in it, rather, the impossibility of spirit, the incapacity for language, the harsh ex-position and suspension of time stands there not as a possibility to come but as a fact.

This verse, "The stone-walls stand / Speechless," says only this: that nothing can answer to it [*entsprechen*], that no cause, no matter, and no meaning can correspond [*korrespondieren*] to it, and that it can say nothing. In it, nothing is communicated but its incommunicability, nothing imparted but its unimpartibility. Yet this incommunicability is nevertheless communicated in it, this unimpartibility is still imparted. That it says nothing is still said in it. Just as language speaks not from possibility but from the *refused* [*verwehrt*] possibility of language, the time of this language is time only from the crude fact that it falters. Incommunicability is the mute resistance in language against which it responds. The caesura—not as "representation itself," but as "standing,"—is the refusal of the time in which it holds itself up and holds itself open. In *parousia* the *para-* remains as the empty and, hence, concealed ground of every *ousia*. The stone-walls stand in *parousia*.

In his letter to Johann Gottfried Ebel regarding the communications needed for spirits to unite and bring forth "the great child of time," the "day of all days," Hölderlin had spoken of the "*advent of the Lord*," the *parousia tou kyriou*, thereby naming the final goal of all communications. Immediately after these words, he breaks off his letter with the sentence: "I must stop, otherwise I'll never stop" (StA 6: 185). This stopping, this *Aufhören*, belongs to the structure of communication, the structure of imparting, and the structure of *parousia*.

Translated by Anthony Curtis Adler

Afterword

Toward a "Non-Metaphysical 'Concept' of Revolution"

This volume brings together Werner Hamacher's two major inquiries into the poetry and thought of Friedrich Hölderlin. The first study, "Version of Meaning," his hitherto unpublished master's thesis, was completed in November 1971 and submitted to the faculty of the Freie Universität-Berlin at the end of that year. The thesis, which was available to the public, circulated among Hamacher's colleagues, students, and friends. Soon after acquiring a copy, I sought his permission to have it translated and published. For several years, he withheld approval. In the last email I received from him, however, mediated by Sophie Hamacher and Johannes Hamacher, who were helping their father communicate from his hospital room, he gave his approval, "even though," he added, "I would have some reservations if it were not at this particular moment."[1] I soon began drafting a return email in the form of a long list of questions about the thesis in particular and his thoughts about Hölderlin in general; but before I had a chance to send the email, word came of his death.

In the absence of any response to the questions generated by the thesis, it seemed appropriate to place it alongside Hamacher's only other major inquiry into Hölderlin, "Parousia, Stone-Walls," which was written some thirty years later and published in the *Hölderlin-Jahrbuch*.[2] As for the title of the volume, it alludes to an essay that Walter Benjamin wrote around 1915, "Two Poems of Friedrich Hölderlin," which Hamacher incisively discusses in two endnotes of his thesis. Like the placement of the two studies in a single volume, its title is an editorial imposition, yet there is reason to suppose that Hamacher would have reluctantly approved of it, for Benjamin's essay, from its title onward, is concerned with a question linking Hamacher's two studies, from their own titles onward: what does "late" mean when speaking of "late Hölderlin"? Hamacher's response to this question is not modeled on Benjamin's essay, nor does he look toward either stylistic considerations or biographical information for an answer, even though the thesis begins by locating Hölderlin's "lateness" in 1802, with his return from France to his native Swabia (21). For Hamacher, however, in 1971 as well as 2004, the degree of the poet's "lateness" is determined primarily by his distance from the competing philosophical systems that came to be known as German idealism: those of Kant and Fichte, on the one hand, and those of Hölderlin's "Tübingen classmates" (39), Schelling and Hegel, on the other. By separating himself from both transcendental and absolute idealism, without reverting to any traditional form of materialism or realism, Hölderlin begins to think and write in such an unprecedented manner that the expression "late Hölderlin" does not function, for Hamacher, as a designation for a certain phase in a developmental process, whether stylistic or biographical, but becomes, instead, something like a category in its own right. This is evident in the subtitle of his later study. The search for the significance of "late Hölderlin" beyond its problematic application to the writings attributed to a relatively young poet during a few years preceding his "madness"—a diagnosis Hamacher never discusses—is the basic element shared by the two studies collected in this volume. As for their difference, it lies, above all, in revolution: the thesis culminates in a provisional theory of revolution, while "Parousia, Stone-Walls" says nothing about revolution after a brief aside in its opening pages. This is the primary question I had wanted to ask the author of these studies in preparation for the publication of his thesis: what happened to its nascent theory of revolution?

When Hamacher submitted "Bild und Zeichen in der späten Lyrik Hölderlins" (Image and sign in Hölderlin's late lyric poetry), in December of 1971, he did not indicate under whose direction it was written nor the academic discipline that it claimed to "master."[3] This was apparently not unusual among master's candidates in the Department of General and Comparative Literary Studies (Seminar für Allgemeine und Vergleichende Literaturwissenschaft, henceforth abbreviated as AVL) at the Freie

Universität.[4] The circumstances under which Hamacher wrote his thesis were, however, unusual. Despite the absence of his name from the title or dedication page, Peter Szondi, who had founded AVL in 1965, would have been the obvious *Referent* ("referee") of Hamacher's thesis. Hamacher matriculated at the Freie Universität two years after the AVL was founded and joined a group of students there who, while studying under Szondi, also became interested in the work of contemporary French philosophers, especially Jacques Derrida, who, as the introduction to this volume describes at greater length, began to visit AVL in 1968.[5] In September of 1970, shortly after the publication of his groundbreaking volume *Hölderlin-Studien*, Szondi informed his students that he had accepted a position at the University of Zurich. In conjunction with his new appointment, he was granted permission to bring along two assistants, one of whom would have been Hamacher.[6] Szondi, however, disappeared in October of 1971. His body was found the following month. "September–November 1971" are the last words of Hamacher's thesis. Readers of this volume also know that its final chapter concerns the failure of mourning in the fading light of a disappearance that itself disappears—"Where the vanishing 'faults' [*fehlt*]" (115). Hamacher briefly explained the circumstances under which he wrote "Image and Sign in Hölderlin's Late Lyric Poetry" in an email to Irene Albers, who was gathering material for a history of AVL, renamed the Peter-Szondi Institute, on the fiftieth anniversary of its founding: "I began to write my master's thesis (on Hölderlin) during the last summer in which Szondi resided in Sils Maria. He never had a chance to see it because it was finished shortly after his death."[7]

Szondi's name is not only absent from the title page of the thesis; it rarely occurs in the subsequent pages. Only once does the name appear in the body of the text, where Hamacher commends a chapter of *Hölderlin-Studien* for identifying "important traces" (46) of certain changes in Hölderlin's concept of history; almost in the same breath, however, he criticizes Szondi for looking in the wrong place for the most significant traces of late Hölderlin's understanding of history. In an endnote, Hamacher's limited criticism of *Hölderlin-Studien* turns into an annihilating critique directed at one of the underlying theses on which it stakes a claim to "philological cognition," to cite the title of Szondi's prefatory essay. Instead of being a thesis seeking the approval of a master, in other words, Hamacher's *Magisterarbeit* examines the master's own thesis. And Szondi is not the only master whom Hamacher subjects to rigorous examination.

This is also true of other twentieth-century *maîtres à penser*, including Adorno and Heidegger, perhaps also Freud via Lacan, and especially Derrida. In the case of Szondi, the thesis in question is readily identifiable: it is the thesis that "philological cognition" can resolve questions of identity, specifically the identity of the one whom Hölderlin calls "he himself, the prince of the festival" despite his use of a bewildering variety of descriptive designations.[8] With respect to Adorno, the thesis is similarly identifiable: it is the thesis of synthesis. In an endnote that matches the critique of Szondi in terms of both its brevity and its annihilating tendency, Hamacher shows that, for Adorno, who otherwise casts Hölderlin and himself as defenders of the "non-identical," the late poetry is governed by the ideal of synthesis, after all: "The fact that Adorno insists on synthesis, even if not a conceptual synthesis, and sees it as distinguished from conceptual synthesis alone through its reflective moment, makes it impossible for him to philosophically articulate the role of withdrawal and of deferral, of double-interpretation [*Doppeldeutigkeit*] and of reversal in Hölderlin" (191). The case of Heidegger is less straightforward: while one endnote adopts the line of criticism with which Adorno begins "Parataxis" and attacks Heidegger for extracting certain words from their syntactical, grammatical, rhetorical, and metrical contexts, and another endnote makes clear that an "imperialist politics" is responsible for Heidegger's miserable misunderstanding of Hölderlin's use of the word "colony," the weight of Hamacher's critique of Heidegger falls on the philosopher's interpretation of *zwischen* (between) as a meaning-generating term. By analyzing a particularly vexing passage of "Celebration of Peace" in which one "between" interferes with another "between," without a third "between" that might mediate between the two, Hamacher shows how Heidegger is nevertheless driven to a synthesis that would make the poet's "betweens" conform with a pre-understanding of between-ness as such. By contrast, in "Celebration of Peace," as Hamacher elucidates the relevant lines, "the between is not a category of meaning, but rather a category that is primarily produced through constellations in such a way that it does not describe the state of 'Beyng,' the 'open,' or 'the expanse' [*das Freie*] without also blocking and hiding [*verstellen*] it. . . . The breaking through, irritation, or negation of the possibility of the opening itself remains unthought in Heidegger. Unproblematically self-identical, its category therefore falls back within the terrain of Idealism and of original synthesis, whose deconstruction is the aim of Hölderlin's texts" (40).

With this passage, Hamacher alludes to other masters who come under examination in his thesis. Neither Freud nor Lacan is named, but from the opening inquiry into the evasive ways of *Hemmung* ("inhibition," "blockage," "obstruction") in "Stimme des Volkes" (Voice of the people) through the passage above, where the critique of Heidegger is condensed into a single word, *verstellen* ("block," "hide," with a suggestion of "displace"), certain psychoanalytic terms and motifs are examined in light of Hölderlin's departure from "the terrain of Idealism," on whose soil Freud and Lacan may have constructed their cardinal concepts.[9] Whereas psychoanalysis remains latent in the passage above and throughout the thesis as a whole, deconstruction is patent in both. To be sure, Derrida's name appears only once, near the end, but the idea of a certain deconstruction guides the thesis from the very beginning. The final sentence of its magisterial opening paragraph sets out the anti- or counter-method by which an interpretation of late Hölderlin does not become a betrayal of the poet's lateness: "in its own process, interpretation will have to be aimed at the suspension of those moments that drive the suppression of the revolt in its object [*die Unterdrückung des Aufruhrs in ihrem Gegenstand betreiben*] and, to the extent that it is logic, it will have to aim at its own deconstruction" (21). This, in abbreviated form, is the farthest-reaching thesis under examination in this master's thesis: deconstruction stands in some as yet unspecified relation to revolution. The relation may at first only be between a deconstruction of certain interpretative logics and the revolt of the interpreted object; but as the thesis develops, starting with its interpretation of Hölderlin's interpretation of the potentially revolutionary, potentially reactionary saying *vox populi vox dei*, the relation between deconstruction and revolution expands and the examination of the master's thesis deepens.

At two moments in the thesis, Hölderlin is shown explicitly in the process of departing from the "terrain of Idealism": first, in the second chapter, where Hamacher describes the transformation of the central stanza of "The Rhine" from a version that bears traces of Hölderlin's encounter with Fichte to its final form, where Idealist preconceptions of Being no longer shape the articulation of divine-human difference; and then again, in the penultimate chapter, where Hamacher distinguishes Hegel's concept of revolution from Hölderlin's. The confrontation between Hölderlin and Fichte is relatively straightforward, insofar as Hamacher shows how the erasure of certain lines indebted to Fichte's philosophy of reflection makes room for a poetic reflection on the permissibility of its own language: "if to say such a thing is / Permitted" (35). The confrontation between Hölderlin and Hegel appears in some respects to be similarly straightforward, yet the master's thesis gives several indications that there may be a difference here—that Hölderlin's separation from Hegel's philosophy of absolute spirit, in other words, is unlike his departure from the "terrain of Idealism" associated with Fichte's *Wissenschaftslehre*. This is arguably the crux of Hamacher's master's thesis, its *experimentum crucis*. In the following passage, Hamacher briefly sketches the course through which Hegel frees himself from the philosophy of reflection that finds its most exacting expression in Fichte's work: "The repression of blindness, infertility, expropriation, and perversity [*Verkehrtheit*] in the philosophy of reflection drives speculative dialectics into the bourgeois phantasm of the self-production of the subject" (108). Hegel, in short—and the thesis is almost telegraphic in its treatment of Hegel—is driven to overdo what he nevertheless has to do: acknowledge what the philosophy of reflection, grounded as it is in the self-positing of the self, must deny. The result, however, is that Hegel thereby becomes entrapped in a phantasm of freedom that expresses itself in a concept of revolution that makes the end into the beginning and thus ultimately rounds history out.

In a famous passage from the *Phenomenology of Spirit* that reverberates throughout the final chapters of Hamacher's thesis, Hegel describes the genesis and structure of self-consciousness, calling death "the absolute master"—which, if unconditionally true, means at the very least that death is the source of power and impotence alike.[10] On this point, for Hamacher, Hölderlin parts ways with Hegel, his former classmate.[11] And it is for this reason that the final chapter of the thesis presents death in Hölderlin's late poems and fragments not in terms of mastery—or its opposites—but as something different: as dissemination, "castration," the fruit of infertility, and "de-interpretation" (*Entdeutung*). If *logos spermatikos*, conceived as dissemination or "castration," were the opposite of the inhibitive obstruction (*Hemmung*) around which Hamacher's interpretation of Hölderlin's interpretation of the old saying *vox populi, vox dei* revolves, the thesis would return to its beginning—with enough added knowledge, perhaps, that it could determine whether the divine-popular "voice" is reactionary or revolutionary, after all. But this is not the case: dissemination, "castration," *logos spermatikos*, and "de-interpretation" are different from one another, and so, too, are the other words, phrases, categories, signs, and images that the master's thesis collects from Hölderlin's latest writings in preparation for a thought of death as something other than the "absolute master," and revolution as something other than a return from impotence to power:

> Only where [spirit and history] have entered the scene of a death that "is" not "theirs" and for that very reason meets them as break, limitation, transgression, infertility, interlude [*Zwischen*], postponement, or deferral; only where [they] accept their impotence as the uncertain and unknowable condition for their efficacy; can there take place that which could only still provisionally be called a revolution. Hölderlin's attempt to sketch out a non-metaphysical "concept" of revolution that does not begin with self-production and self-appropriation designates a *point de suspension* that resists bourgeois idealism and its politics, a point from which a line, though certainly not a straight one, could be drawn to point out the work that could be done to dissolve present systems of coercion, be they economic, political, or philosophical. (108–9)

At this point Hamacher is sure of only one thing: the line leading from the *point de suspension*—otherwise known as "ellipsis," which abbreviates and redirects the theory and practice of parataxis—to a "work" that could be provisionally characterized as revolutionary is neither straight nor straightforward. Beyond its brokenness and crookedness, however, what shape does it take? At the very moment in modern European history at which Hölderlin's works were first being mobilized en masse for "patriotic" goals that ran directly counter to what he meant by "patriotic reversal," Walter Benjamin found himself in a position similar to Hamacher's. "Two Poems of Friedrich Hölderlin" shows how the "poetized" of an early ode about the courage of the poet in the face of death is so fully transfigured in a later version of the ode, renamed almost the opposite of courage, "Blödigkeit," that it comes close to "the pure poetized." Benjamin indicates, however, that the poetized of Hölderlin's very last poems, stretching into the time of his "madness," evinces yet another shape that recedes not only from his commentary but also, perhaps, from commentary in general: "The consideration of the poetized does not lead to myth but, rather—in the greatest creations—only to mythic connections formed by the artwork into a singular, un-mythological, and un-mythic shape [*Gestalt*], which we cannot more closely conceptualize."[12] The unconceptualized shape has the same form as the line described by Hamacher, which leads from a non-metaphysical "concept" of revolution to the work of de-coercion, which, it should be noted, is not the same as "freedom." In an endnote that superficially resembles his critique of Szondi and Adorno, Hamacher thwarts any suggestion that the direction of this line should be identified with what Hölderlin—and Benjamin, in turn—calls "the oriental" (193). Much of the work that Hamacher accomplishes in the central chapters of his thesis is directed against commentators who misconceive of the other, far more prominent directional term in Hölderlin's late writings, namely the Hesperian, and nothing would be achieved by a simple reversal from West to East. Like Benjamin's shape, Hamacher's line functions, rather, as a provocation for a different direction of reading, reflection, and inquiry—a direction that Hamacher begins to explore in the final chapter of his thesis, where, citing Benjamin's *Ursprung des deutschen Trauerspiels* (*Origin of the German Mourning Play*), Hamacher shows how, for Hölderlin, death is not the "absolute master" and mourning is not, in turn, the gaining of mastery over whatever or whoever seems to have disappeared.

"Image and Sign in Hölderlin's Late Lyric Poetry" was supposed to have been only a "seed," so to speak, emerging from the Department of (or "Seminar for") General and Comparative Literary Studies, from which Hamacher would have soon departed, following Szondi to Zurich, where, as an assistant, he would transform his master's thesis into a doctoral dissertation. The seed, however, fell on "fallow lands," to quote the passage from Sigmund von Birken with which Benjamin closes his qualifying dissertation and Hamacher his thesis. Around 1973 Hamacher seems to have completed two supplementary exercises in which he expanded certain parts of the thesis in view of its final transformation into a dissertation. One of the additional texts was probably related to Hölderlin's reception of Fichte, while the other may have culminated in an expanded theory of revolution. Neither of these exercises is extant in Hamacher's literary estate, and they must therefore be considered lost. In the bibliography that Hamacher prepared for his critical edition of Hegel's early writings, he lists under his own name an unpublished text that is probably the second of these exercises, "Diversionen: Zu Hölderlins Geschichtskonstruktion und Sprache" (Diversions: toward Hölderlin's construction of history and language), and this also seems to be the manuscript that Paul de Man briefly discusses in a letter of recommendation he wrote for Hamacher in the summer of 1974.[13] Hamacher wrote to de Man the following fall, expressing some uncertainty about his plans for the expansion of the thesis, but he also notes that he had found a theme for an auxiliary essay: "eating and digesting in Hegel."[14] This was to be finished by the early spring of 1975, at which time Hamacher planned to return to Hölderlin, completing the dissertation by the middle of the summer. Neither of these happened as planned. The Hegel essay simply devoured the Hölderlin project. Writing to de Man in June of 1976, Hamacher concedes that he has not produced a single additional page on Hölderlin but that the essay on Hegel, much to his surprise, has grown far beyond its original conception: "Having now come close to its completion, I am not *entirely* dissatisfied with it, as far as certain argumentative and stylistic achievements and risks are concerned; but I have not yet reworked it and secretly fear that, while ruminating on it—and this is what's at issue—I will become ill."[15]

Thus emerged Hamacher's *pleroma*, which was ultimately accepted as his doctoral dissertation and appeared in print as an exceptionally long introduction to the aforementioned edition of Hegel's early writings. Of Hölderlin there is very little in *pleroma*: Hamacher refutes Dieter Henrich's thesis concerning the influence the young poet exercised over some of the young philosopher's early fragments; he briefly outlines Hölderlin's and Hegel's complementary conceptions of religion circa 1798; and without invoking Hölderlin's name, he quotes three lines from "Patmos" to suggest that the erstwhile Lutheran seminary classmates understood the Last Supper along similar lines.[16] From the perspective of Hamacher's thesis, all of these are surprising, but the last one is especially so, for, according to the general schema adopted for the master's thesis, late Hölderlin—and no one would deny that "Patmos" is late—departed from the "terrain of Idealism" that Hegel ultimately conquered.[17] This is the unresolved and perhaps never quite thematized tension that separates Hamacher's master's thesis from his doctoral dissertation: the germ of the latter lies in those paragraphs of the former where the outlines of Hölderlin's "non-metaphysical 'concept' of revolution" emerge in contradistinction to Hegel's metaphysical concept of the same, which passes from the naming of death in general as "absolute master" to the interpretation of death during the Terror as an incident "without any more meaning [*Bedeutung*] than chopping off a head of cabbage or swallowing a mouthful of water" (108). At this precise point, Hegel is distinguished from Hölderlin: the latter, in a late fragment, says of the "fatherland" that it is "forbidden fruit/ . . . To be tasted last" (109), whereas the former, never content with mere taste, at once incorporates and spiritualizes it into an infinite, reproductive-self-productive cycle: "Metaphorically, though not only metaphorically," Hamacher adds, after quoting the passage from the *Phenomenology* above, "this almost meaningless death must therefore also be brought into connection with acts of reproduction, of drinking and eating, in order to keep the domains of the self and of its meaning unscathed" (108). The phrase calling out for expansion, "not only metaphorically," is the germ from which *pleroma* grew and, as such, the stumbling block upon which Hamacher's extension of his thesis foundered.[18]

Beyond the fragments Hamacher probably produced around 1973, the situation he described in his letters to de Man never changed: not a single page was added to his work on Hölderlin. His last attempt to break the impasse occurred in 1979, when he drafted a brief proposal to revise his thesis in light of recent scholarship on the poet. The proposal begins by emphasizing the reciprocal relation between his thesis and his dissertation: "The results of the recently completed work on Hegel, which were only supposed to have been a sideline to the study of Hölderlin, will play a particularly important role for the new formulation and continuation of this study at the point where it concerns Hölderlin's attempt to develop a 'poetic logic,' in connection with Kant's third *Critique* and Fichte's theory of self-consciousness, which does not succumb to the aporias of the Kantian or Fichtean system, nor to those of speculative ones."[19] After parenthetically criticizing some of the recent attempts to address the problem of Hölderlin's relation to philosophy in the late 1790s, the proposal describes the desiderata that can be satisfied only by further research:

> Beyond a more precise presentation of this problem in terms of its argumentation and systematicity, the work, as the enclosed fragments show to some degree, should contain a discussion of questions connected with a comparativistic aesthetics of production and reception, which, along with references to Kant and Fichte, should have as its object, above all, Rousseau, Herder, and Pindar. As further themes, I should name these: confrontations with psychoanalytic discourse theory, which has recently become interested in Hölderlin; with the existential-hermeneutic confiscation of Hölderlin as the poet of the granting of being; and with those interpretations that immediately stylize Hölderlin into a political allegorist.[20]

In the absence of the fragments from 1973, and with the 1979 project framed only in highly fragmentary form, there is only one indication of how Hamacher would have transformed his master's thesis beyond what he accomplished in 1971, and that can be found in the new title that he gave it. At the top of the list of the questions I wanted to ask him was what "Version der Bedeutung" (Version of Meaning) actually means. Only one thing is altogether clear: "version of meaning" is not "subversion" (20) of meaning. The latter phrase, taken from the introductory paragraph of the thesis, was—and still is—widely taken to be the method and goal of Derrida's so-called disciples. Whatever else "Version of Meaning" may mean, it disputes this widespread misconstrual of deconstruction. In the same stroke, Hamacher may have wanted to shift the framework within which the problem of meaning is posed, from the sphere of structuralist semiotics to which the thesis is partly indebted, toward a theory of meaning associated with Frege's famous essay from the late nineteenth century, "Über Sinn und Bedeutung," generally translated into English as "On Sense and Reference." If *version* were plural, the interpretation of Hamacher's new title, aided by reference to its earlier version as well as its expansion into the unpublished manuscript entitled "Diversions," would be straightforward enough: signs and images are "versions" or "diversions" of meaning insofar as they—somehow both "objectively" and "subjectively"—"turn" toward and away from the referent, that is, the "meaning" (*Bedeutung*) that makes an identity claim meaningful and not simply an empty, tautological formulation. Just as different "incomplete" terms, such as "morning star" and "evening star," turn toward, or direct attention to, the very same referent, namely the planet Venus; and just as every "complete" term, expressed in an indicative assertion, turns toward either truth or falsehood as its mutually exclusive referents, so certain other terms—signs and images in lyric poetry, let us say—turn toward and away from the source of meaningfulness and thus the origin of truth-value pure and simple.[21] This conception of the relations among *version*, *diversion*, and *meaning* would miss, however, what Hamacher, upon reflection, seems to have singled out as the basic thesis of his master's thesis: it is meaning or reference that "verses." And this "version" is indifferent to the distinction between "toward" and "away," both of which are ultimately origin- and goal-oriented. Hölderlin's late poetry, in short, does not involve itself in either subversions or diversions of meaning but, rather, in its mere "turning."

To the extent that this is indeed the thesis that Hamacher ultimately wanted to expand, its outlines emerge in the central chapter, "The Trace of Transgression," where he undertakes with astonishing tenacity an analysis of the three versions of "Der Einzige" (The Only One), reconstructed by Friedrich Beissner for the Stuttgart edition of Hölderlin's writings. In these various versions of the "self-same" poem that names itself as such, the stakes involved in the formulation of identity claims could not be higher. In preparation for his encounter with the second two versions, Hamacher isolates a semantic imperative from the final lines of the first version, which the following ones do not so much subvert or divert as simply—but this is obviously more complicated—"-vert": "to signify [*bedeuten*] the foreignness of that which is close to one another; to meet with the excess in that in which it is limited through measure; to simultaneously secure and relinquish meaning [*Bedeutung*] as that which both misses and strikes its target" (55). The imperative derives from the problem of meaning itself, or more accurately, the problem of meaning, hence referring to, any "only one," which, if the term "identical" applies at all in this unique instance, is identical only with itself. However only-ness may be conceived, to mean "the only one"—and nothing else, no other "God," for example, but also no other poem—seems guaranteed to fail, since "the only one," as a singularity, cannot even be called "a" singularity, insofar as the act of calling it "singular" would compromise its only-ness by making it comparable to others of its putatively unique kind. The "only one" to whom Hölderlin appeals under this heading is called Christ, who, as the poet boldly claims, is the "brother" of certain others, specifically the Greek half-gods Dionysus and Heracles. Meaning happens, reference is attained, while at the same time it is missed and fails to happen, for, in order for the happening to occur in the incomparable case of "the only one," another "brother" will also have been meant. This inflection of reference, or "version of meaning," cannot be understood in terms of logic or law, as long as logic and law recognize an "only one" only in the form of uncontestable power or generative principle, which the "only one" in Hölderlin's three versions cannot fulfill by virtue of his poverty, passivity, and infertility. This transgression of logic and law for the sake of meaning—"the only one"—plots the course of "Hesperian" history under the stringent condition, itself a supplementary law and postulate, that this directional term, "westward," be understood along the same crooked, broken lines: Hesperia, Hamacher shows, is, for Hölderlin, that "opened border" stretching "between the living form of sense and the deadly chaos of what is not sense" (95). From the perspective of the distinction between sense and reference, or *Sinn* and *Bedeutung*, the latter is less like a stationary star blessedly untouched by versions of the former than a planet, hence a "wanderer," like Venus, whose wayward path cannot be plotted with reference to constellated points, since every such point not only wanders, too, but is, in addition, a *point de suspension*—an ellipsis, in other words, pointing toward "the work that could be done to dissolve present systems of coercion, be they economic, political, or philosophical." The question remains, however, whether a version of late Hölderlin along such "Hesperian" lines would be able to expose the revolutionary character of his poetry and thought without in the same stroke stylizing him into a political allegorist.

"Parousia, Stone-Walls" may in fact have been written in response to a question of this kind. In at least one respect, it represents an extension of "Version of Meaning." While the early work is sparing in its engagements with Hölderlin scholarship, the later essay mentions no work of scholarship and contains no scholarly notes whatsoever. This feature of the essay is all the more conspicuous in the context of its original publication, surrounded as it is by essays and notices filled with lengthy and informative footnotes in the pages of a journal, *Hölderlin-Jahrbuch*, that published a large share of standard-setting scholarship, including essays by Szondi and de Man. Nevertheless, "Parousia, Stone-Walls" appears to be a partial fulfillment of the first part of Hamacher's 1979 proposal, for its initial pages are devoted to the explication of the "poetic logic" that Hölderlin developed in conjunction with his critical confrontation with Kantian and Fichtean versions of transcendental idealism. From another perspective, however, the essay has little to do with what Hamacher had earlier proposed. It says nothing about any broader interpretative trends: nothing about Laplanche and "the question of the father," nothing about Heidegger and "the granting of being," and nothing about such politically inclined treatments of the poet as Peter Weiss's *Hölderlin*, which was first performed in the year when Hamacher wrote his master's thesis. The difference between the master's thesis and the essay can also be expressed most effectively in terms of two further absences: just as the name "Benjamin" never appears in the essay, so Hamacher makes only hyphenated reference to revolution. The thesis, meanwhile, closes with a direct reference to a "baroque trait in Hölderlin's late texts" (110), which Hamacher explicates, in turn, through Benjamin's understanding of the relation between mourning and baroque allegory. Far from immediately stylizing Hölderlin into a political allegorist, "Parousia, Stone-Walls" distances the poet both from politics in the conventional sense and from allegory in its perhaps most exacting theoretical formulation.

Along with the absence of footnotes, "Parousia, Stone-Walls" is characterized by another formal lack: there are no divisions, sections, segments, or the like. The sole index of division is the occasional paragraph break, each of which, with one exception, may be only a reluctant concession to journal-enforced conventions. The flow of the argument stands in contrast to its theme, first expressed in the final words of its subtitle, "Late Hölderlin," whose lateness consists in a break with parousia. Such a rupture is, of course, paradoxical, insofar as the absence of presence cannot present itself as such. Never forgetting this paradox, which Hamacher associates, above all, with Hölderlin's fragment "The Meaning [*Bedeutung*] of Tragedies," the essay does not feign a break that would provoke readers into imagining that the argument of the essay, having left "the terrain of Idealism" behind for good, had passed into a fresh field of knowledge or experience that could be stylized or sloganized into, for example, a new realism or a new materialism.

After briefly holding an assistantship at AVL upon the completion of his master's, and then studying for a year at the École Normale Supérieure in Paris, Hamacher was unable for several years to obtain any institutional support in Berlin. Gerhard Goebel, Szondi's replacement at AVL, apparently decided against offering Hamacher an assistantship because his work was based on a mistaken premise: "the identification of method and object."[22] This is a false appraisal of the method pursued in the thesis, which begins with a trenchant critique of mimetic conceptions of interpretation. Yet Goebel's clumsy criticism captures in exact reverse the basic character of "Parousia, Stone-Walls." Method and object are dis-identified. The method is characterized by continuity, the object by discontinuity. Signaled by the comma in the title of the essay—Hamacher was fond of repeating an imperative that Hölderlin was supposed to have uttered during his "benighted" years: "Look, Sir, a comma!" (191)—the break that makes Hölderlin "late" and thus discloses "temporality" traverses the argument at every point, without ever being identifiable with any one point. For a characterization of the method beyond that of dis-identification with the object, there is no better place to turn than the aforementioned clause with which Hamacher concludes the first paragraph of his thesis: interpretation that accords with the appeal of late Hölderlin and, therefore, submits itself to its own critique of interpretative methodology suspends "those moments that suppress the revolt in its object" (21). The revolting object in "Parousia, Stone-Walls" is what follows the comma seen after parousia: walls of stone.

Insofar as the violent destruction of age-old walls—those of a fortress or a "bastille," for instance, suggested perhaps by the etymological and phonological proximity of the German *Mauern* and the French *murs*, which

Hölderlin may have carried with him from his sojourn in France—functions as an outstanding image of revolution, the standing of stone-walls would seem to move in the opposite direction. Such an interpretation, of course, stylizes Hölderlin into a political allegorist, whose poem "Hälfte des Lebens" (Half of Life) would then not only be an expression of his mourning over the demise of his earlier republican-revolutionary hopes; it would also mean that the poem betrays the very walls of which it speaks, for it forces upon them what they do not have: language or speech (*Sprache*). It is this absence, however, that draws them into the second half of Hamacher's argument—after parousia. The stone-walls in "Half of Life" do not speak and have no language. They thus, paradoxically, correspond to the principal thesis of Hamacher's later work: the "philological" thesis that language cannot be owned, appropriated, or in any way acquired. There is, therefore, no such thing as language, if this word is supposed to mean something that one can "have." The supposition, often attributed to Aristotle on the basis of the opening section of *The Politics*, that human beings "have" language or speech (*logos*) is, for Hamacher, the *proton pseudos* of "politics" in the broadest terms.[23] Uncoerced by the force of this falsehood, the stone-walls in Hölderlin's short poem are the revolting object *kat' exechon*. Hamacher would perhaps refuse the "are" in this last sentence, insofar as it lends the walls a little language. Nevertheless, the stone-walls, along with the second half of "Half of Life" as a whole, can still be called "non-human" under the assumption that the Aristotelian understanding of "being human" remains standing. By virtue of their language- and speech-less character, the stone-walls in "Half of Life" cannot even be called walls, built as they are—unlike hills or mountains—by human hands; thus do the stone-walls deconstruct. Consonant with the cosmic revolution designated by "winter," they are an earthly "revolt" or, better yet, a planetary "uproar" (*Aufruhr*), which may not herald a revolution of the earth; but still, in their adamant refusal to stand for anything—above all, to stand for the interdiction, whether silent or vocal, "here is mine, over there is yours, and I am the product of a coercive force separating one domain from another"— Hamacher finds certain *points de suspension*.

—Peter Fenves

Appendix

Friedrich Hölderlin, "The Only One" (Third Version)[1]

What is it that
To the ancient happy shores
Fetters me, so that I love them
Still more than my own fatherland?
For as though in heavenly
Captivity cowering, speaking in accordance with the day
I am where, as the stones say, Apollo walked
In the shape of a king
And Zeus condescended
To innocent youths, and sons in a holy fashion
Begot, and daughters,
Mutely whiling away amid humankind?

Yet of lofty thoughts
Many have nevertheless
Come from the Father's head
And great souls
Come down from him to mortals.
And of Elis and
Olympia I have heard, and stood
Forever at the sources, on top of Parnassus
And up above hills of the Isthmus
And over there
By Smyrna too, and down

By Ephesus I have walked.

Much that is lovely I have seen
And sung the image of God
As here among the human kind
It lives. For very much like space
In youth the Heavenly in plenty
Is numerable   and yet
You old gods and all
You valiant sons of gods,
Still another I search for whom
Within your ranks I love,
Where hidden from the alien guest, from me
You keep the last of your race,
The treasured gem of the house.

My Master and Lord!
O you, my teacher!
Why did you keep
Away? And when
I saw, among the spirits, the ancients
The heroes and
The gods, why were you
Not there? And now my soul
Is full of mourning as though
You Heavenly yourselves excitedly cried
That if I serve one I
Must lack the other.

And yet I know, it is my
Own fault, for too greatly
O Christ! I am attached to you;
Although Heracles' brother
And boldly I confess, you
Are the brother also of Evius, who prudently, in ancient times,
Judged the sullen madwoman,

The god of the earth, and granted
A soul to the animal, which roams
In living from its own hunger and followed the shape of the earth,
But the right paths he commanded all at One time and places,
Things, too, he cultivated of each one.

Hindering me is however shame
From comparing you with
Worldly men. And yet know I
The one who made you, your father is
The same as theirs. For Christ also stood alone
Beneath the visible heaven and stars, visible
To those who freely dispose over what's constituted as law, with permission from God,
And the sins of the world, the incomprehensibility
Of cognitions, namely, when what persists the industrious overgrows,
The courage of men and of the stars was above him. For the world always rejoices
Away from this earth, that it
Bares the earth; where what is human does not hold the world. There remains, though, a trace
Yet of a word; this a man perceives. But the place was

The desert. So these are equal to each other. Full of joy, plentiful.
Gloriously green turns
A cloverleaf. Shapeless this would be, if for the sake of the spirit one were
Not allowed to say, as one instructed in the knowledge of bad prayer, that they
Are like commanders to me, heroes. This the mortals are allowed to do because
Without hold God is without comprehension. But as on chariots
Humble   with violence
Of the day or
With voices God appears as
Nature from without. Mediately

In holy writings. The Heavenly
And men are together on earth the whole time. A great man and similarly a great soul
If equal in heaven

Desires toward one on earth. Forever
This remains, that the world is always wholly chained
Every day. Often however appears
A great one not to be altogether fit for
Great things. But they stand every day, as at an abyss, one
Next to the other. Those three, however, are
This, that they are under the sun
Like hunters are to the hunt, or
A farmer who, taking a breath from work,
Bares his head, or a beggar. Beautiful
And lovely it is to compare. Good does
The earth. To cool. Always however

Translated by Julia Ng

Notes

Introduction

1. See Jacques Derrida, "Culture et écriture: la prolifération des livres et la fin du livre," *Noroit* 130 (1968): 5–12.

2. Jacques Derrida, *Of Grammatology*, trans. Gayatri Spivak (Baltimore and London: The Johns Hopkins University Press, 1997), 3.

3. Derrida, "Culture et écriture," 11.

4. Gert Mattenklott, in a speech delivered on the occasion of the 30th anniversary of the Szondi Institute; cited by Irene Albers in her foreword to *Nach Szondi: Allgemeine und vergleichende Literaturwissenschaft an der freien Universität Berlin, 1965–2015*, ed. Irene Albers (Berlin: Kadmos, 2016), 9.

5. See Samuel Weber and Irene Albers, "Screen Memories," 299–309; the sequence of letters between Weber, Derrida, and Szondi, 44–50; Sima Reinisch's summary "Derrida in Dahlem," 51–53; and the "Chronik," 451–519; all in Albers, ed., *Nach Szondi*.

6. For this and other biographical details I am grateful to the Deutsches Literaturarchiv Marbach, which houses Hamacher's literary estate, for making available Hamacher's "Curriculum Vitae" from March 12, 1990, and to Dr. Robert Zwarg for supplying us with a facsimile.

7. Peter Szondi, *Hölderlin-Studien. Mit einem Traktat über philologische Erkenntnis* (Frankfurt am Main: Insel Verlag, 1967). Republished in Szondi, *Schriften II* (Frankfurt am Main: Suhrkamp, 1978), 263–412.

8. Norbert von Hellingrath, "Hölderlin und die Deutschen," in *Hölderlin: Zwei Vorträge* (Munich: Bruckmann, 1921), 17 and 21.

9. Pierre Bertaux, "Hölderlin und die französische Revolution," *Hölderlin-Jahrbuch* 15 (1967/68): 1–27; 2.

10. Bertaux, "Hölderlin," 1.

11. Bertaux, "Hölderlin," 7.

12. Bertaux, "Hölderlin," 9.

13. Bertaux, "Hölderlin," 13.

14. Pierre Bertaux, *Friedrich Hölderlin: Eine Biographie* (Frankfurt am Main: Suhrkamp, 1978).

15. For this point and many of the other historical details in the previous two paragraphs, I was fortunate to rely on Robert Savage's illuminating epilogue to his book *Hölderlin after the Catastrophe: Heidegger, Adorno, Brecht* (Rochester, NY: Camden House, 2008), 194–214.

16. Günter Mieth, "Ein Rückblick auf öffentliche Hölderlin-Ehrungen 1970," in Mieth, *Friedrich Hölderlin: Zeit und Schicksal. Vorträge 1962–2006* (Würzburg: Königshausen & Neumann, 2007), 216–26; 220.

17. Renate Böschenstein-Schäfer, "Bericht über die Diskussion," *Hölderlin-Jahrbuch* 15 (1967/68): 318.

18. Bertaux, "Hölderlin," 26.

19. Böschenstein-Schäfer, "Bericht,"319.

20. Martin Walser, "Hölderlin zu entsprechen," *Hölderlin-Jahrbuch* 16 (1969/70): 6.

21. Hölderlin, "On the Procedure of the Poetic Spirit" (StA 4: 257; EL 281, mod.) and "Ground of the *Empedocles*" (StA 4: 152; EL 261, mod.).

22. Walser, "Hölderlin zu entsprechen," 17. What Walser has in mind in terms of contemporary German politics is the stagnation of parliamentary democracy brought about by two-party politics and the necessity of recognizing socialism—especially as "actualized" in the GDR—as presenting a genuine alternative to this impasse. Cf. Mieth, "Ein Rückblick," 220.

23. Walser, "Hölderlin zu entsprechen," 18.

24. "Euch ist nicht / Zu helfen, wenn ihr selber euch nicht helft," Hölderlin, "Tod des Empedokles, Erste Fassung" (StA 4: 63).

25. Mieth, "Ein Rückblick," 222.

26. Peter Szondi, "Hölderlin's Overcoming of Classicism," trans. Timothy Bahti, *Comparative Criticism* 5 (1983): 261.

27. Walser, "Hölderlin zu entsprechen," 4.

28. Peter Szondi, "Er selbst, der Fürst des Festes," in Szondi, *Hölderlin-Studien*; reprinted in Szondi, *Schriften* 2 (Frankfurt am Main: Suhrkamp, 1978), 339.

29. Bertaux, "Hölderlin," 3.

30. Heraclitus, Fragment B50, as cited in Bertaux, "Hölderlin," 3; my translation.

31. Thus continues Fragment B50. Cf. Heraclitus, *The Art and Thought of Heraclitus*, ed. Charles H. Kahn (Cambridge: Cambridge University Press, 1979), 44–45 (= XXXVI); I've modified the translation of *homolegein* in such a way as to make apparent that the "agreement" is achieved by way of a "homology" to the *logos* being "listened to."

32. Pierre Bertaux, *Hölderlin und die französische Revolution* (Frankfurt am Main: Suhrkamp, 1969), 126.
33. Heraclitus, Fragment B51, 64–65 (= LXXVIII), translation modified.
34. Bertaux, *Hölderlin*, 126.
35. Bertaux, *Hölderlin*, 125.
36. Cf. Wilhelm Michel, *Hölderlins abendländische Wendung* (Jena: Diederich, 1923).
37. Szondi, "Hölderlin's Overcoming of Classicism," 256.
38. Beda Allemann, *Hölderlin und Heidegger* (Zürich: Atlantis Verlag, 1954), 30.
39. This is captured in Heidegger's 1941/42 lecture course on *Andenken*, which is also the subject of the essay first published in a Tübingen memorial volume compiled in commemoration of the hundredth anniversary of Hölderlin's death.
40. Martin Heidegger, "Logos (Heraklit, Fragment 50) (1951)," in *Vorträge und Aufsätze* (Frankfurt am Main: Vittorio Klostermann, 2000), 211–35.
41. Heidegger, "Logos," 230.
42. Martin Heidegger, "Remembrance," in *Elucidations of Hölderlin's Poetry*, trans. Keith Hoeller (New York: Humanity Books, 2000), 116–18.
43. Szondi, "Hölderlin's Overcoming of Classicism," 251, 257.
44. Szondi, "Hölderlin's Overcoming of Classicism," 256.
45. Szondi, "Hölderlin's Overcoming of Classicism," 262; cf. Theodor Adorno, "Parataxis: On Hölderlin's Late Poetry," *Notes to Literature* (New York: Columbia University Press, 1991), 2: 119.
46. Szondi, "Gattungspoetik und Geschichtsphilosophie" (Poetics of genre and philosophy of history), in *Hölderlin-Studien*; reprinted in *Schriften* 2: 402ff.
47. Adorno, "Parataxis," 133ff.
48. Walter Benjamin, "Zwei Gedichte von Friedrich Hölderlin," in *Gesammelte Schriften*, ed. Rolf Tiedemann and Hermann Schweppenhäuser (Frankfurt am Main: Suhrkamp, 1972–1991), 2: 112.
49. Benjamin, "Zwei Gedichte," 2: 112.
50. Szondi, "Gattungspoetik," 400.
51. Szondi, "Er selbst," 339.
52. Adorno, "Parataxis," 136; cited by Hamacher in the opening paragraph of "Version of Meaning" (20).
53. Szondi, "Er selbst," 331.
54. Hamacher cites from the Snell edition of Heraclitus in German, according to which the fragment also bears the number 92; the English translation is in Heraclitus, *The Art and Thought of Heraclitus*, 71 (= XCII).
55. Adorno, "Parataxis," 123.
56. Werner Hamacher, "Ein Brief," in *Nach Szondi*, 293–298.
57. In fact, there seem to have been two such expansions of themes from the master's thesis, and Hamacher lists one of these expansions in the bibliography

for the German edition of *pleroma*—that is, his critical edition of Hegel's early writings on Christianity—under the title "Diversionen: Zu Hölderlins Geschichtskonstruktion und Sprache" (Diversions: Toward Hölderlin's construction of history and language), noting next to it that it is "unveröffentlicht" (unpublished). See Werner Hamacher, *pleroma—zur Genese und Struktur einer dialektischen Hermeneutik bei Hegel*, in *Kritische Ausgabe von G. W. F. Hegel: Der Geist des Christentums—Schriften 1796–1800* (Berlin: Ullstein 1978), 7–333, 537; the English edition appeared under the title *pleroma—Reading in Hegel* (Stanford: Stanford University Press, 1997), but does not include the critical bibliography. Thanks goes to Markus Hardtmann for bringing to our attention the reference to "Diversions," and thus to another valence of Hamacher's alteration of the title of his master's thesis from "Image and Sign" to "Version of Meaning," a topic that is addressed in some detail in the afterword.

58. For an illuminating discussion of Taubes's relation to Schmitt, see Bruce Rosenstock, "Palíntropos Harmoníē: Jacob Taubes and Carl Schmitt '*im liebenden Streit*,'" *New German Critique* 121.41 (2014): 55–92.

59. Letter from Werner Hamacher to Jacob Taubes, Nov. 2, 1981; Leibniz-Zentrum für Literaturforschung zu Berlin.

60. "NOW. Walter Benjamin on Historical Time," in *The Moment: Time and Rupture in Modern Thought*, ed. Heidrun Friese (Liverpool: Liverpool University Press, 2001), 161–96; "Guilt History: Benjamin's Sketch 'Capitalism as Religion,'" trans. Kirk Wetters, *diacritics* (Fall–Winter 2002): 81–106; "Das Theologisch-Politische Fragment," in *Benjamin-Handbuch*, ed. Burkhardt Lindner (Stuttgart: Metzler, 2006): 175–92; "Lingua Amissa: The Messianism of Commodity-Language and Derrida's Specters of Marx," trans. Kelly Barry, in *Ghostly Demarcations: A Symposium on Jacques Derrida's "Specters of Marx,"* ed. Michael Sprinker (London and New York: Verso, 1999), 168–212; "Uncalled. A Commentary on Kafka's 'The Test,'" in *Reading Ronell*, ed. Diane Davis (Urbana: University of Illinois Press, 2009), 74–93; "The Relation/The Aphora," in *The New Centennial Review* 8 (2008): 29–70; "Ou, séance, touche de Nancy, ici," in *The Sense of Philosophy: On Jean-Luc Nancy*, ed. Darren Sheppard, Simon Sparks, and Colin Thomas (London and New York: Routledge, 1997), 38–60; "The Right Not to Use Rights: Human Rights and the Structure of Judgments," trans. Tobias Boes, in *Political Theologies: Public Religions in a Post-Secular World*, ed. Hent de Vries and Lawrence E. Sullivan (New York: Fordham University Press, 2006), 671–90; "The One Right No One Ever Has," trans. Julia Ng, *Philosophy Today* 61 (2017): 947–62; *Sprachgerechtigkeit* (Frankfurt am Main: Fischer, 2018).

Version of Meaning

1. The master's thesis was submitted to the Free University of Berlin with the title "Bild und Zeichen in der späten Lyrik Hölderlins" (Image and sign in

Hölderlin's late lyric poetry). Hamacher later crossed out this title and added a new one: "Version der Bedeutung: Studie zur später Lyrik Hölderlins" (Version of meaning: a study of Hölderlin's late lyric poetry). In keeping with the protocols of the master's thesis, Hamacher included an *Übersicht* ("overview" or "general plan"). His model seems to have been the "Contents" page with which Benjamin begins his *Origin of the German Mourning Play*. Hamacher's "Overview" reads as follows:

I. Interpretation [*Auslegung*]: Interpretation of Yearning, Yearning for Interpretation—A Voice in Ruins—Laying Out in Interpretation.

II. Crooked [*Krumm*]: Fichte's Original Synthesis—Taking Part—In Between, the Celebration—Parenthesis: Deferred Syntax—Inclination

III. The Trace of Transgression: Greek Sculpture, Logos—The Subject's Hubris—Lack—Syntactic Secession—Hesperian Reversal I—Negation of Death—Of One—History: Perversion [*Verkehrung*] of the Signifier—Double Economy—"Islands"—Positivity—Trace, Desert, Niobe—Shapeless [*Ungestalt*]—Homburg Poetology—Next to, Abyss—Supplementation of the Lack

IV. " . . . Almost/Backwards . . . ": Hesperian Reversal II—Platonic *Epistrophē*—The Fall of the Gods—Hesiod's Evening—God Transplanted—"ISTer" [IS he]—Deferral of Reflection, Infertility [*Unfruchtbarkeit*]—Hegel's "Glorious Sunrise"

V. Dissemination, Mourning: Fruit of the Infertile [*Frucht der Unfruchtbaren*]—Logos Spermatikos—Interpretation as "Castration"—Measurelessness, End of Mourning—trans.

2. Stéphane Mallarmé, "Parenthèse," in *Oeuvres complètes* (Paris: Pléiade, 1945), 323; "Parenthesis," in *Divagations: The 1897 Arrangement by the Author*, trans. Barbara Johnson (Cambridge: Harvard University Press, 2007), 154.

3. Hamacher inserted the following marginal comment concerning "its" in the phrase "its status": "grammatically ambivalent."—trans.

4. See for instance Ulrich Gaier's interpretation of "The Only One" in *Der gesetzliche Kalkül* (Tübingen: Niemeyer, 1962).

5. Cf. Peter Szondi's proof in "Gattungspoetik und Geschichtsphilosophie" in *Hölderlin-Studien* (Frankfurt am Main: Suhrkamp, 1970).

6. Theodor Adorno, "Parataxis: Zur später Lyrik Hölderlins," in *Noten zur Literatur, III* (Frankfurt am Main: Suhrkamp, 1965), 192; "Parataxis: On Hölderlin's Late Poetry," in *Notes to Literature* (New York: Columbia University Press, 1991), 2: 136.

7. Hamacher underlines "unattainable" and adds an exclamation point in the margin.—trans.

8. In the first version it is in the middle but, of course, it is no longer so in the second. [Hamacher underlines *work*, *follows*, and *is* in "is shattered."—trans.]

9. This reconstruction of an intralingual reference is also supported by one other, not altogether insignificant link: the positioning of the strophes. The strophe in which the "lying" beneath the stars is described is the last of the first

group of six; the last strophe of the second group of six speaks of the "legend [*Sage*] [that] . . . , Travelling on from the East, has reached us"; and the last strophe of the third group of six is concerned with the "interpretation" [*Auslegen*] of holy *legends* [*Sagen*].

10. Cf. Rolf Zuberbühler, *Hölderlin's Erneuerung der Sprache aus ihren etymologischen Ursprüngen* (Berlin: Schmidt, 1969), 29. He refers to the etymology given by Wilhelm Heinse in his novel *Ardinghello*: "Comprehension/Understanding [*Verstand*] comes from standing [*Stehen*]."

11. Hamacher underlined *same* and added in the margin, "X instant [*X Augenblick*]."—trans.

12. Hamacher changed "lays itself out into that which the first version calls" to "lays itself out into one that the first version calls."—trans.

13. See "In Lovely Blueness . . . " (StA 2: 374).

14. Cf. B. Böschenstein, *Hölderlins Rheinhymne* (Zürich: Atlantis, 1959), 78.

15. Fichte's term is *Schranke*, but Hamacher also uses *Grenze* in the same sense, as "limit."—trans.

16. Both the "name" [*Nahmen*] and the verb "to take" [*nehmen*] and "to participate" [*teilnehmen*] are spelled with an "h" in the original poem.—trans.

17. Heraclitus, *Fragmente*, ed. and trans. by Bruno Snell (Munich: Artemis, 1965), 23; Fragment 92, D. 62; Heraclitus, *The Art and Thought of Heraclitus: An Edition of the Fragments with Translation and Commentary*, ed. and trans. Charles H. Kahn (Cambridge: Cambridge University Press, 1979), 71.

18. Cf., for instance, Peter Szondi, *Hölderlin-Studien*, 71, 78, etc. Szondi even speaks emphatically about an epiphany of God "*in the* poem" (80), as though the fictional moment in the hymn "Celebration of Peace" at which its poet thinks he sees the prince "with eyes dusk-dim" (l. 18) were not constitutive for the poem's entire course and for the philosophical history of the festival that it presents.

19. "Verhängt" means both "doomed" and "covered."—trans.

20. Martin Heidegger, *Erläuterungen zu Hölderlins Dichtung* (Frankfurt am Main: Klostermann, 1951), 43–44; *Elucidations of Hölderlin's Poetry*, trans. Keith Hoeller (Amherst, NY: Humanity Books, 2000). 63–64; Beda Allemann, *Hölderlin und Heidegger* (Zürich: Atlantis, 1954), 128ff.

21. See "The Voice of the People," second version, PF 243, mod.—trans.

22. Heidegger, "Das Ende der Philosophie und die Aufgabe des Denkens," in *Zur Sache des Denkens* (Tübingen: Niemeyer, 1969), 75; "The End of Philosophy and the Task of Thinking," in *On Time and Being*, trans. Joan Stambaugh (New York: Harper & Row, 1972), 68; emphasis added.

23. Hamacher changed "rather, it is a sign of something that itself has the structure of a sign" to "rather, with it, as such a sign, it points toward something that has the structure of a sign."—trans.

24. Cf. Jean-Jacques Rousseau, *Essai sur l'origine des langues* (Paris: Bibliothèque du Graphe, 1970). The relation of Hölderlin's philosophy of language to that of Rousseau, as well as the connection between their historical-philosophical and social-philosophical theories, no doubt belongs thematically to this discussion. The breadth with which these connections would need to be treated, however, requires its own study.

25. Here in the sense of the first letter to Böhlendorff; see StA 6: 426; EL 207, mod.

26. Walter Benjamin uses this description in his Hölderlin essay in *Illuminations* (Frankfurt am Main: Suhrkamp, 1961), 32; "Two Poems of Friedrich Hölderlin," trans. Stanley Corngold in the first volume of *Selected Writings*, ed. Marcus Bullock and Michael Jennings (Cambridge, Mass.: Harvard University Press, 1996), 25.

27. Theodor Adorno, "Parataxis," *Noten zur Literatur, III*, 186; *Notes on Literature*, 2: 136. On the other hand, Adorno describes the synthetic-asynthetic syntax that his concept of parataxis does not cover; specifically: "The paratactic revolt against synthesis attains its limit in the synthetic function of language as such. What is envisioned is a synthesis of a different kind, language's critical self-reflection, while language retains synthesis" (186; 2: 136). The fact that Adorno insists on synthesis, even if not a conceptual synthesis, and sees it as distinguished from conceptual synthesis alone through its reflective moment, makes it impossible for him to philosophically articulate the role of withdrawal and of deferral, of double-interpretation and of reversal in Hölderlin.

28. The importance of the use of causal prepositions when attacking the logical syntax of language can be seen by comparing this phrase with one from fragment 80 (in Beissner's ordering): "No Poles are we/Of the learned half" (StA 2: 339). The terrain of poets is not *halved*, as Poland was, by the claims of scholars to know the truth.

29. The gesture of that which has been embedded in writing, which is characterized by a remark such as the one recorded by Waiblinger: "Look, Sir, a comma!" no doubt already informs the punctuation of Hölderlin's "classical" period. Thus, the horizontal dash after the end of the verse "Day now inclines to the present Earth.—" appears to carry out his interpretation (graphically), as it were, and anticipate the "levelling out" that occurs three lines later; Waiblinger's citation derives from Wilhelm Michel, *Das Leben Friedrich Hölderlins* (Darmstadt: Wissenschaftliche Buchhandlung, 1963), 546.

30. "A while" [*Weile*] is in the fourth verse and "hurry" [*eilen*] is in the fourth-to-last verse of the thirteenth strophe of "The Rhine."

31. Peter Szondi, "Gattungspoetik und Geschichtsphilosophie," in *Hölderlin-Studien*.

32. Allemann, *Hölderlin und Heidegger*, 61.

33. Robert Stoll, *Hölderlins Christushymnen* (Basel: Schwabe, 1952), 156; Beissner, StA 2: 755; Allemann, *Hölderlin und Heidegger*, 53n26.

34. In the 1970 Insel edition—and this is characteristic of the dominant Hölderlin reception—his editors, Beissner and Schmidt, who are more intent on unambiguousness than Hölderlin, have placed a comma, going against the objective tendency of the text, between "me" and "you." In this and most other editions, such interventions are legion. They indicate, to the same degree, both incomprehension and a feeling of danger in the face of the splintering of one meaning [*Bedeutung*] into several.

35. The version Hamacher cites incorporates corrections from the H1a version in StA 2: 745, ll. 30–31 and 746: ll. 1–2.—trans.

36. Beda Allemann is right to criticize the naïve misunderstanding of the hymnic self-accusation; the large gap in the manuscript that immediately precedes the confession indicates that this confession was ascribed a very specific function in the architecture of the hymn; see Allemann, *Hölderlin und Heidegger*, 60.

37. G. W. F. Hegel, *Wissenschaft der Logik*, ed. Eva Moldenhauer and Karl Markus Michel (Frankfurt am Main: Suhrkamp, 1969), 45; *Science of Logic*, trans. A. W. Miller (London: Routledge, 2002), 416; II.2 ("Identity").

38. Cf. Allemann, *Hölderlin und Heidegger*, 60–61.

39. Jochen Schmidt was probably the first in recent Hölderlin scholarship to point out this trait of Hölderlin's texts, although this insight did not leave the slightest trace in either his method or the results of his interpretations; see Schmidt, *Hölderlin's Elegie "Brod und Wein"* (Berlin: de Gruyter, 1968), 124.

40. Allemann, *Hölderlin und Heidegger*, 36.

41. Cf. Szondi's commentary in *Versuch über das Tragische* (Frankfurt am Main: Suhrkamp, 1964), 171–73; *Essay on the Tragic*, trans. Paul Fleming (Stanford: Stanford University Press, 2002), 11–14.

42. "Greek art is foreign to us because of the national convenience and bias it has always relied on, and I hope to present it to the public in a more lively manner than usual by bringing out further the oriental element it has denied and correcting its artistic bias wherever it occurs" (StA 6: 434; EL 215).

43. Cf. Friedrich Beissner, *Hölderlins Übersetzungen aus dem Griechischen* (Stuttgart: Metzler, 1961), 168.

44. In "Two Poems of Friedrich Hölderlin" Walter Benjamin was probably the first to point out the double meaning of the word *geschickt* (sent, skillful): "The poet appears among the living, determining and determined" (*Illuminationen*, 35; *Selected Writings*, 1: 27). Benjamin was likely also the first to notice the *double* tendency of the poetic language of Hölderlin's late work. He avoids explicitly formulating the ambiguity, which in the summative sentence was between measure and excess and which, in the second ode, describes how the images as well as the ideas "all . . . arise as unlimited against the formed, limited appear-

ance resting in itself" (*Illuminationen*, 46; *Selected Writings*, 1: 35) He calls this unlimitedness "oriental." Precisely this concept, however, remains controversial in Benjamin's study. Insofar as it stands with equal justification for the opposite of unlimitedness—"Again the rigidity and inaccessibility of the image must remind one of oriental vision" (*Illuminationen*, 40; *Selected Writings*, 1: 31)—it refers to the dissolution of "the difference between form and the formless" (*Illuminationen*, 40; *Selected Writings*, 1: 31) rather than a difference between distinct things.

45. The word "Gestalt" is crossed out and replaced by "Figur."—trans.

46. The word "Schiklichkeit" itself is not translated in EL.—trans.

47. Cf. Bernard Böschenstein, *Konkordanz zu Hölderlins Gedichten nach 1800* (Göttingen: Vandenhoeck und Ruprecht: 1964), 77.

48. The agonal moment of the metaphor may have led to the reference to the "heroes of the Iliad," who are named in the sentence that follows. Otherwise, this "hitting upon" [*Treffen*] and "grasping" [*Fassen*] cannot be read other than in the context of determining what is factically deadly and what factically kills, of apprehending the more or less sensible or spiritual body, and thus again in the context of the metaphorics of the agon.

49. In the first version of "The Only One," the strophe containing the comparison between Christ and Evius refers to his having "first planted the vineyard" [*Den Weinberg stiftet*] (StA 2: 154; PF 537). One of Hölderlin's best-known verses, from the end of "Remembrance" (*Andenken*), is, of course, "what remains, however, the poets grant" [*Was bleibet aber, stiften die Dichter*] (StA 2: 189; PF 579, mod.).—trans.

50. On the arrangement of the verses here, which is preserved against Beissner's recommendation, see Allemann's justification, *Hölderlin und Heidegger*, 61–62n31.

51. Hamacher added "appearance" by hand.—trans.

52. See Heidegger's remark on *doxa* in *Einführung in die Metaphysik* (Tübingen: Niemeyer, 1966), 78–79; *Introduction to Metaphysics*, trans. Ralph Manheim (New Haven: Yale University Press, 1959), 104–5.

53. Hölderlin plays with the connection between "islands" [*Inseln*] and "are" [*sind*] almost excessively at the end of the "Elegy" (StA 2: 74, ll. 110–16) and "Menon's Lament for Diotima" (StA 2: 79, ll. 122–30; PF 293–301).

54. Unfortunately, I am not aware of a name other than this customary one [*Hilfsverb*, "helping verb"], which the fascistic language of the Duden grammar has sanctioned in line with its general project of naming all linguistic functions as much as possible after the master-slave dialectic; see *Duden Grammatik der deutschen Gegenwartsprache* (Mannheim: Dudenverlag, 1966), 71.

55. Cf. G. W. F. Hegel, *Phänomenologie des Geistes* (Hamburg: Meiner, 1952), 564; *Phenomenology of Spirit*, trans. Terry Pinkard (Cambridge: Cambridge University Press, 2018), 467.

56. The capitalized "One" designates a numeral.

57. Matthew 4:3–4 (King James Version).

58. Cf. John 1:1.

59. See Sophocles, *Antigone*, Act 3, scene 2, ll. 823–38 in the Loeb edition (New York: MacMillan, 1912).—trans.

60. How precisely the etymon of this word is calculated from the context of the other words cited here can be seen most evidently from the fact that it is used instead of "damage" or "defect" [*Schade*]; cf. StA 2: 763, l. 7 and 2: 752, l. 15.

61. Momme Mommsen has shown that "the treasured gem of the house" is a citation from Aeschylus's *Agamemnon*; see Mommsen, "Dionysos in der Dichtung Hölderlins," *Germanisch-Romanische Monatsschrift* N.F. 13.4 (1963): 378.

62. Hamacher added in the margin: "grammatically unclear relation."—trans.

63. Plato, *The Statesman* 270d–e; *Sämtliche Werke* (Reinbek 1969), 5: 27; trans. C. J. Rowe, in Plato, *Complete Works*, ed. John W. Cooper (Indianapolis: Hackett, 1997), 312.

64. Plato, *The Statesman*, 269e; *Sämtliche Werke*, 5: 26; *Complete Works*, 311.

65. Plato, *The Statesman*, 273c–e; *Sämtliche Werke*, 5: 29–30; *Complete Works*, 311–15.

66. Plato, *The Statesman*, 311c; *Sämtliche Werke*, 5: 72; *Complete Works*, 358.

67. Cf. Plato, *The Statesman*, 311a-c; *Sämtliche Werke*, 5: 72; *Complete Works*, 357–58.

68. For passages in the Old Testament, see the article on "conversio / Umkehr" in the first volume of the *Historisches Wörterbuch der Philosophie*, ed. J. Ritter (Darmstadt: Wissenschaftliche Buchgesellschaft, 1971).

69. See, for instance, Matthew 3:2; 4:17; 18:3 ["Repent ye" (King James Version)—trans.]

70. "Prooemium habendum d. 27. Dec. 1785. die Ioannis, in caput primum epistolae ad Ebraeos" (StA 4: 171)—trans.

71. Hesiod, *Theogony*, ll. 215–16, in *Werke*, trans. Thomas von Scheffer (Wiesbaden, 1947), 17; *Theogony*, trans. Glenn Most (Cambridge, Mass.: Loeb Classical Library, 2006), 21.

72. Hesiod, *Theogony*, l. 275, *Werke*; *Theogony*, 25.

73. Hesiod, *Theogony*, l. 518, *Werke*; *Theogony*, 45.

74. Hesiod, *Theogony*, ll. 748–53, *Werke*; *Theogony*, 64–65.

75. Cf. Plato, *The Statesman*, 273e; *Sämtliche Werke*, 5: 30; *Complete Works*, 315.

76. What might blossom from an interpretation that focuses on the "meaning" [*Sinn*] of a word without consideration for how it might be determined by its context, without reading meaning itself as a demonstrative term to which "its" reference [*Bedeutung*] is subsequently added through its convergence or divergence from other meanings, can be seen most clearly in Heidegger's *Elucida-*

tions on the "colony" as a "daughterland" subjected, as it were, to an imperialistic politics; cf. Heidegger, *Erläuterungen zu Hölderlins Dichtung*, 88; *Elucidations of Hölderlin's Poetry*, 117. Jochen Schmidt was the first to describe, in his study of "Bread and Wine," the connection between the "transplant [*verpflanzet*]" of verse 54 (StA 2: 599) and the colony as a (plant) nursery [*Pflanzstätte*]; see Schmidt, *Hölderlins Elegie*, 180 and 201. The interpretation here differs from Schmidt's in all other respects.

77. Cf. Hesiod, *Theogony*, ll. 734–35 and ll. 769–74, *Werke*, 49 and 51.

78. Cf. "but now he names his most treasured possession, / Now for it words like flowers originating he must find" (StA 2: 93; PF 325, mod.).

79. Georg Christoph Lichtenberg, Notebook D, Aphorism 201 (1773–1775), in Lichtenberg, *Gedankenbücher. Mit einem Nachwort von Franz H. Mautner* (Frankfurt am Main: Fischer, 1963), 63; *Philosophical Writings*, trans. Steven Tester (Albany: SUNY Press, 2012), 55.

80. StA 2: 191, ll. 36–40.

81. See Friedrich Hölderlin, *Sämtliche Werke*, ed. Norbert von Hellingrath, Ludwig von Pigenot, and Friedrich Seebass (Berlin: Propyläen, 1923), 4: 368.

82. There is no doubt that the semblance is, at the same time, also a "subjective" semblance: "He seems to *me*. . . . " Yet only the context, which also refers to the reflective sense of semblance, explains the exposed position of the "seems" at the beginning of the verse. And in this connection it becomes visible for the first time what "subjectivity" means in "The Ister."

83. G. W. F. Hegel, *Jenenser Logik, Metaphysik und Naturphilosophie*, ed. G. Lasson (Hamburg: Meiner, 1923), 195.

84. Hegel, *Phänomenologie des Geistes*, 558–59; *Phenomenology of Spirit*, 462.

85. Though certainly not immediately in the sense intended in the letter to Sinclair of December 24, 1798.

86. Hegel, *Phänomenologie des Geistes*, 30; *Phenomenology of Spirit*, 21.

87. Hegel, *Phänomenologie des Geistes*, 418–19; *Phenomenology of Spirit*, 343.

88. G. W. F. Hegel, *Vorlesungen über die Philosophie der Geschichte*, ed. Eva Moldenhauer and Karl Markus Michel (Frankfurt am Main: Suhrkamp, 1970), 529; *Philosophy of History*, trans. J. Sibree (New York: Dover, 1956), 467, mod.

89. "There is no philosophy other than Hegel's that is so much and so thoroughly a philosophy of revolution, all the way down to its innermost drives" (Joachim Ritter, *Hegel und die französische Revolution* [Frankfurt am Main: Suhrkamp, 1965], 18). This statement by Ritter needs to be supplemented with the observation that it is a philosophy of the *bourgeois* revolution and, furthermore, that it is able to work with the complexes of ideas and figures of thought that, as I have tried to show, have belonged to the set of instruments available to philosophical Idealism at least since Plato's cosmology. Even Marx's definition of the proletarian revolution as the negation of negation (e.g. Karl Marx, *Das Kapi-*

tal, vol. 1, *Marx-Engels Werke* (Berlin/DDR: Dietz, 1962), 23: 791) belongs in formal terms to the context of Idealism, whereas the material expositions within the critique of political economy evince implications of the Hegelian formula diverging from metaphysical ones.

90. Pierre Bertaux has remarked that "patrie" and "Vaterland" were polemical concepts used by the German Jacobins against feudalism; see Bertaux, *Hölderlin und die französische Revolution* (Frankfurt am Main: Suhrkamp 1969), 52–53.

91. As Werner Kirchner has convincingly shown in his book on the *Hochverratsprozeß gegen Sinclair*, Hölderlin and his friends must have turned against France under Napoleonic rule by 1804 at the latest; see Kirchner, *Hochverratsprozeß* (Frankfurt am Main: Insel, 1969), 29.

92. This significantly modifies the traditional definition of the boundary [*Grenze*] found for instance in Aristotle's *Metaphysics* (1022a).

93. Sigmund von Birken, *Fried—erfreueten Teutonie*, cited in Walter Benjamin, *Ursprung des deutschen Trauerspiels* (Frankfurt am Main: Suhrkamp, 1963), 264; *Origin of German Tragic Drama*, trans. John Osborne (London: Verso, 1998), 233.

94. John 1:4 (King James Version).

95. The phrase *von selbst* means "by itself" in the sense of "automatically"—and, thus, ostensibly without the intervening act of a "self."—trans.

96. Jacques Derrida, "La double séance," *Tel Quel* 42 (1970): 41; "The Double Session," in *Dissemination*, trans. Barbara Johnson (Chicago: University of Chicago Press), 1981, 268n67. [Barbara Johnson's translation contains a couple of elaborations of "comprend" and "signifié," neither of which is in the (French) version cited by Hamacher. To maintain fidelity to the rhythm of Hamacher's text, I have omitted these elaborations, marking their places with ellipses.—trans.]

97. Cf. Jacob Grimm and Wilhelm Grimm, *Deutsches Wörterbuch* (Stuttgart: Hirzel, 1893), 8: 2473.

98. For instance, Friedrich Beissner in his commentary (StA 2: 830) and Jochen Schmidt, *Hölderlins letzte Hymnen* (Tübingen: Niemeyer, 1970), 70.

Parousia, Stone-Walls

1. The original version of this essay, "Parousie, Mauern. Mittelbarkeit und Zeitlichkeit, später Hölderlin," appeared in *Hölderlin-Jahrbuch* 34 (2006): 93–142.

2. *Zukunft* ("future" in contemporary German) is translated as "advent" whenever it refers directly to the biblical phrase, and intermediary formulations are used to establish a linkage with the more purely temporal sense. Hamacher's use of the phrase *zukünftige Zukunft* ("futural ad-vent") remains untranslatable unless both these senses of *Zukunft* are brought into play.—trans.

3. *Übermaß* is an ordinary word that, depending on context, can be translated as "excess," "immoderation," or even "overkill." Here and elsewhere, it is rendered as "over-measure" to preserve the connection with "measure" (*Maß*).—trans.

4. As Hamacher soon notes with respect to the relevant line from "The Rhine," "Ein Räthsel ist Reinentsprungenes," *rein-* ("purely") and *Rhein* are homophones.—trans.

5. Hamacher plays on the near homophony of *Zeit* ("time") and *Seite* ("side").—trans.

6. The verb *aufhören*, which means "to stop" in contemporary German, is a compound of the prefix *auf* ("on," "up," "upon," "in") and the verb *hören*, whose primary sense is "to hear."—trans.

Afterword

1. Werner Hamacher, email to Peter Fenves, June 25, 2017.

2. Despite the fact that Hamacher would often discuss Hölderlin in conversations, he is very sparing in his remarks about the poet beyond the texts collected into this volume. The epigram drawn from Hölderlin that is used for the master's thesis appears in the introductory essay to *Premises*, as do some of the aphorism from a prose text often called "Reflection" in the final essay of the volume; see Werner Hamacher, *Premises: Literature and Philosophy from Kant to Celan*, trans. Peter Fenves (Stanford: Stanford University Press, 1999), 20, 341–42. His reticence is evident even in *pleroma*, which is discussed below. In his late reflections on philology, also discussed briefly below, Hölderlin's name occasionally appears, but here, too, reticence is the basic attitude.

3. Among the questions I compiled for Hamacher about his thesis was one concerning its changing title. Below is a brief discussion of the title used for this edition; in a CV prepared in 1990, Hamacher listed yet a third title: "Sprache und Geschichte in der Lyrik Hölderlins" (Language and history in Hölderlin's lyric poetry).

4. For this entire paragraph I want to reiterate my thanks to Irene Albers, who also helped me both resolve some typographical problems with the manuscript of the master's thesis and determine the circumstances under which it was written, as several of the following notes attest.

5. For the circumstances of Derrida's first visit to AVL, which involved a comic mix-up, see Samuel Weber and Irene Albers, "Screen Memories: Samuel Weber in Conversation with Irene Albers and Sima Reinisch," in *Points of Departure: Samuel Weber between Spectrality and Reading*, ed. Peter Fenves, Kevin McLaughlin, and Marc Redfield (Evanston, IL: Northwestern University Press, 2016), 269–85.

6. See the chronology complied by Irene Albers at the conclusion of *Nach Szondi: Allgemeine und vergleichende Literaturwissenschaft and der freien Universität-Berlin, 1965–2015*, ed. Irene Albers (Berlin: Kadmos, 2016), 475.

7. Werner Hamacher to Irene Albers, email of September 21, 2015.

8. Peter Szondi, "Er Selbst, der Fürst des Fests. Die Hymne *Friedensfeier*," in *Hölderlin-Studien*, reprinted in Szondi, *Schriften* (Frankfurt am Main: Suhrkamp, 1978), 1: 315–42. Hamacher's critique, also discussed in the Introduction, can be found in note 18 to "Versions of Meaning" (190).

9. Beyond tracking the thematic importance of *Hemmung* in his reading of "Voice of the People", Hamacher borrows the term *Entstellung*, here translated as "distortion" (see, for instance, 20), from Freud, Lacan, and perhaps also Benjamin (in his reading of Kafka); more directly, the theme of repression (*Verdrängung*) enters into several of the readings, if not the basic framework through which Hamacher understands the work of deconstruction in the thesis. Several years after he completed his thesis, and perhaps only for pecuniary reasons, Hamacher translated into German two volumes of Lacan's writings; see Jacques Lacan, *Freuds technische Schriften (Seminar I)*, trans. Werner Hamacher (Olten, Freiburg: Walter Verlag, 1978); Jacques Lacan and Jean Hyppolite, *Schriften über die Verneinung*, trans. Werner Hamacher and Ursula Rütt-Förster, in Jacques Lacan, *Schriften III* (Olten, Freiburg: Walter Verlag, 1979).

10. Georg Wilhelm Friedrich Hegel, *Phänomenologie des Geistes*, reprinted in *Werke*, ed. Eva Moldenhauer and Karl Markus Michel (Frankfurt am Main: Suhrkamp), 3: 115; *Phenomenology of Spirit*, trans. Terry Pinkard (Cambridge: Cambridge University Press, 2018), 115; § 194.

11. Schelling, the third classmate, never appears by name in Hamacher's thesis, which indicates the degree to which its reference to "Tübingen classmates" is problematic, pointing toward a larger study. The absence of Schelling, whose work Hamacher knew very well, can also be seen, to some extent, in Derrida, whose early work contains important traces of late Schelling that then gradually disappeared.

12. Walter Benjamin, "Zwei Gedichte von Friedrich Hölderlin," in *Gesammelte Schriften*, ed. Rolf Tiedemann and Hermann Schweppenhäuser (Frankfurt am Main: Suhrkamp, 1972–91), 2: 106.

13. See Georg Wilhelm Friedrich Hegel, *"Der Geist des Christentums": Schriften 1796–1800*, ed. Werner Hamacher (Berlin: Ullstein, 1978), 537. I would like to thank Markus Hardtmann for alerting me to this title, which, so far as the editors of this volume have been able to discover, remains the only trace of the text. Its potential significance can be gauged by the words that de Man uses to describe it: "a methodological and exegetic contribution of major importance" (Paul de Man, letter of recommendation for Hamacher, dated July 15, 1974). Hamacher probably first met de Man when the latter first visited

AVL in June, 1971, giving a paper on Nietzsche's *Birth of Tragedy*; see Albers, ed., *Nach Szondi*, 474. Hamacher sought to publish this paper for his edition of *Nietzsche aus Frankreich* (Berlin: Ullstein, 1986); but it was ultimately published in the abbreviated German translation of de Man's *Allegories of Reading*, which Hamacher edited, co-translated, and introduced; see Paul de Man, *Allegorien des Lesens*, trans. Werner Hamacher and Peter Krumme (Frankfurt am Main: Suhrkamp, 1987).

14. Hamacher to de Man, letter of November 22, 1974; MS-C004–B016–F012, UC-Irvine Special Collections.

15. Hamacher to de Man, letter of June 17, 1976; MS-C004–B016–F015, UC-Irvine Special Collections. In the same letter, Hamacher asks de Man whether he would "play the Doktorvater" for this dissertation.

16. See Werner Hamacher, "pleroma—zu Genesis und Struktur einer dialektischen Hermeneutik bei Hegel," in Hegel, "Der Geist des Christentums," 56–58, 188–90, and 127, respectively; Hamacher, *pleroma—Reading in Hegel*, trans. Nicholas Walker and Simon Jarvis (Stanford: Stanford University Press, 1998), 44–45, 166–68, and 109.

17. From the perspective of his master's thesis, the proximity between Hölderlin and Hegel in *pleroma* is surprising. De Man may have been responsible, at least in part, for this change. Consider the conclusion to de Man's essay on Heidegger's "elucidations" of Hölderlin's poetry: "[Beda] Allemann has fallen victim to an error that Heidegger's influence may indeed induce: to preserve the historical perspective which requires that Hegel remain short of the superseding of Western metaphysics while Hölderlin is already on the far side of it" (Paul de Man, "Heidegger's Exegesis of Hölderlin," trans. Wlad Godzich, in *Blindness and Insight: Essays in the Rhetoric of Contemporary Criticism* [Minneapolis: University of Minnesota Press, 1983], 266). One of the questions I wanted to ask Hamacher in conjunction with the publication of his master's essay was whether he agreed with de Man in this regard; and if so, whether he, too, had fallen victim to this error; and more broadly, whether de Man was one of the "masters" under examination in his thesis. Hamacher's thesis gives several indications that circa 1971 he was unaware of de Man's writings on Hölderlin. This is especially true of a passage where he draws attention to the problem of Hölderlin's relation to Rousseau (41), a passage that includes no endnote to de Man's essay on this very topic, even though it had been recently translated into German; see Paul de Man, "Hölderlins Rousseaubild," trans. Renate Böschenstein-Schäfer, *Hölderlin-Jahrbuch* 15 (1967–68): 180–208. (On the typescript of the master's thesis I received from Eva Geulen, there is a large question mark at this point but no indication of whose hand made it; I suspect that the mark came from de Man.) The relation between Hamacher and de Man was not, however, altogether unilateral in this respect. During the years in which Hamacher was intent on ex-

panding his thesis, de Man was seeking to develop the aforementioned essays on Hölderlin into a larger project on the history of Romanticism after Rousseau. This never came to fruition either. It is as though, around 1975, de Man and Hamacher had destroyed each other's future Hölderlin projects.

18. As with Hegel, so with Kant: Hamacher's essay "Ex tempore—Zeit als Vorstellung bei Kant" (Ex tempore—time as representation in Kant), written in close conjunction with "Parousia, Stone-Walls," makes Kant and Hölderlin into companions in tearing apart certain prevailing conceptions of homogeneous temporality; the essay can be found in *Politik der Vorstellung*, ed. Joachim Gerstmeier und Nikolaus Müller-Schöll (Munich: Verlag Theater der Zeit, 2006), 68–94.

19. Undated fragment from Hamacher's literary estate; the year is established by the fact that the opening sentence indicates that it was written six years after 1973, which is presumably the date at which Hamacher had last reviewed his thesis and written "Diversions."

20. Ibid. Hamacher adds the following coda, expressing an attitude toward the questions under discussion that should be kept in mind while reading the thesis as a whole: "There is little to find in the enclosed passages; they should give an example of the style of my, in the narrow sense, literary-scientific work." The relentlessly critical attitude toward the work of others is anything but a sign of scholarly triumph.

21. Gottlob Frege, "Über Sinn und Bedeutung" (1892), in Frege, *Funktion, Begriff, Bedeutung: Fünf logische Studien*, ed. Günther Patzig (Göttingen: Vandenhoeck & Ruprecht, 1986), 40–65.

22. Letter from Hamacher to de Man, November 22, 1974; MS-C004-B016-F012. Goebel, a Romanist who produced editions of Mallarmé's writings, may have been incited to this judgment in reaction to Hamacher's references to Derrida's "Double séance." Writing to de Man, Hamacher calls Goebel's criticism "truly childish silliness." Yet something of its sting may have stuck, for he was not averse to asking kindred questions, as he does, for example, at the beginning of his first essay on Walter Benjamin: "And why is every reading of Benjamin, hardly less explicitly than this one, instead of keeping its distance from his idiom, inclined to make itself, entirely without ironic intention, into a pastiche of [that idiom] by adopting the cadences of his language, his syntactical gestures and his words?" (Werner Hamacher, "The Word *Wolke*—If It Is One," trans. Peter Fenves, *Studies in Twentieth-Century Literature* 11 [1986]: 133–62).

23. The opening section of Aristotle's *Politics*, where he defines the human being—and the human being alone, in contrast with certain passages in his later works, especially his *Historia animalium*—as the "animal having language," is an essential element of Hamacher's later presentation of philology as well as his corresponding inquiries into the theory of justice, law, and politics; see especially Werner Hamacher, *Ninety-Five Theses on Philology*, in *Minima Philologica*, trans.

Catherine Diehl and Jason Grove (New York: Fordham University Press, 2015), 8; thesis 6. Hamacher developed the theme of *point de suspension* in his early study of Friedrich Schleiermacher's ellipses; see *Premises*, 44–80.

Appendix

1. The "Third Version" of Friedrich Hölderlin's poem "Der Einzige" (The Only One) derives from Friedrich Beissner's reconstruction (StA 2: 161–64). When Hamacher wrote his master's thesis, the Stuttgart edition was the standard critical one, although he also consulted the earlier critical edition begun by Norbert von Hellingrath (100, 195). As is evident from "Parousia, Stone-Walls," Hamacher continued to use the Stuttgart edition, even as newer critical editions became available, including the so-called Frankfurt edition under the direction of D. E. Sattler. In a 1975 letter to Paul de Man, Hamacher, having acquired the introductory volume of the Frankfurt edition, lauded the "grandiosity" of its "polygraphic transcription" (MS C004-B016-F014, UC-Irvine Special Collections).—eds.

Name Index

Title Index

Letters

First Line Index

MERIDIAN

Crossing Aesthetics

Giorgio Agamben, *Creation and Anarchy: The Work of Art and the Religion of Capitalism*

Giorgio Agamben, *What Is Real?*

Giorgio Agamben, *Karman: A Brief Treatise on Action, Guilt, and Gesture*

Giorgio Agamben, *What Is Philosophy?*

Ethan Kleinberg, *Haunting History: For a Deconstructive Approach to the Past*

Giorgio Agamben, *The Omnibus* Homo Sacer

Giorgio Agamben, *The Mystery of Evil: Benedict XVI and the End of Days*

Giorgio Agamben, *The Fire and the Tale*

Eyal Peretz, *The Off-Screen: An Investigation of the Cinematic Frame*

Giorgio Agamben, *The Use of Bodies*

Giorgio Agamben, *Stasis: Civil War as a Political Paradigm*

Paul North, *The Yield: Kafka's Atheological Reformation*

Giorgio Agamben, *Pilate and Jesus*

Kevin McLaughlin, *Poetic Force: Poetry after Kant*

Barbara Johnson, *A Life with Mary Shelley*

Giorgio Agamben, *Opus Dei: An Archaeology of Duty*

Giorgio Agamben, *The Highest Poverty: Monastic Rules and Form-of-Life*

Giorgio Agamben, *The Kingdom and the Glory: For a Theological Genealogy of Economy and Government*

Paul Celan, *The Meridian*

Bernard Stiegler, *Technics and Time, 3: Cinematic Time and the Question of Malaise*

Giorgio Agamben, *The Sacrament of Language: An Archeology of the Oath*

Peter Fenves, *The Messianic Reduction: Walter Benjamin and the Shape of Time*

Giorgio Agamben, *Nudities*

Hans Blumenberg, *Care Crosses the River*

Bernard Stiegler, *Taking Care of Youth and the Generations*

Ruth Stein, *For Love of the Father: A Psychoanalytic Study of Religious Terrorism*

Giorgio Agamben, *"What Is an Apparatus?" and Other Essays*

Rodolphe Gasché, *Europe, or the Infinite Task: A Study of a Philosophical Concept*

Bernard Stiegler, *Technics and Time, 2: Disorientation*

Bernard Stiegler, *Acting Out*

Susan Bernstein, *Housing Problems: Writing and Architecture in Goethe, Walpole, Freud, and Heidegger*

Martin Hägglund, *Radical Atheism: Derrida and the Time of Life*

Cornelia Vismann, *Files: Law and Media Technology*

Jean-Luc Nancy, *Discourse of the Syncope: Logodaedalus*

Carol Jacobs, *Skirting the Ethical: Sophocles, Plato, Hamann, Sebald, Campion*

Cornelius Castoriadis, *Figures of the Thinkable*

Jacques Derrida, *Psyche: Inventions of the Other*, 2 [MD1]volumes, edited by Peggy Kamuf and Elizabeth Rottenberg

Mark Sanders, *Ambiguities of Witnessing: Literature and Law in the Time of a Truth Commission*

Sarah Kofman, *Selected Writings*, edited by Thomas Albrecht, with Georgia Albert and Elizabeth Rottenberg

Arendt, Hannah, *Reflections on Literature and Culture,* edited by Susannah Young-ah Gottlieb

Alan Bass, *Interpretation and Difference: The Strangeness of Care*

Jacques Derrida, *H.C. for Life, That Is to Say . . .*

Ernst Bloch, *Traces*

Elizabeth Rottenberg, *Inheriting the Future: Legacies of Kant, Freud, and Flaubert*

David Wills, *Matchbook: Essays in Deconstruction*

David Michael Kleinberg-Levin, *Gestures of Ethical Life*

Jacques Derrida, *On Touching—Jean-Luc Nancy*

Jacques Derrida, *Rogues: Two Essays on Reason*

Peggy Kamuf, *Book of Addresses*

Giorgio Agamben, *The Time That Remains: A Commentary on the Letter to the Romans*

Jean-Luc Nancy, *Multiple Arts: The Muses II*

Alain Badiou, *Handbook of Inaesthetics*

Jacques Derrida, *Eyes of the University: Right to Philosophy 2*

Maurice Blanchot, *Lautréamont and Sade*

Giorgio Agamben, *The Open: Man and Animal*

Jean Genet, *The Declared Enemy*

Shoshana Felman, *Writing and Madness: (Literature/Philosophy/Psychoanalysis)*

Jean Genet, *Fragments of the Artwork*

Shoshana Felman, *The Scandal of the Speaking Body: Don Juan with J. L. Austin, or Seduction in Two Languages*

Peter Szondi, *Celan Studies*

Neil Hertz, *George Eliot's Pulse*

Maurice Blanchot, *The Book to Come*

Susannah Young-ah Gottlieb, *Regions of Sorrow: Anxiety and Messianism in Hannah Arendt and W. H. Auden*

Jacques Derrida, *Without Alibi*, edited by Peggy Kamuf

Cornelius Castoriadis, *On Plato's 'Statesman'*

Jacques Derrida, *Who's Afraid of Philosophy? Right to Philosophy 1*

Peter Szondi, *An Essay on the Tragic*

Peter Fenves, *Arresting Language: From Leibniz to Benjamin*

Jill Robbins, ed., *Is It Righteous to Be? Interviews with Emmanuel Levinas*

Louis Marin, *Of Representation*

J. Hillis Miller, *Speech Acts in Literature*

Maurice Blanchot, *Faux pas*

Jean-Luc Nancy, *Being Singular Plural*

Maurice Blanchot / Jacques Derrida, *The Instant of My Death / Demeure: Fiction and Testimony*

Niklas Luhmann, *Art as a Social System*

Emmanual Levinas, *God, Death, and Time*

Ernst Bloch, *The Spirit of Utopia*

Giorgio Agamben, *Potentialities: Collected Essays in Philosophy*

Ellen S. Burt, *Poetry's Appeal: Nineteenth-Century French Lyric and the Political Space*

Jacques Derrida, *Adieu to Emmanuel Levinas*

Werner Hamacher, *Premises: Essays on Philosophy and Literature from Kant to Celan*

Aris Fioretos, *The Gray Book*

Deborah Esch, *In the Event: Reading Journalism, Reading Theory*

Winfried Menninghaus, *In Praise of Nonsense: Kant and Bluebeard*

Giorgio Agamben, *The Man Without Content*

Giorgio Agamben, *The End of the Poem: Studies in Poetics*

Theodor W. Adorno, *Sound Figures*

Louis Marin, *Sublime Poussin*

Philippe Lacoue-Labarthe, *Poetry as Experience*

Ernst Bloch, *Literary Essays*

Jacques Derrida, *Resistances of Psychoanalysis*

Marc Froment-Meurice, *That Is to Say: Heidegger's Poetics*

Francis Ponge, *Soap*

Philippe Lacoue-Labarthe, *Typography: Mimesis, Philosophy, Politics*

Giorgio Agamben, *Homo Sacer: Sovereign Power and Bare Life*

Emmanuel Levinas, *Of God Who Comes to Mind*

Bernard Stiegler, *Technics and Time, 1: The Fault of Epimetheus*

Werner Hamacher, *Pleroma—Reading in Hegel*

Serge Leclaire, *Psychoanalyzing: On the Order of the Unconscious and the Practice of the Letter*

Serge Leclaire, *A Child Is Being Killed: On Primary Narcissism and the Death Drive*

Sigmund Freud, *Writings on Art and Literature*

Cornelius Castoriadis, *World in Fragments: Writings on Politics, Society, Psychoanalysis, and the Imagination*

Thomas Keenan, *Fables of Responsibility: Aberrations and Predicaments in Ethics and Politics*

Emmanuel Levinas, *Proper Names*

Alexander García Düttmann, *At Odds with AIDS: Thinking and Talking About a Virus*

Maurice Blanchot, *Friendship*

Jean-Luc Nancy, *The Muses*

Massimo Cacciari, *Posthumous People: Vienna at the Turning Point*

David E. Wellbery, *The Specular Moment: Goethe's Early Lyric and the Beginnings of Romanticism*

Edmond Jabès, *The Little Book of Unsuspected Subversion*

Hans-Jost Frey, *Studies in Poetic Discourse: Mallarmé, Baudelaire, Rimbaud, Hölderlin*

Pierre Bourdieu, *The Rules of Art: Genesis and Structure of the Literary Field*

Nicolas Abraham, *Rhythms: On the Work, Translation, and Psychoanalysis*

Jacques Derrida, *On the Name*

David Wills, *Prosthesis*

Maurice Blanchot, *The Work of Fire*

Jacques Derrida, *Points . . . : Interviews, 1974–1994*

J. Hillis Miller, *Topographies*

Philippe Lacoue-Labarthe, *Musica Ficta (Figures of Wagner)*

Jacques Derrida, *Aporias*

Emmanuel Levinas, *Outside the Subject*

Jean-François Lyotard, *Lessons on the Analytic of the Sublime*

Peter Fenves, *"Chatter": Language and History in Kierkegaard*

Jean-Luc Nancy, *The Experience of Freedom*

Jean-Joseph Goux, *Oedipus, Philosopher*

Haun Saussy, *The Problem of a Chinese Aesthetic*

Jean-Luc Nancy, *The Birth to Presence*